People of the Middle Fraser Canyon

The Middle Fraser Canyon contains some of the most important
archaeological sites in British Columbia, including the remains of
ancient villages that supported hundreds, if not thousands, of people.
How and why did these villages come into being? Why were they
abandoned?

In search of answers to these questions, Anna Marie Prentiss and Ian
Kuijt take readers on a voyage of discovery into the ancient history of
the St'át'imc or Upper Lillooet people, from eight thousand years ago
to the present. Drawing on evidence from archaeological surveys and
excavations and from the knowledge of St'át'imc people as acquired
in interviews, they follow the human occupation of the region from
the early peopling of the Interior to the emergence of the first villages.
Explanations for the villages' establishment and collapse, they argue, lie
in the evolution of food-gathering and -processing techniques, climate
change, the development of social complexity, and the arrival of
Europeans.

Prentiss and Kuijt's wide-ranging vision of culture and ancient history
in British Columbia is brought to vivid life through photographs,
illustrations, artist renderings and fictionalized accounts of life in the
villages, a glossary and pronunciation guide for the St'át'imc language,
and sidebars on archaeological methods, theories, and debates.

Anna Marie Prentiss and Ian Kuijt

People of the Middle Fraser Canyon
An Archaeological History

WITH ILLUSTRATIONS BY ERIC S. CARLSON

UBCPress · Vancouver · Toronto

20 19 18 17 16 15 14 13 12   5 4 3 2 1

Printed in Canada on acid-free paper.

Library and Archives Canada Cataloguing in Publication

Prentiss, Anna Marie
   People of the middle Fraser Canyon: an archaeological history /
Anna Marie Prentiss and Ian Kuijt; with illustrations by Eric S. Carlson.

Includes bibliographical references and index.
Issued also in electronic formats.
ISBN 978-0-7748-2168-1

   1. Lillooet Indians – Antiquities. 2. Fraser Canyon (B.C.) – Antiquities. 3. Antiquities, Prehistoric – British Columbia – Fraser Canyon. 4. Excavations (Archaeology) – British Columbia – Fraser Canyon. I. Kuijt, Ian II. Title.

E99.L4P74 2012   971.1'37004979   C2012-901449-4

Canadä

UBC Press gratefully acknowledges the financial support for our publishing program of the Government of Canada (through the Canada Book Fund), the Canada Council for the Arts, and the British Columbia Arts Council.

This book has been published with the help of a grant from the Canadian Federation for the Humanities and Social Sciences, through the Aid to Scholarly Publications Program, using funds provided by the Social Sciences and Humanities Research Council of Canada.

We also gratefully acknowledge the International Council for Canadian Studies' financial contribution through its Publishing Fund.

UBC Press
The University of British Columbia
2029 West Mall
Vancouver, BC V6T 1Z2
www.ubcpress.ca

Contents

Illustrations

Acknowledgments

For over twenty years, we have enjoyed a wonderful relationship with many members of the St'át'imc Nation. They have been the most gracious of hosts to us and our occasional groups of college students. A number of people have been particularly instrumental in the development of archaeological fieldwork and in the research and writing of this book. We thank the following (in no particular order): Desmond Peters Jr., Desmond Peters Sr., Marie Barney, Bradley Jack, Vivian Jack, Gerald "Bobo" Michel, Saul Terry, Rodney Louie, and Art Adolph. Gerald Michel graciously permitted us to use his photograph of salmon processing in the Fraser Canyon.

Archaeology is never a solo endeavour. We build on the labours of our colleagues and our forebears. This book would not have been possible without the important Mid-Fraser archaeological investigations undertaken in the Fraser Canyon by David Sanger, Arnoud Stryd, Mike Rousseau, and Brian Hayden. We also want to acknowledge the contributions and support of our friends and colleagues Mike Blake, Ken Ames, Dana Lepofsky, Jeanne Arnold, Walter Aufrecht, Geordie Howe, Richard Brolly, Dave Crellin, Karla Kusmer, Cathy Carlson, George Nicholas, Eldon Yellowhorn, Suzanne Villaneuve, Tanja Hoffman, Nadine Gray, Natasha Lyons, Jon Driver, Dave Burley, Knut Fladmark, Jim Chatters, Jim Spafford, Tom Foor, John Douglas, Kelly Dixon, Paul Goldberg, Mike Richards, Dongya Yang, Camilla Speller, Dave Schaepe, Michael Lenert, Nathan Goodale, Guy Cross, Lucy Harris, Naoko Endo, and undoubtedly others whom we have inadvertently left out. We thank Eric Carlson for his commitment to produce the best artistic reconstructions of ancient cultures we have ever seen. We thank Leora Bar-El for her excellent contribution on linguistics. And we also thank Robert C. O'Boyle for his excellent artifact drawings.

This book draws heavily on ethnographic research in the Mid-Fraser Canyon since the time of James Teit's important research over a century ago. We thank, in particular, Dorothy Kennedy, Randy Bouchard, Nancy Turner, Stephen Romanoff, Michael Kew, and Diana Alexander for their significant contributions.

We thank Darcy Cullen at UBC Press for working with us to develop the manuscript and seeing it through the peer review and editorial processes. Finally, we thank the anonymous peer reviewers for their careful engagement with this material and useful comments and advice.

Anna Prentiss

I thank my family for enduring more hot days, cold nights, bears, wild horses, and wilder crew members in archaeological field camps than anyone should have to experience. Their good cheer and good ideas were always essential to the smooth running of our field projects. Duggan Backhouse-Prentiss provided several photographs for this book and served as our project filmmaker during the 2009 campaign at Bridge River. I also thank my parents, Bill and Sally Prentiss, for their always enthusiastic support and for delivering cold beer to my hot, dry field camp at Keatley Creek in 1999.

I would like to extend a special thank you to my crews from various field seasons between 1999 and 2009 in the Mid-Fraser region for their dedication and hard work. Research at the Keatley Creek and Bridge River sites was conducted in collaboration with the St'át'imc Nation, the Pavilion Band (Keatley Creek), and the Bridge River Band (Bridge River). Field and laboratory research was generously funded by the National Science Foundation (Grants BCS-0108795, BCS-0313920, and BCS-0713013), the Wenner-Gren Foundation for Anthropological Research, and the University of Montana. Simon Fraser University's Department of Archaeology generously provided laboratory space for analyses of artifacts, faunal remains, and paleoethnobotanical materials from 1999 to 2004.

A sabbatical from the University of Montana provided time to write this book. Funding for Eric Carlson's travel and research in 2006 was generously provided by Dan Dwyer, vice president for research and development, University of Montana, and Gerald Fetz, dean of the College of Arts and Sciences, University of Montana.

As always, it has been a joy to work with my old friend and partner in crime Ian Kuijt. Although our careers have often taken us in different directions, we always seem to find time to team up again for worthwhile projects, particularly those associated with British Columbia archaeology. Cheers to you, Ian.

Ian Kuijt

I would like to thank Meredith Chesson, wife, editor, and partner, and our eight-year-old daughter, Kaatje Dianne Chesson (who is more of a Kuijt than she knows), for their support over many years of fieldwork in different countries. The "girls" have been partners in the writing of this book. Thanks also to Chris Rodning, Department of Anthropology, Tulane University, who provided a home away from home for writing over the Christmas holidays of 2007 and 2008. Coupled with the warm hospitality of Ralph and Diane Chesson, Chris made it possible to balance the need to write, spend time with the family, and enjoy New Orleans. I would also like to thank my father, Job Kuijt, who over the years has been a great source of inspiration and support and at an early age instilled a strong interest in the people, history, and cultures of British Columbia. While growing up in British Columbia and Alberta, I was deeply interested in the prehistoric and historical past of British Columbia, and this interest was fuelled by my parents, Jean and Job, taking me and my siblings to museums and by our family drives through southern British Columbia each summer.

I would also like to thank numerous field crews, most notably the Slocan Narrows field crew of 2000, who further fuelled my interests in the archaeology and First Nations of Canada. Finally, I would like to thank Anna Prentiss. We have known each other for twenty-four years (we first worked together as graduate school teaching assistants for a physical anthropology class) and have co-directed field projects and edited books together. It continues to be a pleasure to work cooperatively on research and publication projects. Although I now live far away from western North America, working with Anna has served as an important lifeline to British Columbia. My continual thanks for actively involving me in your work and for taking me back, at least intellectually, to where I grew up.

The research and writing of this book was supported by the Social Sciences and Humanities Research Council of Canada; the University of Lethbridge, Alberta; an Alberta Learning Research Excellence Envelope Research grant; and, most recently, the Department of Anthropology, University of Notre Dame.

People of the Middle Fraser Canyon

1
Introduction

We were at our field camp at the ancient housepit village of Keatley Creek, located above the Fraser River near the town of Lillooet, British Columbia. It was a warm and dry evening. The wind gently rustled the cottonwood trees, and the day was finally cooling off. Students sat around the campfire discussing some of the day's work. The day's excavation had been hard but productive. As temperatures crossed into the triple digits (Fahrenheit), the crew exposed remnants of a small house floor that had last been occupied about 1,600 years ago: a shallow cooking feature, a hearth, surrounded by a scattering of salmon and deer bones, a few small stone flakes produced by sharpening a tool, and a single spear point. The students had many questions. How did the ancient ones collect and hunt their food? Where did it come from? Who were the people who lived in this village? How did they come to live here?

Sitting with the students was Desmond Peters Sr., a highly respected elder from the St'át'imc Nation, the indigenous people of the Middle Fraser Canyon area. The students, all around 21 years old and hailing from suburban communities in the United States, automatically looked to him for insight. Where did they find their food? Desmond's eyes scanned the landscape: "This is my refrigerator ... my fish comes from down there ... my deer from over there." His hand waved from west toward the river to the mountains in the east.

Desmond's words and gestures conjured up images of a time long past, a time when the St'át'imc Nation controlled the land and water of the Middle Fraser Canyon around Lillooet, a time when the people collected food, traded, married, feasted, danced, and lived their lives without interference from

Euro-Canadian powers, a time that, in some ways, remains lost in the mists of the past yet is deeply important to members of the St'át'imc Nation.

People are interested in the past for many reasons. Some people seek to understand our collective histories, our origins, and our connections with the land. Where did we come from? How did we get here? Others seek explanation. How did the ancient villages of the Middle Fraser Canyon grow to the point where they supported hundreds if not thousands of people? Why were some of the villages abandoned? Others want to know what the past was like. What was it like to live in the ancient world of the Middle Fraser villages? Still others seek wisdom. Does the record of past cultures hold secrets that could help us today and our children in the future?

This is a book about the archaeology of the Mid-Fraser area. We are archaeologists, and in this book we flesh out an archaeological history that answers some of these questions. We recognize there are other pathways to knowledge of the past, such as oral history, but we leave these approaches and topics to other scholars to explore in greater detail. Our interpretations of archaeological data derived from surveys and excavations are, however, strongly enhanced by reference to ethnographic and oral historical sources, and we reconstruct through prose, photography, and art our visions of culture and ancient history in this area of British Columbia. Throughout the book, we draw upon the knowledge and insight of the St'át'imc people, related to us during interviews and recorded by ethnographers, to aid us in portraying their traditional culture in the recent and more distant past. We address a number of significant cultural developments in the Mid-Fraser Canyon and wider Pacific Northwest region. Some of these topics include the archaeological evidence for early peopling of the region, major changes in hunting and gathering strategies, and the development of permanent villages; the emergence of social status inequality; and the collapse and repopulation of major settlements.

Because archaeological research is ongoing in this region, this book is but another step forward in an exciting process. We hope to offer new information about the past and to stimulate the next generation of research on the long-term history of the St'át'imc people and their ancient lands.

The Middle Fraser Canyon

For those of us who did not grow up in the Middle Fraser Canyon, the first visit to this place generates a lasting impression. This is a land of extremes. Ancient villages, surrounded by mountain peaks, perch on the edge of precipices high above the Fraser River (Figure 1.1). The Mid-Fraser region includes the Fraser River and its flood plains, adjacent talus slopes and terraces, and surrounding mountains and high valleys. The Bridge River empties into the Fraser within

FIGURE 1.1 The Mid-Fraser Canyon north of Lillooet, showing the narrow river valley, high benches, and mountains.

Photograph by Ian Kuijt

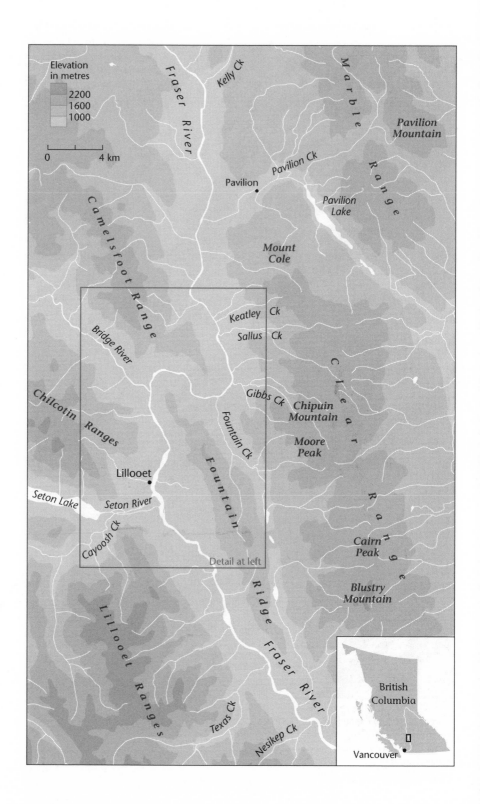

Elevation
in metres

2200
1600
1000

0   4 km

Fraser River

Kelly Ck

Marble Range

Pavilion Mountain

Pavilion Ck

Pavilion

Pavilion Lake

Camelsfoot Range

Mount Cole

Keatley Ck

Sallus Ck

Bridge River

C l e a r

Chilcotin Ranges

Gibbs Ck

Chipuin Mountain

Fountain Ck

Moore Peak

Lillooet

Fountain

R a n g e

Seton Lake

Seton River

Cairn Peak

Cayoosh Ck

Detail at left

Blustry Mountain

Lillooet Ranges

Ridge Fraser River

British Columbia

Texas Ck

Nesikep Ck

Vancouver

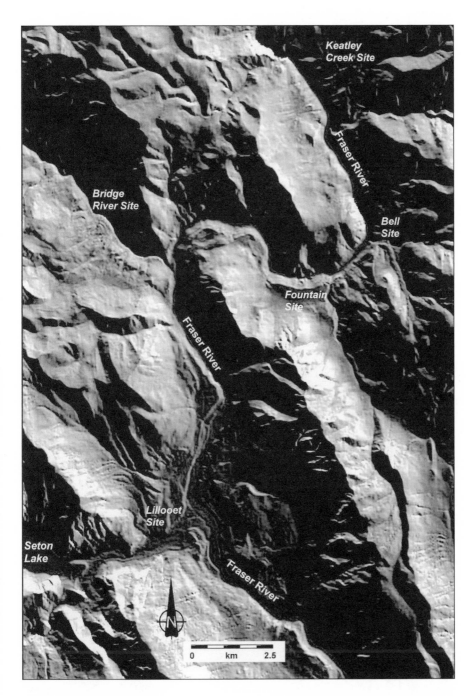

FIGURE 1.2 Map of the Middle
Fraser Canyon with aerial
photograph showing major
archaeological sites.

this area, adding to the rushing flow of water and creating the most famous St'át'imc fishing spot. The Fraser River is also fed by a multitude of creeks, including Cayoosh, Lochnore, Nesikep, Texas, Gibbs, Fountain, Sallus, Keatley, Pavilion, and Kelly. Collectively, this flow of water travels several hundred miles south toward Vancouver and empties into the Pacific Ocean. A number of mountain peaks – including Blustry Mountain, Cairn Peak, Chipuin Mountain, Fountain Ridge, Moore Peak, Mount Cole, and Pavilion Mountain – dwarf the canyon's steep wall (Figure 1.2).

Visitors immediately feel the effects of the dry, hot, summer air. Technically, the climate is semi-arid. Vegetation ranges from sagebrush and bunch grass on the river terraces to pine forests on the mountain slopes, from open grasslands in higher elevation meadows to dense Douglas fir and spruce in mountain forests and alpine tundra on the highest peaks. The region supports a remarkable range of edible plant resources, including a wide range of berries, roots or geophytes, greens, seeds, nuts, and edible bark. Rich berry species grow along the dry river terraces and well into the montane forests. Forests and meadows produce tree bark, seeds, nuts, and many greens. Open mountain slopes, meadows, and grasslands contain large quantities of root foods. Within all of this bounty, the river held the most appeal for human inhabitants in the past.

A first-time visitor to the Mid-Fraser Canyon, touring on higher terraces or hiking in the mountains, would likely fail to recognize many cultural features hundreds of metres below. Deep in the canyon, scattered along the riverbanks, are hundreds of traditional fish-drying racks, still used today. By drawing attention to the landscape's vast fish resources, they serve as cultural iconography. In fact, the Fraser River is rich with a variety of fish (Figure 1.3), the most famous being salmon, which pass through the Mid-Fraser region during their annual spawning runs. Four species are known to have made their way up to this region in the past: spring or chinook salmon in the early warm season, sockeye in mid- to late summer, and coho in the early fall. Pink salmon rarely made it much past the mouth of the South Thompson. The river is also home to some large sturgeon and a variety of smaller fish. And although they lie outside of viewing range from the canyon, nearby lakes, rivers, and larger creeks are home to trout.

With a little luck, a hiker in the forests of the mountain slopes may see a number of familiar land mammals. Deer, scattered through much of the landscape, live at higher elevations in summer and lower elevations in the winter. Bighorn or mountain sheep and elk still exist in the area, but their numbers have dropped since ancient times (Figure 1.4). Moose were never common, though a rare one is seen on occasion. Mountain goats can still be found in the higher mountains west of the Fraser Canyon. The Mid-Fraser region continues to be home to black and brown bears, mountain lions, bobcats, and coyotes.

FIGURE 1.3 Fish-drying racks
along the Fraser River.

Photograph by Ian Kuijt

FIGURE 1.4 Bighorn sheep
feeding near Lytton.
Photograph by Ian Kuijt

Beavers inhabit forested areas, and a variety of smaller rodents and rabbits live
in the area.

The St'át'imc Nation

Although many people now live along the Mid-Fraser Canyon, the St'át'imc
people have lived here the longest. (*St'át'imc* is a recent transcription syn-
onymous with a number of other spellings, including *Stl'átl'imx, Stla-Sli-muk,*
and *StlatlumH.*) The St'át'imc are Salish-speaking people (see Appendix) and
are typically identified as Upper Lillooet in many books and academic articles.
The term *Lillooet* is derived from *Lilwat,* a name used in the past to identify the
Lower Lillooet people or those who lived to the south between Anderson and
Harrison lakes. On a practical level, the St'át'imc Nation is subdivided into a
number of bands that have their own chiefs, councillors, lands, resources, and

traditions. These bands include Cayoosh Creek (Selcw'el'was), Lillooet (T'itq'et), Shalalth (Tsal'alh), Bridge River (Xwisten), Fountain (Xa'xlip), and Pavilion (Tsk'way'laxw).

Drawing upon the perspective of archaeology and ethnography, we attempt to understand some of the ancient history of the St'át'imc people and their ancestors. The archaeological record, as material evidence, provides a window into the past. It is, however, only one of several sources of knowledge on the history of indigenous peoples. Other sources include traditional knowledge in the form of passed-down stories about actual and mythical figures and recorded history since the coming of Europeans. Ethnographers such as James Teit and writers such as Trefor Smith also recorded traditional knowledge.

Traditional stories tell of a time when powerful transformers walked the earth. According to one story, transformers were sent to Earth by Old Man to make it habitable. In this story, Coyote, Mink, and the Black Bears travelled up from Lower St'át'imc territory on Lower Lillooet Lakes into Upper St'át'imc lands. While doing so, they taught the people how to do essential tasks such as catching and processing fish. They established peaceful relations between the Lower and Upper St'át'imc people. In another story, Old Man visited Earth to finish the work of the transformers. He turned bad people into birds, rocks, and animals and provided the others with places to live. Still other stories describe the development of traditional villages and activities. In the story of Nkolstem, for example, an abandoned boy helped by the sun eventually gains the powers of a transformer, marries into a new village, and teaches the people how to make and use nets and traps.

Historical literature records the more recent history of the St'át'imc. The history of Native and European interaction in Canada is both tragic and transcendent. Newcomers brought early economic opportunity in the form of trade. This was not to last, however. Epidemics wiped out villages, and government restrictions – for example, those mandated by the Indian Act of 1876 – forced the St'át'imc people from the land and denied them access to traditional cultural practices and resources. Today, times are changing, but it is still an uphill battle for First Nations to redress old wounds, fight for control of traditional resources, and revitalize their rich culture.

Archaeology offers an important complementary perspective on ancient history and plays a role in today's cultural developments. At its most basic level, an archaeological perspective is based upon the recovery, description, and interpretation of material evidence such as stone tools, cooking features, and animal bones. Working closely with First Nations groups, archaeologists today provide insight into cultural developments from hundreds to thousands of years ago in the Mid-Fraser Canyon. The results of archaeological research have been useful in providing hands-on educational opportunities for a range of people, from children to elders, from people living along the Fraser River to university students living in cities. This research also offers hard data on traditional settlement and subsistence, which can be used in the legal arena.

Archaeological research will be essential for overcoming some of the obvious and not so obvious effects of the Indian Act. This early piece of Canadian legislation and its subsequent amendments had a wide variety of deleterious effects on Aboriginal people. The act provided the government with the exclusive privilege to define who was an Indian, and although it permitted Indian people to hunt and fish in traditional ways, it required them to obtain permission to leave government-defined reserves. Further, Indians were denied Canadian citizenship and were prevented from governing themselves. Government agents controlled most of the actions and activities on reserves, including access to and use of government money. Finally, the act furthered a process known today as ethnocide by making many traditional activities such as the potlatch illegal.

The Indian Act also had more surreptitious effects, the most critical being the consequences of its power to define Indian bands as social and bureaucratic organizations and to determine who qualified as a Status Indian. By redefining Indianness, the government altered traditional social relationships that had been defined by membership in a wide range of organizations, including families, multifamily house groups, clans or clan-like groups, villages, and possibly even multivillage polities. An unanticipated effect of the act's definitions of *bands* was its impact on early anthropologists, who often borrowed the term to describe contemporary and past groups without questioning the term's validity or meaning. James Teit, for example, subdivided the St'át'imc into four bands, which he named Lillooet River, Pemberton, Lake, and Fraser River. In this book, we avoid these terms and seek evidence of traditional social organization that predates the Indian Act.

Archaeology of the Middle Fraser Canyon

The archaeology of the Middle Fraser Canyon, which is scattered throughout the landscape, is one of the world's most valuable records of the human past. In some places, evidence consists of little more than a stone tool dug up in a flower bed; in other places, it is manifested in rock art, ancient paintings, or incised depictions on rock walls. Evidence of the past is also spectacularly visible in the form of ancient villages, as seen at the Bridge River or Keatley Creek sites.

The significance of the Mid-Fraser archaeological record is not measured merely in the frequencies of sites: many of these sites provide a spectacular record of human occupation. The preservation of organic materials such as bark baskets is outstanding, an extremely rare occurrence in most archaeological sites.

FIGURE 1.5 Aerial view of a housepit in the Stein River Valley.

Photograph by Ian Kuijt

Normally it is in sites that are under water or located in permanently dry rock shelters or caves that materials are well-preserved. Dry caves and water-logged sites do not favour the growth of organisms associated with the decay of organic materials. It is not unusual to find bones, roof timbers, and even fragments of basketry in some dry deposits in Middle Fraser canyon villages.

The villages are composed of large numbers of pithouses: round-shaped residences sunk into the ground and between 5 and 20 metres in diameter (Figure 1.5). Houses generally contain the remains of living floors, which preserve evidence of activity areas associated with the day-to-day activities of household members. The floors are surrounded by rim middens (refuse heaps) composed of discarded food, broken tools, and old hearth and roof materials. These middens are invaluable time capsules that reflect the histories of the houses.

Housepit villages such as Keatley Creek and Bridge River developed over hundreds of years. The archaeological record of many housepits formed through regular reoccupations organized around cleaning and rebuilding activities. An early researcher in this area, Teit recorded that people constructed them by first digging a pit and then acquiring wood for upright posts and horizontal beams (Figure 1.6). The wood superstructure was then built by using strong upright posts to support the horizontal beams. Layers of timbers and matting covered the roof, and in some cases sediments sealed the construction, offering extra insulation (Figure 1.7). People dug pits indoors and lined them with birch bark to store food. They constructed hearths and made benches and storage platforms. Aside from regular cleaning, a family could live in such a house for 10 to 20 years without significant architectural modification.

At some point, however, wood would become dangerously old, and vermin could infest portions of the roof and floor. In these cases, good timbers would be salvaged and the old roof burned down. Families returning from late warm-season food-gathering trips would then rebuild roofs and floors before they re-inhabited the houses. Sometimes rebuilding involved removing all of the burned roof materials and scraping out the old floors. At other times, as with many Bridge River houses, the people would remove burned and collapsed roof materials but not the floors. Instead, they would import new sediments and dump them over the old floors, thereby preserving an even more detailed record of household life over multiple generations.

The materials found at Mid-Fraser villages are invaluable. But even more important is the potential of archaeology and ethnography to answer questions about past human cultures and the processes of culture change. Early archaeological researchers sought answers to historical questions such as when did First Nations people first come to the region? What kind of tools and features did they use, and when did the pithouse villages emerge? What relationships did

▲ FIGURE 1.6 Cross-section
view of a housepit.
Illustration by Eric S. Carlson

▼ FIGURE 1.7 Historical
photograph of a Plateau
pithouse, ca. late nineteenth
century.

these people have with their neighbours? Building upon this descriptive foundation, archaeologists during the 1980s and '90s began to address new questions, questions on the social and economic world of these villages. Why did the villages evolve? Could the Mid-Fraser villages be explained in relation to changes in ancient environments? Alternatively, was the development of the large villages and their large houses the work of social changes, for instance, the result of actions by emerging leaders and their followers? Archaeologists working in the region continue to explore these questions and many more specific ones. Do the Mid-Fraser villages reflect the emergence of larger sociopolitical units such as chiefdoms? Did shamans live in the villages and, if so, what was their role? Were the early villages organized around clan-like social groups?

Creating an Archaeological History of the Mid-Fraser

This book offers a long-term history of continuity and cultural change in the Mid-Fraser Canyon, a voyage into the past via a crude time machine. We recognize that although our primary focus is the archaeological record, the indigenous peoples of the region did not exist in isolation. Developments in the larger region sometimes had profound effects on the Mid-Fraser cultures. We therefore provide significant archaeological background on regional developments for the period before the emergence of the great Mid-Fraser villages some 2,000 years ago. But before we travel to the ancient past, we must develop some appreciation for how the past is reconstructed using archaeological information. How is archaeological research undertaken, and how are different terms used?

Archaeological Basics

Archaeological research has many goals. One is to understand the past in the sense that archaeological studies can help bring to life images, stories, and objects of ancient cultures. Archaeologists can describe these cultures in a myriad of ways, ranging from simple inventories of artifacts to complex reconstructions of settlement and subsistence, social organization, and even elements of belief systems. Once archaeologists place these cultures in time using radiocarbon dating, they can construct their cultural history. Cultural histories provide basic information, which leads to explanatory research. Since the 1960s, archaeologists have been engaged in understanding the reasons that various cultural forms developed, persisted, and sometimes failed or disappeared. This type of research requires extensive collaboration with other scientists such as paleoecologists, who reconstruct ancient environments. Explanations for change range from those focused on external factors, such as environmental conditions, to internal factors, such as human technological developments. Culture change over the long term requires an understanding of both.

FIGURE 1.8 A cache pit
feature from 1,250 years ago.
This feature was partially
excavated in Housepit 16 at
the Bridge River site in 2009.
Photograph by Anna M. Prentiss

Reconstructing past cultures from material remains begins with artifacts, portable items made by people. Artifact function tells us about activities; their shape, style, and design can provide insights into past social organization and identity. Artifacts in the Mid-Fraser Canyon range from stone tools and debris from their manufacture to fragments of birch bark baskets. Artifacts differ from ecofacts, natural items such as animal bones and plant remains that are recovered from archaeological sites. Ecofacts tell us about subsistence, technologies (roof beams, for example), and past environments. Features are nonportable items made by people. Hearths and cache pits (Figure 1.8) are features, as are housepits and rock art. Features tell us about shelter and the built environment, about cooking techniques, and about any intangible elements of culture that may be embodied in artistic images painted on or pecked from stone walls. Archaeological sites are made up of spatially clustered sets of artifacts or features. Sites can range in scale and complexity from a small cluster of stone artifacts, perhaps the result of a brief episode involving stone tool manufacturing, to an immense housepit village such as Keatley Creek, which has more than 115 houses and nearly endless artifacts and smaller features.

▲ FIGURE 1.9 Graduate student Lisa Smith conducting excavations in Housepit 20 at the Bridge River site in 2009. Notice the large cache pit feature to her right.
Photograph by Anna M. Prentiss

▶ FIGURE 1.10 Students Cynthia Kazanis and Duggan Backhouse-Prentiss screen for artifacts and animal bones at the Bridge River site in 2009.
Photograph by Anna M. Prentiss

When archaeologists excavate an archaeological site, they destroy the spatial context of the archaeological materials. It is therefore critical that they record the site in significant detail so they can reconstruct it in three dimensions back in the laboratory. Archaeologists therefore excavate sites slowly (Figure 1.9). An old archaeology professor once remarked, "Archaeology is not a spectator sport." Archaeologists remove sediments in each layer carefully to expose cultural materials. They sieve sediment to collect artifacts and bones (Figure 1.10) or save it for further laboratory analysis. Although slow and methodical, the long-term results of this painstaking work can be amazing. Over weeks, months and, in some cases, years, archaeologists map artifacts and features as they are exposed. They collect artifacts and sample features for further laboratory studies.

In general, systematic documentation generates two types of spatial recordings, one horizontal and one vertical. Plan view maps show horizontal spatial

relationships between artifacts and features. A horizontal plan map of a housepit floor, for example, illustrates several activity areas from above and highlights clusters of artifacts associated with a hearth feature and food storage pits. The second kind of map is known as a vertical profile. Much like a cut birthday cake, this view of archaeological deposits reveals the layers excavated in an archaeological site. Vertical profiles of the Mid-Fraser villages can be complex. A single profile, for example, may illustrate dozens of superimposed layers, including a series of housepit floors and a complex set of roof and rim midden layers (see Figures 4.8 and 7.2 for examples).

Dating and Cultural Chronologies

One of the first questions people ask when they visit archaeological sites is, "How old is it?" Archaeologists answer this question using a variety of creative methods. A quick and easy approach is to compare artifacts of known ages. For example, if a specific type of shaped projectile point, dated to 3,000 years ago at one village, is found at a second village, then it is likely that the second projectile point also dates to 3,000 years ago. However, the occupants of the second village might have scavenged the artifact from an older site. To get around problems associated with the reuse of artifacts, archaeologists examine stratigraphy (or layering) in sites to determine which layers are shallower (and presumably younger) and which are deeper (and likely older).

Neither of these techniques, however, provides a precise estimate of age. To accomplish this, Mid-Fraser archaeologists rely on radiocarbon dating. Radiocarbon (or carbon-14) dating is predicated on the knowledge that unstable radioactive isotopes such as carbon-14, which are found in all living things, will break down at a known rate when an organism dies. In the case of carbon-14, it takes about 5,730 years for half of the carbon isotope to disappear (known as a half–life) and another 5,730 years for the next half to go, and so on. Scientists can use charcoal or bone to measure how much carbon-14 remains and calculate the age when the creature or plant died. Unfortunately, the starting amount of carbon-14 varies, depending on how much carbon-14 is in the environment during the life span of the organism. As a result, there can be a mismatch between the radiocarbon date and the actual calendar year of the organism's death. Scientists can use a mathematical procedure that compares the results of radiocarbon testing to tree-ring chronologies to arrive at an adjusted, calibrated calendar date. We rely on the latter method throughout this book.

Once they have analyzed all artifacts, ecofacts, and features in the laboratory, archaeologists can start to reconstruct archaeological chronologies. When a general cultural pattern is recognized to persist for a significant period of time, archaeologists define it as a tradition. They have identified two traditions on the Canadian Plateau: the Nesikep and Plateau Pithouse traditions. Archaeologists also identify horizons. A horizon consists of a geographical distribution of similar cultural materials for a particular area and for a much shorter period of time than a tradition. For example, the Plateau Pithouse tradition is subdivided into three horizons: the Shuswap, Plateau, and Kamloops. Traditions may also be subdivided on a more local level into phases. The late cultural chronology of the Mid-Fraser Canyon, for example, was originally divided into the Kettlebrook, Lillooet, and Fountain phases.

Interpreting the nature of archaeological cultures can be challenging. Generally speaking, archaeological cultures are based on distinctive artifacts and features that reflect a common cultural heritage. This does not necessarily mean that an archaeological culture is the same thing as a linguistic or socio-ethnic group: people who spoke different languages often used the same items.

Likewise, the Shuswap horizon does not refer to the Shuswap (or Secwepemc) people, though it is entirely likely that Secwepemc ancestors did participate in cultural activities that led to the formation of an archaeological record that might be lumped into the Shuswap horizon. But it is equally possible that Lillooet and Thompson ancestors also played a role in the Shuswap horizon. The inhabitants of the Mid-Fraser villages during the last 2,000 years were likely ancestral St'át'imc, though individuals and groups from other areas might have contributed as well. Continuity and consistency in artifact styles and technologies, settlement patterns, and the remembrances of knowledgeable elders support this argument.

Archaeological Analysis: Reconstructing Ancient Cultures

Archaeological research is a complex collaborative process. Gone are the days when archaeologists excavated a site and merely collected and photographed the best tools and art forms. Today, archaeologists collect an enormous range of data that require an almost endless array of analytical specialists. The ultimate goal of modern archaeological work is to develop a detailed understanding of the organization of ancient communities. But to get there we must first figure out the site, as one archaeologist put it. This means sorting out the myriad natural and cultural processes that affected the distribution of materials found in any archaeological site.

People often ask, how do archaeologists know where to dig? Archaeologists use a range of approaches – from probabilistic sampling (driven by statistics) to simple judgmental approaches ("this looks like a likely spot") – to define excavation areas. Archaeologists can now employ sophisticated research methods that allow them to look below the ground surface (Box 1.1). Termed geophysical research, these methods provide a rough method for identifying the location of larger features but not individual objects. These methods offer new ways to learn about what is below the surface and to target specific areas for excavation. Excavations at the Bridge River village, for example, have been guided by the use of techniques such as magnetometry, electrical conductivity, and ground-penetrating radar, all designed to provide insight into the distributions of buried cultural features such as floors, hearths, and storage pits without having to dig anywhere (see Figure 4.12 in Chapter 4). Once geophysical signatures have been defined, excavation units can be more carefully situated to excavate areas thought to reflect particular activities such as cooking, food storage, or tool manufacture.

The archaeological record of housepits is complicated. Archaeologists must sort out how stratigraphy, the layers of sediments in an archaeological site, were formed. For example, archaeologists commonly expose what they interpret to be housepit floors. These floors typically are made of clay-rich sediments that contain artifacts, animal bones, and features such as hearths, post-holes (places where house posts were sunk), and cache pits (storage features). The investigators then face a number of questions. What are the floor sediments, and where did they come from? How did they come to be distributed on the house floor? Is there evidence for particular activities embedded within the sediments themselves? To answer these questions, we rely on careful studies of sediment contents and structure or fabric. The best researchers are those with geological and archaeological training, those who can study microscopic layers through micromorphology. Micromorphological analysis requires collecting intact blocks of sediment, impregnating them with resin, sectioning the blocks into thin layers invisible to the human eye, and carefully inspecting the layers under a high-powered microscope.

The collection of archaeological sediments enhances our understanding of other aspects of village life. Soil chemists look for evidence of cultural activities that involved food processing by measuring variations in chemical characteristics (calcium and organic phosphorus, for example). Soil chemists can also use a technique known as flotation to sort sediments and find small botanical remains. They mix sediments with water to separate light botanical materials from heavy soils. The botanical remains are then identified by a paleoethnobotanist, who

BOX 1.1 ARCHAEOLOGICAL SPECIALTIES

What are some of the different subfields of archaeology? The field of archaeology includes many areas of specialization, and each area has its own unique approach to data collection and analysis. The following are relevant to this book.

Archaeological geophysics is the study of archaeological sites and sediments using techniques of applied geophysics. Archaeogeophysicists use a variety of techniques to image buried materials in archaeological sites before excavation. Magnetometry (or, more technically, magnetic susceptibility) allows the investigator to find anomalies or interruptions in the earth's magnetic sphere. These anomalies are normally magnetized sediments that resulted from high temperatures, for instance, from

hearths, burning roofs, or roasting ovens. Electrical conductivity and resistivity studies rely on instruments that measure interruptions to electrical currents passed through sediments on archaeological sites. These techniques are useful for finding buried house foundations, floors and, on occasion, graves. Ground-penetrating radar allows the researcher to create images or profiles of sedimentary cross-sections similar to those created by archaeologists who map layers of sediment in the wall of an excavation unit.

Geoarchaeology is the study of the formation of sediments in archaeological sites. Geoarchaeologists collect data on the form, structure, composition, and chemical characteristics of sediments to figure out the natural and can provide insights into the use of plants for food, cooking, bedding, and architecture in ancient housepits (see Box 1.1).

A wide range of animal bones are recovered from excavated sediments during archaeological research projects. Zooarchaeologists (see Box 1.1) study these remains to identify species and anatomical parts. In addition, they examine each bone for marks that reveal something about how the animal died, whether it was butchered or cooked by people, and how it came to be deposited in the archaeological record. Archaeological chemists may also measure variation in bone chemistry to determine what the animal was eating. Zooarchaeologists provide important information on ancient diets and, along with paleoethnobotanists, insight into the ecological contexts of housepit occupations.

Stone tools and chipping debris, or debitage, are probably the most common items derived from housepit excavations. Lithic technologists study how ancient stone artifacts were made and used. These specialists collect information on the techniques of tool manufacture. They may, for example, identify the stages through which an ancient knapper (stoneworker) designed and crafted a tool. The analyst then looks at the edges of a tool under a microscope to define patterns of use-wear – scratches, abrasions, and polishes – that reflect how a tool was used. Lithic technologists not only want to understand tool technology and use patterns, they also seek to explain what archaeologists call the organization

cultural processes that affected their development. One particularly advanced approach to geoarchaeology is the study of sediment micromorphology. Investigators collect intact blocks of sediment (for example, from an excavation unit wall), impregnate it with resin, and use a thin, polished section to look at the microscopic structure or fabric of the sediment. When applied to Mid-Fraser housepits, this method allows investigators to come to conclusions about how floors or rim middens were created or came into being.

Paleoethnobotany is the study of plant remains from archaeological sites. These items are normally recovered from sediment samples, but they can also include much bigger elements such as house posts or roof beams.

Paleoethnobotanists analyze data sets collected from diverse sources: macrobotanical items, burned seeds, plant pieces, pollen, and even phytoliths or silica "skeletons" from plant cells. These researchers reconstruct elements of past foodways, technologies, and environments.

Zooarchaeology is the study of animal remains from archaeological contexts. Zooarchaeologists analyze animal bones, shell, hair, and other remains of past animal life. Complementing the work of paleoethnobotanists, zooarchaeologists reconstruct how people acquired, processed, and consumed animal foods. They also use animal remains to enhance our understanding of past ecosystems.

of lithic technology, or the underlying cultural and economic logic behind tool production and use. Did the ancient ones have particular tools designed for specific functions? Did they set aside particular raw materials for particular tool types? Were tools made from rare and coveted materials? Is there evidence for trade in tools or raw materials between villages?

Artifacts made from soft organic materials are also recovered from Mid-Fraser archaeological sites, but they are less common than stone artifacts. Production of artifacts from wood, hide, feather, and plant fibres was probably common in the ancient past. These materials were essential for the creation of such things as nets, clothing, furniture, decorations, baskets, trays, and utensils. Yet they are not common in the archaeological record because they decompose far more easily than substances such as stone and bone. They tend to be found in places where sediments are dry and chemically neutral or nonacidic. When found, such items provide priceless insight into facets of ancient cultures less easily reconstructed than from stone and bone.

In today's scientific world, our understanding of the past is advanced daily. Geneticists, for example, are working with archaeologists to extract genetic material from animal bones and, potentially, soil. This research is in the earliest stages but will offer profound insight into patterns of human and animal migration and evolution.

Archaeological Inference: What Was It Like in the Past?

Because we cannot physically go back in time and observe the actions of ancient peoples, we must draw inferences from materials excavated in archaeological sites. Archaeological inferences can be a tricky business. Archaeologists must first work from what we call frames of reference. How do we recognize an activity area associated with normal day-to-day family food preparation and tool manufacture on a housepit floor? How do we know whether there is evidence of status distinctions among families or houses? To answer these questions, we seek to understand the links between human behaviour and its archaeological residue. Drawing upon other work, in this book we explore a number of indicators of behaviours, ranging from tool manufacture to food preparation to social relations. To do this, we examine ethnographic accounts of human practice, such as construction of housepits, to develop their likely archaeological hallmarks. If this information is not available, we rely on experimental archaeological studies designed to fill in gaps in our knowledge. The trick is to maintain an open mind so we can recognize when patterns from the past differ from predictions drawn from ethnographies. Cultures of the ancient past were not always organized quite like those of recent times.

Because similar archaeological signatures can develop from more than one process, we must be careful to consider a wide range of alternative explanations for patterns in the archaeological record. This need for care is nowhere more evident than in the study of animal bones. Archaeologists, for example, debate how dogs were used in Mid-Fraser villages. During excavations at Keatley Creek village, Brian Hayden, an archaeologist from Simon Fraser University, exposed a set of dog bones in a deep cache pit. All told, the bones included the remains of at least one dog that had been killed by a blow to the back of the head. Canine tooth marks on many of the bones indicated that the dog had then been ravaged by other dogs. Archaeologists offer two interpretations. Some argue that the dog had been killed as part of a ritual sacrifice and left to decompose outside the housepit. The bones were then collected and placed in the cache pit. Others argue that the villagers had dealt with a problem dog by killing it and disposing of its body in the pit. To date, the debate has not been settled, though the latter hypothesis carries fewer assumptions. Resolution of such debates requires careful analysis of animal bones to define the post-mortem history of individual animals. It leads archaeologists to collect data on bone breakage, gnawing from other animals, and butchery and cooking marks.

Another important discussion centres on social status distinctions in the past and how they are reflected in artifact distributions on housepit floors. Archaeologists generally assume that status differences among family groups are reflected in some people having more and others having less. For instance, some researchers argue that variations in the numbers of ornaments such as beads, high-cost tools such as ground-stone bowls, rare raw materials such as obsidian or nephrite jade, or the use of special foods such as dog, mountain goat, or elk reflect status differences within communities. But it is not always clear whether some are clustered because of status, the functional use of a given area, or tool and food refuse disposal patterns. On the floor of Housepit 7 at Keatley Creek, for example, high counts of deer bones tend to be associated with relatively low numbers of salmon bones and vice versa. Does this difference mark social distinctions (for example, wealthy folks ate deer and poorer folks ate fish), or does it reflect variability in consumption or discard contexts (for example, dried salmon was eaten in most areas but deer only in certain spots)?

The lesson learned from these discussions is that archaeologists must develop arguments and make conclusions based on many independent sources of information. Explaining the development of animal bone assemblages requires the careful assessment of the formation processes associated with each bone. Likewise, at the more grand scale of sociopolitical inference, multiple categories of artifacts, animal bones, and plant remains must be examined in the hope that all, or at least most, will point to a single coherent conclusion. Otherwise, we must think further about the nature of these patterns.

Finally, it is important to recognize that there is substantial cultural continuity between the ancient past and the present in the Mid-Fraser area. The cultural memory of St'át'imc elders reaches back deep into time, providing an incredibly valuable and complementary resource for interpreting the archaeological record. Yet we must also watch out for what archaeologist Martin Wobst (1978) calls the tyranny of the ethnographic record. Cultures change over time, and there might have been cultural traditions and structures that differ from the contemporary ethnographic record.

Archaeologists often use an interpretive strategy known as the direct historical approach to understanding the past. Proponents of this approach assume that knowledge of recent cultural patterns can be used to interpret older materials. We can rely on this approach to a degree in the Mid-Fraser context. We must beware, however, of making simplistic analogies between the recent historical period and the more ancient past. There have been significant opportunities for change, and much traditional knowledge has been lost with the passing of earlier generations, particularly when European diseases affected Mid-Fraser peoples so badly.

The archaeological record of the Mid-Fraser Canyon demonstrates that communities were considerably larger in the ancient past. The arrangement of houses in some communities might have been substantially different from more recent arrangements. Their arrangement may imply variation in social groups, ritual practices, and sociopolitical units unknown to 20th-century ethnographers and their informants. These patterns call for alternative interpretations and remain a fundamental challenge for archaeologists working in the region. By acknowledging that many cultural systems might have been even more complex in the past, and by recognizing the unique histories of these people, we affirm our opposition to theoretically and ethically bankrupt concepts of primitivism and progress. We join many of today's archaeologists in rejecting concepts of cultural evolution as a simple march of progress.

Visions of the Past: Art and Prose

There are many ways to convey interpretations of the past. The standard approach taken by professional archaeologists is through technical writing in excavation and survey reports and in scholarly journals and books. Fewer archaeologists have tried to synthesize their research into works for a more general audience. Fewer yet have tried to integrate prose and artistic images. Our hope is that this book transports readers into the past through the use of artistic reconstructions and two forms of prose: discussions of archaeological research and fictional accounts of life in the Mid-Fraser villages.

What did people, villages, and the insides of the pithouses look like? With such a rich archaeological and oral history record as exists today, we can visualize how past peoples gathered together, ate, shared, fought, and worked in different places over time. Art is an effective and powerful means of bringing the past to life, but doing so is surprisingly complicated and challenging. The most challenging issue facing would-be illustrators is identifying unconscious biases about what the past should look like. Our understanding of the past is by necessity coloured in some measure by contemporary ideas about both the past and the present and the relationship between the two. For example, in many artistic reconstructions of the ancient past, women are rarely seen, and when they are present, they are generally depicted in passive roles in the background of the main action.

As we developed the drawings for this book, we sought to overcome as many biases as possible while developing archaeologically informed but ethnographically sensitive views of the past. To accomplish this, we engaged artist Eric Carlson to develop the drawings in collaboration with the St'át'imc people. Carlson travelled to the Mid-Fraser region during fishing season in August 2005. He met with elders and other knowledgeable persons such as Gerald "Bobo" Michel (Figure 1.11) and was taken to a number of critical cultural sites, including the Six Mile Rapids' fishing rocks and ancient villages such as Keatley Creek and Bridge River. He photographed and sketched these places and, interacting with his tour guides and elders, began to develop ideas for the illustrations.

Following his visit, Carlson came to us for our input, and he began to create sketches. Once the first round of drawings was produced, we sent them back to participants in the Mid-Fraser communities for their comments. This process was repeated until everyone was satisfied with the depictions. The illustrations provide a rich addition to the text; they convey images of a past long gone yet in many ways still alive in the knowledge, words, and actions of the St'át'imc people. We do recognize, however, that the illustrations are contemporary creations that will be subject to critique and modification as new information and interpretations come to light.

We also include fictional (yet archaeologically accurate) snapshots of life in the Mid-Fraser Canyon and elsewhere to complement Carlson's images. These vignettes draw on the ethnographic record and our own time spent with St'át'imc people. Like the drawings, they are modern depictions of the past and no doubt refect the assumptions of their creators. They too will inevitably take on new meanings, depending on the perspective of the viewers. We believe, however, that the vignettes create a sense of immediacy with the past. Some may criticize the vignettes and drawings for failing to reflect ancient Aboriginal mindsets or logic. Our response is that this is an impossible task because we are not those

FIGURE 1.11 Gerald "Bobo"
Michel demonstrates trad-
itional salmon processing for
photographer Eric Carlson.

people. We instead seek to set a stage upon which the reader's own imagination can operate. We also seek to convey a sense of some of the realities that people likely faced in the past. Sometimes food was abundant and the weather was good; at other times, food sources failed, and the people faced tough choices.

Debating Archaeology and the Goals of This Book

This is a book about the long-term history of the indigenous peoples of the Middle Fraser Canyon and their immediate environs, as reconstructed primarily from the archaeological record. The Mid-Fraser peoples did not live in isolation. Therefore, to effectively reconstruct their ancient history, we must examine the surrounding areas, particularly elsewhere on the Plateau and the Northwest Coast. We must also address some of the biggest topics of debate in the archaeological community. How and why does culture change? What caused ancient population movements? Why did permanent villages develop? What were the underlying causes of social inequality?

Archaeologists of the Pacific Northwest have paid significant attention to questions about village development and the emergence of ranked societies, as well as the broader problem of general culture change and human migrations. Because archaeologists bring different theoretical perspectives to the archaeological record, interpretations can vary, sometimes significantly, and lead to disagreement and debate. Constructive debate and discussion are good because they drive science forward. Archaeology is no exception to this rule. Debates allow us to resolve differing opinions, or at least draw attention to a range of possible points of view. Throughout this book, we outline what we consider to be the facts of archaeological research and then review current debates. Obviously, we have our own perspectives on the record and, consequently, on the history of ancient Mid-Fraser cultures. Although we present this book as a series of arguments, ones that we think are convincing (see Box 1.2), we recognize that some positions are likely to change as more data become available. We try to identify for the reader when we feel there is strong evidence for our interpretations; in other cases, we draw attention to where more work is needed.

Our primary goal in writing this book is to convey the rich archaeological heritage of the people of the Middle Fraser Canyon, the St'át'imc. Although we rely substantially on archaeological knowledge, we also illustrate how that knowledge is informed by our understanding of traditional St'át'imc culture. For, indeed, the past has not been forgotten in the Mid-Fraser Canyon. The people have seen much change. They live in yet another phase of what we will demonstrate is a long and distinctive history.

BOX 1.2 CONCEPTUALIZING THE PAST: THEORETICAL FRAMEWORKS

Throughout this book, we offer arguments about the activities of ancient human groups and the processes of long-term cultural change and stability. At times, anthropological archaeologists use a bewildering array of theoretical approaches in their research. Some view culture as an adaptive system that evolves from one state to another, much like stages of succession in ecosystems. From this perspective, the shift from a hunting and gathering to an agricultural system is similar to the transformation of an open pine forest to a dense hardwoods ecosystem in the sense that outside forces (such as climate change) precipitate changes to the ecosystem. For cultural contexts, the transformation may mean shifts in human birth and death rates, changes in food production systems, and even alterations in human belief systems and ritual practices. This approach has been critiqued for its lack of interest in the activities of individual persons. Other researchers see culture as simply the byproduct of a seemingly endless stream of interpersonal actions and negotiations. People using this approach are less interested in the underlying economics of human organization and more interested in the thoughts of individual cultural agents. A different group of scholars known as evolutionary archaeologists see culture as an inheritance system much

like that of biology. Whereas genetic codes are inherited in biology, in the cultural context, it is cultural information that is inherited and subsequently manifested as variability in human behaviour.

The framework employed in this book relies on the assumption that individual humans and human groups play an active role in the creation and transmission of cultural concepts and meaning. We also recognize, however, that the cultural process is complicated and that persistent patterns of human behaviour can have social and ecological consequences. At best, the application of efficient economic strategies can lead to success as measured in the continuation of that associated lifeway or growth in the human population. At worst, some strategies lead down blind alleys to historical dead ends and, unfortunately, we cannot always know whether we are in one of those places. Consequently, we expect the long-term history of Pacific Northwest cultures to reflect significant variation in cultural practices as expressed in both short-lived and longer-term archaeological signatures. Human history in every part of the world has been dynamic, filled with starts and stops, and there is no reason that the cultures of the greater Pacific Northwest were not characterized by this same pattern.

2
Before the Villages
Middle Period Occupation of the Plateau

Early evening on a terrace above the Fraser Canyon, 4,100 years ago.
It's the beginning of another cold night. The wind blows hard out of the north, and the air holds a crisp hint of snow. The leaves are gone from the willows by the river, the same willows the families had used to construct their temporary shelters of bent poles and hides. Trying to conserve their only source of heat, the adults move glowing coals from the outdoor fire pit between the huts into shallow depressions indoors. Later, protected from the wind and warmed by a small fire, the people work, rest, and discuss recent events.

The girl overhears the hunters talking about the poor weather and the scarcity of game. One hunter, in a whisper, retells the story of two hunters from another family who got caught in a snowstorm last winter, miles from their families. Had they not found shelter in a small rock overhang, they would have died. The girl wonders what would have happened to the families if they had not returned. Each day, she notices the hunters bringing home less and less large game. During the last warm season, she and the other older children were asked to help catch small mammals, birds, and fish. They even ate reptiles. Their trips for berries and greens got longer and longer. She remembers the tart taste of berries on her tongue and the feel of sticky juice on her fingers. She recalls how they feasted on salmon earlier in the year, when the fish moved in great numbers through the big river.

The hunters stop talking and make the best of the waning light. They sharpen stone spear tips, press new blades from small cone-shaped cores, and mount them on hafts. The girl watches her mother repair clothing and then pack dried food. The girl knows that if the hunters do not come back with more food this time, the families will pack up and move. Grandmother, who is preparing a meal, starts to sing the old songs. For a moment, the girl forgets her hunger.

British Columbia's Middle Period ended about 4,100 years ago. Increasingly cold conditions made life for people in the Interior untenable and forced them to abandon the area after 4,000 years of relative success. These people had moved into the region around 8,000 years ago, when they likely encountered a landscape empty of human occupants. People who lived in the Early Period or Paleoindian Period probably visited the Canadian Plateau at even earlier dates, from 11,000 to 8,000 years ago, but did not linger. All that is known about these people comes from the occasional sparse scatter of stone artifacts found on the surface of the land. Thus, there is little we can say about these earliest travellers.

In contrast, we know considerably more about the people of the Middle Period. In this chapter, we address a number of questions concerning occupation of the area between 8,000 and 4,000 years ago. Who were the people of the Middle Period? What was their lifestyle? What permitted them to successfully live in the Interior for such a long time span and yet still succumb to climatic cooling? Finally, did they have any form of ancestral relationship to the pithouse-using peoples of the Late Period?

The period defined as the Middle Holocene (ca. 6,000 to 3,000 years ago) has until recently been poorly understood by archaeologists of the Pacific Northwest. Fortunately, archaeological research in the past two decades has provided a much-improved base for understanding the processes of culture change. We know that this was a time of dramatic cultural transformation as the region's people shifted from mobile hunting and gathering to a sedentary lifestyle centred on harvesting and storing selected plant foods (for example, roots), fish, and sea mammals. This transition was followed by cultural elaboration in the years before the appearance of the first Europeans. Archaeologists working in the Pacific Northwest generally favour an implicit explanatory model in which the latter adaptation evolves gradually throughout the region. In contrast, we support the argument that change was punctuated, that is, it took place at different rates in different areas and was sometimes associated with population movements. This argument draws on innovative archaeological and paleoecological research by

FIGURE 2.1 View of the Fraser River, looking north toward Lytton, 1986.

Photograph by Ian Kuijt

Jim Chatters and the theoretical modelling of paleontologist Niles Eldredge. From our perspective, the ethnographic record from the Northwest Coast and Interior offers direct evidence of conflict, the rise and fall of villages, the exchange of ideas, and group mobility. The record of early human life across the region illustrates similar periods of rapid change and the movement of people.

Archaeological Discoveries

Under the direction of Charles Borden and David Sanger in 1961, teams of archaeologists from the University of British Columbia were excavating several sites near Lochnore Creek, South of Lillooet, and discovered several ancient human burials. These excavations were the first systematic attempt to reconstruct the early cultures of the region. The researchers focused on several sites in the Lochnore-Nesikep area, located about halfway between Lytton and Lillooet. As with most areas in the Fraser Canyon, this area is characterized by open forests, isolated terraces along the edges of the valley, and deeply incised river drainage (Figure 2.1).

After years of research, Sanger eventually reported that there was tantalizing evidence of past hunter-gatherer cultures in the Interior. He argued that large spear points, tiny knife-like slivers called microblades (used to arm arrow points), and pecked stone hammers indicated that people had lived in the area from recent centuries to just after 7,000 BP (before the present). Older deposits held no evidence of even the most ephemeral of dwellings, but we assume that the people must have constructed temporary shelters from brush and hides. The people likely lived in small temporary camps. Named after Nesikep Creek, one of Sanger's original excavation localities, the Nesikep tradition was identified as the dominant cultural pattern within the Middle Period.

As Sanger and Borden laboured in the Mid-Fraser Canyon during the 1960s, another archaeologist named B. Robert Butler was conducting excavations on the Columbia and Snake River Plateaus to the south in the United States. Butler likewise associated large spear points with small hunter-gatherer camps that dated to between 9,000 and 5,000 years ago. He called the culture the Old Cordilleran tradition to suggest its context in the western-most mountains of North America. Since the 1960s, many Old Cordilleran sites have been found and excavated primarily in the southern Interior and up to the central Northwest Coast. Today, when archaeologists refer to the interior version, they typically call it the Cascade phase. On the Coast, the term *Old Cordilleran* is inter-changeable with Olcott tradition and *Pebble Tool Culture*. Like the people of the Nesikep tradition, Old Cordilleran folks moved frequently and lived in small communities.

The Old Cordilleran were not, however, the first to people the Pacific Northwest. In a recent study, archaeologists Charlotte Beck and Tom Jones effectively argue that two population expansions from Alaska may have preceded the entry of the Old Cordilleran peoples. The first expansion most likely resulted in what archaeologists call the Pre-Clovis and Clovis cultures, now known through much of North America (south of the ice sheets that covered much of Canada during this era). The second expansion appears to have brought the Western Stemmed tradition, another early Paleoindian cultural pattern associ-ated primarily with what is now the western United States. Like the Clovis and Pre-Clovis peoples, the Western Stemmed folks were residentially mobile and focused on large game when available. These people, however, also left behind abundant evidence that they harvested the rich food resources of the marshes and lakes of the Columbia Plateau and western Great Basin. Drawing from a wide range of archaeological and osteological data, archaeologist Jim Chatters and colleagues argue that incoming Old Cordilleran groups may have displaced the last of the Western Stemmed populations (at least in the Colum-bia Plateau and northern Great Basin). The first Nesikep tradition groups on

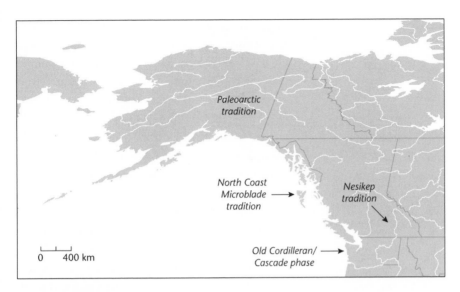

FIGURE 2.2 Early (5,000 to 10,000 years ago) cultures in the Pacific Northwest.

the Canadian Plateau may have encountered and likely displaced some of these early Old Cordilleran peoples.

The people of the Old Cordilleran and Nesikep tradition maintained a way of life characterized by foraging and frequent residential moves from some time shortly after 10,000 years ago to about 5,000 to 4,000 years ago. Their cultural traditions did not favour formal villages with large architecturally complex houses. After about 3,600 years ago, however, new peoples lived in rather elaborate houses dug partially into the earth, often in permanent winter villages. Inside these houses were various cooking pits and what appear to be food-storage facilities. Clearly, there had been significant cultural change since that early period. Later archaeologists, studying the Mid-Fraser context and other localities elsewhere on the Canadian Plateau, would come to recognize this pattern of change and wonder how and why it had occurred.

The Nesikep Tradition

The Nesikep tradition consisted of three similar cultural adaptations, sometimes called phases, which overlapped in time (see Figure 2.2). Many archaeologists who work in the Mid-Fraser area believe that these peoples differed from those of the late prehistoric, historic, and present periods. The earliest phase, the Early Nesikep, dates from about 8,000 to just under 6,000 years ago.

The Early Nesikep peoples had several tactics for making chipped-stone tools (Figures 2.3 and 2.6). They produced large bifacial spear points (meaning

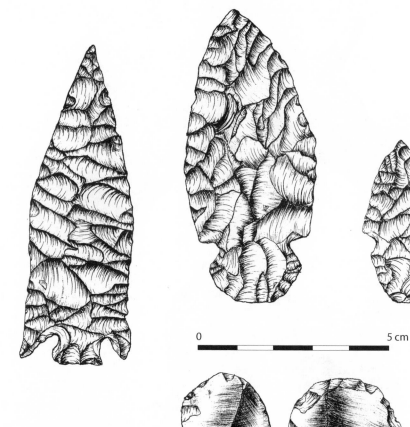

0   5 cm

▲ FIGURE 2.3 Artifacts
of the Nesikep tradition.
Upper row, left to right:
Early Nesikep projectile point,
Lehman projectile point, and
Lochnore projectile point.
Lower row, left to right:
unifacial scraper notched
for hafting and oval scraper.

Illustrations by Robert O'Boyle

▶ FIGURE 2.4 An artist's
conception of prehistoric
Canadian Plateau artifacts
in preparation and use.
Upper image: digging
stick handle, Plateau
Pithouse tradition.
Middle image: hafting
a projectile point, Early
Nesikep phase.
Lower image: slate knife is
used as a salmon-processing
tool, Locarno Beach phase.

Illustration by Eric S. Carlson

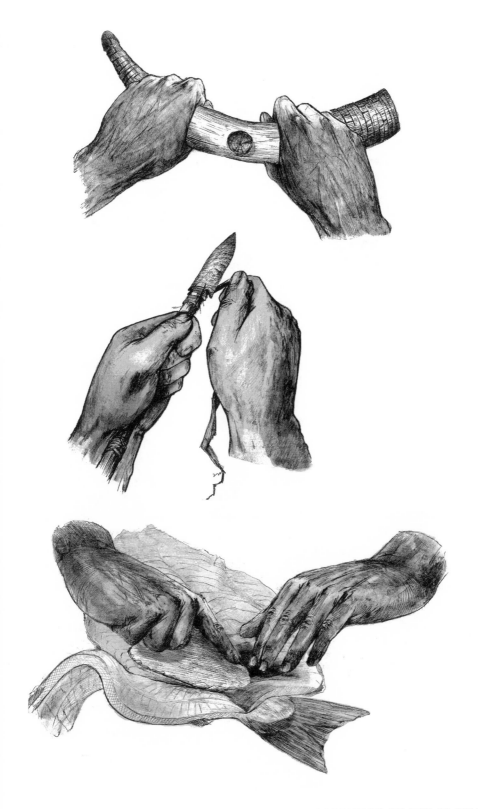

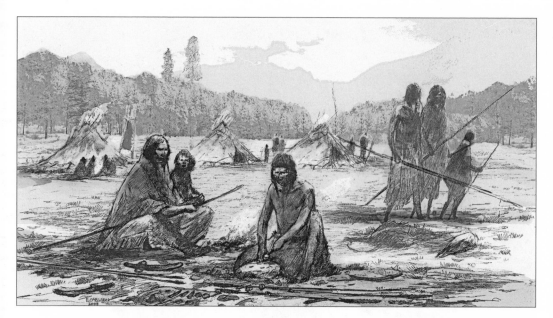

FIGURE 2.5 Artist's conception of a Nesikep tradition camp.

Illustration by Eric S. Carlson

the tools were chipped on both sides). Small notches in a flat base or corners of the blades were used for hafting, attaching the point to a spear shaft. They made these tools by chipping a larger flake from a core, a larger block of stone. People then used various tools to chip these objects into new shapes: a small hammer stone (pebble) for rough shaping, a soft hammer or an antler billet for further shaping and thinning, and a sharpened antler tip to complete the finishing details. Pressure flaking involved literally pressing flakes off the edges of the stone tool. The spears might have comprised several parts, including a foreshaft that contained the actual point, which was in turn slotted into a thicker main shaft. We presume that people used these spears primarily to hunt medium- to large-sized game such as elk and deer.

Early Nesikep people also produced round- to oblong-shaped flakes from which unifacial (or single-sided) chipping produced a tool useful for tasks such as scraping hides or planing wood. They also began to experiment with a range of scraper shapes, including a triangular form, commonly known as an end scraper, and crudely circular forms.

These ancient people also produced microblades, razor sharp slivers of stone common to early sites in the region. Microblades were produced over 20,000 years ago in Siberia, and the technology travelled with early immigrants to Alaska

FIGURE 2.6 The Walachine site along the Thompson River. As with many pre-pithouse and early pithouse period sites, this site contains eroding shellfish and bone remains, rocks that were once part of fire hearths, and a few chipped stone tools and waste materials.

Photograph by Ian Kuijt

and then into British Columbia at some point after 10,000 years ago. It may seem silly to draw such grand conclusions from such small and scattered artifacts, but there are many ways to produce microblades, and the peoples of the Paleo-Arctic tradition used a specialized process that required several distinct stages of production. They began by manufacturing a tool that resembled a bifacial knife. They then split the biface and shaped the broken surface to create a striking platform (the place where blades would be pressed off). They then pressed microblades from the platform down one edge. As the technique spread from central Alaska down the Northwest Coast, it diversified into a wider range of techniques.

Early Nesikep knappers generally chose to produce a small core with a flattish top for a platform. They then carefully shaped the faces of the core to allow for blade removals and used a pressure flaker to press the slivers from the face. The result was often hundreds of microblades. The flakes were two to five centimetres long, had parallel sides, and had a width of about a half centimetre. Studies of the wear traces on the edges of these tiny artifacts suggest that people used them as cutting tools. In many ways, they were an early Exacto blade system. The microblades were probably mounted on the margins of antler handles for fine-cutting operations such as clothing manufacture, or they might have been hafted along the margins of spear shafts to add an extra cutting edge to already formidable hunting weapons.

There is no evidence for Early Nesikep housing. We can assume, however, that they did construct temporary lodges, perhaps from timbers and hides. Early Nesikep sites frequently contain shallow fire hearths, which were used for cooking meals and to provide heat. Evidence for subsistence is sparse, but it indicates that these people frequently ate deer and relied on a wide range of foods, including salmon, birds, and mollusks. We have no evidence for their preferred plant foods, but it probably included a range of berries and greens. There is no evidence such as storage pits to suggest that these people routinely stored foods.

What can we say about Early Nesikep lifestyles? Comparing the archaeological record to that of more recent hunter-gatherers around the world, we suspect that these people lived in small family groups. The lack of permanent villages, cemeteries, and storage systems suggests that they moved around a lot and that there were no significant status differences among people. Sharing was probably mandatory, and everyone benefitted from foraging within the group. Small sites that lack houses or storage indicate that people moved frequently, probably timing their moves to access new food resources at different times of the year.

By around 6,500 years ago, another cultural pattern emerged. Although part of the longer-lived Nesikep tradition, this period is called the Lochnore phase. Lochnore people were culturally similar to the Early Nesikep. They appeared late in the Early Nesikep era but persisted until about 4,000 years ago. Lochnore stone knappers used the same three tactics for making chipped-stone tools. They made large bifacial spear points, similar in function to the Early Nesikep forms, but different in style. Instead of a lengthened triangular shape, they were bipointed or laurel leaf–shaped, often with small notches for hafting located near the bases. Lochnore knappers expanded the repertoire of scrapers seen in Early Nesikep times, producing triangular end scrapers, oblong side scrapers, circular scrapers, circular scrapers with notches for hafting, and crescent moon-shaped scrapers. Archaeologists are not yet entirely clear on the full range of functions for these tools, but it is generally held that they were used in a wide variety of scraping activities. Finally, Lochnore folk continued the tradition of microblade manufacture begun during the Early Nesikep phase.

We have better evidence about Lochnore subsistence patterns. People continued to hunt deer and elk, but they also consumed a much wider range of mammalian species, including bear, beaver, marmot, and muskrat. They hunted birds ranging from raptors to ducks. Finally, they harvested a wide array of fishes (from salmon to turbot) and mollusks. There is no evidence that these people had house structures or food storage systems. And, similar to the Early Nesikep, their sites comprise a small scattering of artifacts and hearths spread across the Canadian Plateau. We conclude that the Lochnore and Early Nesikep peoples shared a similar social and economic organization. Given Lochnore's technological similarities to Early Nesikep and their overlapping dates, we can also conclude that Lochnore was probably a descendent culture. The change in spear-point style could be attributed to either independent invention or cultural borrowing since other groups dating to the same time frame used similar styles in the Columbia Basin to the south and on the Northwest Coast to the west.

The final members of the Nesikep tradition are associated with the Lehman phase, which began around 6,000 years ago and ended about 4,500 years ago. Archaeologists know and understand little about the Lehman phase. The phase is represented by only a few site components, which are usually mixed with Lochnore materials. Lehman spear points lie stylistically about halfway between the Lochnore and Early Nesikep types. They can be described as semi-triangular in shape with a convex base and side notches. Lehman knappers also produced a variety of long chipped-stone knives and a similar array of triangular and circular scrapers. It is not clear whether people in the Lehman phase manufactured microblades. What does the Lehman phase represent? We suggest two possibilities. One is that the people of the Lehman phase do reflect a separate cultural branch from the Early Nesikep, perhaps a splinter group that modified

FIGURE 2.7 The Fraser River near the Milliken site. Excavations by Charles Borden at several sites within this area uncovered evidence of early occupation in the interior of British Columbia.

Photograph by Ian Kuijt

its tool kit but remained in the same area. Another possibility is that Lehman tools reflect a specialized activity set within the Lochnore phase. This would not be a surprise, given that the two phases overlap and that their artifacts often comingle.

The Nesikep tradition was not the only cultural pattern on the Plateau and nearby central Northwest Coast. Since it is possible that some of these other cultures were ancestors of the more recent Mid-Fraser people, it is important to consider developments in these other areas.

The Old Cordilleran

The Old Cordilleran tradition of the Plateau and adjacent Northwest Coast represents an early adaptation by people who moved into the plateau nearly 10,000 years ago. The current consensus among archaeologists is that the Old Cordilleran folk were descendants of Paleo-Arctic peoples who moved through eastern Siberia and Alaska between 16,000 and 10,000 years ago and eventually moved down the Northwest Coast into what is now the interior of Washington and surrounding regions.

During the Cascade phase, Old Cordilleran peoples of the Plateau produced stone tools that included leaf-shaped (or bipointed) bifacial knives and spear points that were similar to those made by Lochnore knappers, but without side notches. They also relied on a generalized core and flake technology to produce simple flake and stone tools that lacked any formal shaping. Although people produced microblades, the tools did not play the same role as they did among Early Nesikep or Paleo-Arctic people. Sometime after 7,000 BP, Cascade peoples began to use ground sandstone slabs and hammers made from river cobbles to process coarse seeds and other materials acquired in the arid steppes and grasslands of the Columbia Basin. Like Early Nesikep people farther north, Cascade peoples were broad-spectrum foragers: they hunted animals of all sizes – especially deer, birds, fish, and molluscs – and gathered a wide range of plant foods. They left few formal dwellings and evidently did not employ storage strategies.

On the Coast, Old Cordilleran peoples used few formed tools such as end scrapers and opted, instead, to use large flakes driven from river cobbles. Despite the frequent use of this expedient technology, they continued to produce elaborate leaf-shaped spear points and, occasionally, microblades. Subsistence in the coastal zone meant reliance on medium to large game (including seals), shellfish and, not surprisingly, fish. Old Cordilleran groups made the first shell heaps, or middens, along the Fraser River. These middens were a product of intense use of salmon on a seasonal basis, as well as mussels and small fish such as sticklebacks and eulachon. Some places – such as Namu on the central Coast,

FIGURE 2.8 The north end of
Fountain Ridge, 2008. This is
a good example of what landscapes could have looked like
during periods of intense
drought and frequent fires.

Photograph by Anna M. Prentiss

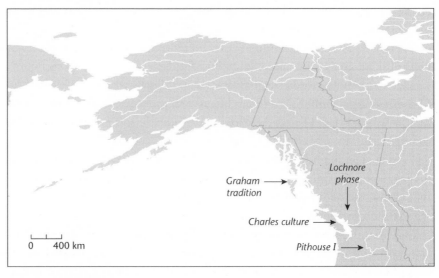

Graham
tradition →

Lochnore
phase

Charles culture →

0   400 km

Pithouse I →

FIGURE 2.9 Cultures of the
Pacific Northwest around
4,000 to 5,000 years ago.

the Milliken site in the Lower Fraser Canyon, and The Dalles of the Lower Columbia – might have functioned as aggregation localities for multiple groups during fishing season (Figure 2.7). Given access to the rich resources of the Coast, Old Cordilleran peoples might have lingered for slightly longer times in their camps than did their relatives on the Columbia Plateau or the people of the Canadian Plateau. Nonetheless, they still left few indicators of houses or the employment of food storage.

Between about 5,000 and 4,000 years ago, groups began to change through-out the region, creating a period of dramatic cultural diversity. It was this period of cultural evolution that began to set the stage for the emergence of the basic cultural pattern that would typify later cultures in the Mid-Fraser region.

Cultural, Environmental, and Technological Change

Culture and Environment

The Nesikep and Old Cordilleran traditions emerged as adaptations to generally warm and dry conditions. Summers and winters differed little from those of today. Summers were long and hot, and winters were relatively mild. Dry condi-tions meant frequent forest fires, which, in turn, created relatively open pine forests in more mountainous areas (Figure 2.8). Bunch grass and sagebrush overran valleys and open basins. People probably ate a balanced range of foods. Because of sea level instability, salmon runs were smaller and far less predictable than they are today. But dry conditions in the Interior also had an adverse effect on spawning. Salmon require cold clear water. Dry conditions probably increased the amount of sediment in the waters, thereby delaying or reducing the number of fish that arrived each spawning season. High amounts of sediment were also unhealthy for eggs and young salmon.

Dry conditions also meant that deer were probably less accessible in more arid areas. Their numbers, however, might have increased at higher elevations. The same is true for other large mammals such as elk and bear. Fires at higher elevations also facilitated the expansion of patches of berry bushes and edible roots such as spring beauty and balsamroot on the Canadian Plateau. Most of the region's root plants require dry meadows and grow better in drier climates. In contrast, the most important root resource of the Columbia Plateau, camas, required wet meadows and was never abundant.

On the Coast, forests were probably much more open than today and likely favoured larger game populations. Fluctuating sea levels and warm sea surface temperatures made marine resources somewhat unpredictable from year to year. It is no surprise that archaeologists have found little evidence of many species of shellfish and fish in food middens until after about 5,000 years ago.

For hunter-gatherers, the Pacific Northwest between 4,000 and 5,000 years ago would have been a good place to live. Paleoenvironmental research illustrates there was an increase in annual rainfall about 5,000 years ago. Winters were still mild, but they were increasingly moist. The sea level had stabilized, and shellfish beds were expanding, bringing more fish and marine predators such as seals and dolphins to the region. The salmon runs expanded as spawning became more successful, and deer and other game populations flourished in the wetter climate.

Why Was There a Change in Hunting and Gathering Societies?

To the untrained eye, hunter-gatherers seem to move about almost randomly through the landscape, crisscrossing valleys and mountains in search of new food and tool-making materials. This apparent randomness is actually an illusion, for their behaviours are both purposeful and planned. When viewed from the standpoint of annual movements and food gathering, hunter-gatherers lived within a seasonal cycle that was as scheduled as those of wheat farmers, ranchers, and fruit growers today. They made decisions about local hunts or forays for fish or berries in response to immediate short-term needs. But their decision making also incorporated long-term advance planning. People likely asked themselves where they needed to be in a week, a month, or six months to take full advantage of the annual salmon run, deer migrations, or berry ripening.

As in today's world, people in the past were concerned about social networks and connections. Even the far-flung ancient people of the Pacific Northwest operated within social networks defined by marriages, trade relations, and the like. Families and groups of families had to coordinate where to meet for important gatherings, for instance, an annual salmon-fishing ground. The knowledge of generations, passed down from elders to children, ensured that things would happen as they always had. Because breaking the annual cycle would likely cause more problems than it would alleviate, it probably did not happen often. People lived together for good reason: living together provided protection, labour, and help. Those who broke the rules faced social isolation, and the severance of social ties with the larger group and the protection it afforded brought greater risks. In extreme cases, death could come at the hands of other groups, but it could also come from natural causes such as starvation brought on by scheduling mistakes.

People lived in a conservative cultural context, one in which new generations were socialized primarily by their elders (Box 2.1). What would make these social bonds come so unglued that people changed not only their standard way of cooking but also their yearly schedule, key technologies, and standard social obligations? Surely, this change would not come from someone simply deciding to do things differently. Changing social and environmental conditions must also have played a role. The changes associated with the optimal conditions of the Middle Holocene period of 4,000 to 5,000 years ago (more moisture and greater fish and shellfish stocks) might have provided an ecological trigger for just such a shift. Greater productivity in areas that were previously marginal meant that groups could linger for longer periods of time in places that had previously permitted stays of only a few days. Now they could stay longer, perhaps even several weeks. But doing so would have brought about other changes. A long stay in one place might begin to foreclose opportunities elsewhere. Severe interruptions of annual cycles could require the development of drastic new measures for food harvesting and processing. To make matters worse, intergroup or interpersonal social obligations could be affected, resulting, for example, in missed trade opportunities. But more critically, this shift might mean severing the social ties that had ensured survival in bad times. This is a critical point. In today's society, we have costly insurance policies to protect us from disaster. There is little doubt that ancient people of the Pacific Northwest relied heavily on a system of social bonds, such as maintaining close family connections, and favours that acted as insurance during times of need. Without these bonds and social connections, groups faced greater risk and an inability to secure food for the following year.

If a group (or groups) found themselves camped in a new geographical area, a location with unrecognized hunting or fishing opportunities, then this might have influenced band members to convince others to stay longer during one season. Repeating this pattern over many years would eventually have required people to rearrange their social commitments and their basic economy to such a degree as to render their old system unrecognizable. Hard times would reinforce old strategies, while rich resource conditions would reward new adaptations. Change would also be more likely to occur outside of the social pressure of a larger dominant population, thus in smaller more isolated groups. Change occurs only when people are ready. New ideas only take hold when things become practical and part of prevailing wisdom. From this standpoint, radical change comes about either through the stimulus of altered environmental conditions and human responses or through independent actions by specific persons, which, intended or not, produce a process of change that ripples through the entire group.

Diversification: New Regional Adaptations

The archaeological record of the Pacific Northwest indicates that cultural diversification likely happened in at least three places and resulted in three new and quite different approaches to hunting and gathering (Figure 2.9). One of the most radical changes occurred in the Columbia Basin of Washington State and western Idaho, the traditional home of a number of Salish- and Sahaptian-speaking groups. Just after 5,000 BP, highly mobile foragers of the Cascade phase suddenly (from an archaeological standpoint) became sedentary foragers, that is, people started to live in the same place for much of the year. Archaeologist Jim Chatters called the new culture Pithouse I because of its semi-subterranean houses, which are among the oldest dated in the Plateau region. That older housepits have been excavated in different parts of the Great Basin (California, Oregon, and southwest Wyoming) suggests that knowledge of pithouse construction might have originated elsewhere and been transported into the area by the literal movement of peoples or transmission of ideas.

Whatever the case, people in Pithouse I rarely built housepits over 7 metres (about 21 feet) in diameter. These pithouses probably had superstructures made

BOX 2.1 LEARNING FROM PARENTS AND OTHER RELATIVES

Learning systems in hunter-gatherer societies are often organized around strict elder-to-child teaching practices, and these practices can result in remarkably stable and constant sharing of knowledge between generations. This reality is illustrated humorously in a story told by elder Laura Thevarge:

> "I'm going to tell a story about what my mother did when she was raising us. She brought a machine like that (tape recorder). She wanted to know, she was learning what they call "psychology." I don't know that word, but you people must know what psychology is.
>
> Then Lorna Williams told a story about what her mother did to her. I said, "My mother did that too, she never teaches us. It's our aunts and our grandfathers and other women that teach us. Our parents never taught us." That's what I said.
>
> Lorna told what her mother did. Her mother told her, "You are going to cook

today." That girl was maybe 10 years old, and she's the one that's going to fix their meal. They were going to work in their garden.

> She ran around to all her relatives to see what she was gonna cook. They didn't know either. Then one of her aunts said to her. "What did your mother tell you, what do you know how to cook?" Then she (Lorna) told her (aunt) what she was going to cook. "Oh good, you can cook like that and it will be good."
>
> So I told my daughter, "My mother did the same thing to me." She told me, "You're gonna cook." "Oh my," I said. That's the way they did things before. I didn't know what I was gonna do with this. Potatoes and meat, I was gonna cook outside.
>
> "Oh," I said. I went there, I made a fire there. I didn't know what I was gonna do with the pot she had given me. *Lhvnkaya* (cast iron pot) we call them,

from thin timbers set in a conical form, a bit like a flattened teepee. It is not clear what covered the structures, but it might have included woven mats and hides. People entered the houses from the side, and the interior was organized into activity zones: places for sleeping, food preparation, and stone tool making. People who lived at Pithouse I sites made the same tools as the earlier Cascade peoples. This included leaf-shaped spear points, flake tools, small grinding stones, and microblades. However, there were no storage pits. The presence of houses implies that these people had a greater investment in particular places than the earlier and far more mobile Cascade people. They probably stayed longer at particular camp spots. Indeed, analysis of animal bones from Pithouse I sites suggests that the people harvested foods in both the warm and cold seasons.

Many archaeologists believe that Pithouse I people became sedentary for significant portions of the year, quite a change from the ever-moving people of

lhvnkaya. "Oh," I said. I went to look for rocks. I made a sort of a fire.

Oh, where I was fixing was too small. I wasn't gonna be able to put it there. So I had to push rocks over to where it was burning more. "Oh, I'll just use a little bit of water," I thought. I didn't know what to do to make it cook faster. I was thinking, "I'm already getting behind."

So then I was in a hurry, I cooked fast. And then my cooking got burnt. "Oh my," I said. So I called my mother. "My cooking is cooked!" I called. So she called the man who was ploughing for us. They came. Still he ate it. It was really burnt, the potatoes and meat. (laughs)

Oh, I was scared, but then he said, "Oh, this is very good Laura." He said. "What you cooked is really good," he told me. (laughs) So my mother didn't get mad at me. (laughs) Oh, it was very funny. I was scared because it was burnt ... so then she asked me, "How come there was a little

bit of water?" So I said, "Oh, so it would cook faster!" "If there's a little bit of water ... there should have been a little more water, so it wouldn't get burnt" (my mother said). But it was so it would boil faster, that's what I'd been thinking. (laughs)

We were so pitiful! That's what we call "psychology," I think. We are supposed to watch what our parents do. [Matthewson 2008:62]

It is easy for us to imagine the same story playing out in a camp or pithouse hundreds of years ago. The cast iron pot might have been a basket for boiling water using hot stones; the potatoes could have been spring beauty or Indian potatoes; the meat, freshly killed deer. Regardless, the story provides insight into traditional learning systems, particularly the ways young people learned proper behaviour in St'át'imc society.

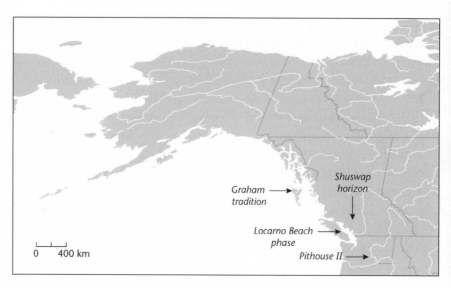

FIGURE 2.10 Cultures of the
Pacific Northwest around
2,500 to 3,600 years ago.

the Cascade phase. But how did they pull this off without storage? Surely, they needed to put some things away for the long winter. Winter at this point was mild and resources abundant, even in the Columbia Basin, especially along major river valleys and in the uplands. To survive without significant storage, these foragers had to plan carefully where to live.

Archaeological evidence suggests that Pithouse I peoples placed their houses in what ecologists call ecotones, places adjacent to multiple ecosystems (riparian zones, river terraces, forested mountain sides, and so on). From this base, optimally positioned to access the widest range of resources, the group would systematically target food sources as they became available throughout the year. Animal bones, the most diverse in the history of the region, support this interpretation. In addition, it appears that no food source dominated over the others. Pithouse I people therefore foraged throughout multiple ecological contexts and favoured no particular food or group. Jim Chatters has shown that they sometimes undertook extended foraging trips that required the creation of specialized camps. There is evidence for some of these camps in the Chief Joseph Dam area. Once the number of critical game species was reduced around the base camps, the groups moved on to other locations. It was a clever system, one well suited to the environment.

Out on the Pacific Coast, Old Cordilleran foragers adopted another hunter-gatherer strategy suited to their environment. With salmon and many other marine resources on the rise, stretches of the rivers and coastline provided enhanced opportunities for intensified harvests. At least some people of the central Northwest Coast, now known to archaeologists as the Charles culture, appear to have adopted an economic strategy called serial foraging, which involved moving through a series of well-known localities and targeting a specific resource in each. Evidence suggests that salmon streams were targeted during major runs in the summer and early fall. Other evidence suggests that marine mammals and shellfish determined the schedule at other times. Many middens – shell heaps containing a wide range of discarded food remains, broken tools, tool-making debris or debitage and even, sometimes, human burials – first appeared during this period, and they were increased substantially by these people. There is, however, little evidence of residential dwellings or signs of food storage on the Gulf Islands and along the Mainland coast.

Food storage is difficult to reconstruct in coastal settings because, traditionally, Native people did not always use storage pits but, rather, wooden boxes and racks in houses. Archaeologists study fish-processing techniques to determine how and why fish was stored. Salmon processed for storage were typically cleaned close to the fishing site. Heads were removed and meat smoked. Once ready for consumption, the fully processed fish were introduced to houses, and the remains were disposed of in trash dumps near buildings. It is generally assumed that mostly postcranial elements ended up in these dumps, because the heads were discarded and left at the location of fishing and processing. This pattern generally holds true in the archaeological record of Late Period villages on the Coast. In contrast, middens produced by people of the Charles culture typically do contain frequent head parts, which supports the conclusion that fish were harvested not for storage but for immediate consumption.

It appears that these people employed a pattern of intensive salmon harvesting that was similar to that employed by people of later times. Yet they likely consumed the fish shortly after capture and moved on to the next place to fish and eat. This strategy was productive as long as winters remained mild and resources were available year round. Indeed, this subsistence pattern appears to have rewarded Charles culture folk to such a degree that they had the time to create artwork in the form of carvings on wood and antler along with several new tool forms, including ground slate knives and points.

Archaeological investigations in the Fraser Valley east of Vancouver, home of today's Stó:lō, who speak Coast Salish, have uncovered an inland version of the Charles culture, which has been named the Eayam phase. Although subsistence remains are rarely preserved at the Eayam sites of X̱á:ytem (previously known as Hatzic Rock) and Maurer, excavations revealed large house structures similar to those of much more recent inhabitants. Like Pithouse I, these sites are located in ecotone contexts with optimal access to a wide range of potential food resources. Unfortunately, we know relatively little about the foods these people ate or their food-processing strategies, for animal bones do not preserve well in this context. Features at Xá:ytem include large outdoor roasting ovens, which suggest that the people might have engaged in a form of outdoor cooking associated with gatherings and feasting. A number of shallow pits suggest some degree of limited storage, though the nature of the storage remains unclear. The limited excavations at Maurer did not focus on extramural (outside of house) features. The ecotone context associated with these sites suggests that their inhabitants employed strategies similar to those of the Pithouse I sedentary foragers of the Columbia Basin. It is even possible that these could be winter occupations for groups ranging more widely out into the Gulf of Georgia during the warm season.

Clearly, the archaeological record of the Charles culture is complex and contains evidence of both mobile serial foraging and more sedentary adaptations. More research is necessary to determine whether these adaptations reflect different parts of a single annual cycle or distinctly different strategies undertaken by different groups.

A final cultural form emerged farther up the Northwest Coast. Current evidence suggests that a dramatic change in technology, settlement, and subsistence occurred on Haida Gwaii (the Queen Charlotte Islands) between 5,000 and 5,500 years ago. This shift was possibly followed by a similar transition on the Mainland near what is now Prince Rupert Harbour about 4,500 years ago. A similar cultural transition could have occurred at other outer coast places such as the Yuquot area of Vancouver Island or in the neighbourhood of Bella Bella on Campbell Island; however, the archaeological record is not sufficient to explore this possibility further.

Data from several sites associated with an archaeological culture called the Early Graham tradition, located in northern Haida Gwaii, suggest the operation of a new approach to hunting and gathering, the collector strategy. This strategy differed from both the mobile forager model and that of the sedentary foragers of the Columbia Plateau and the serial foragers of the Gulf Islands. Collectors tend to live in more permanent villages and employ what archaeologists call logistical or task-group mobility to acquire large amounts of food that can be stored for longer periods of time. The strategy is a logical way to feed large numbers of people during long winters. It is, therefore, no wonder that this strategy eventually became the economic basis of all later Pacific Northwest cultures.

Current evidence from the Early Graham tradition sites, such as Blue Jackets Creek and Cohoe Creek, suggest that residential bases began to include large house floors, perhaps reflecting aboveground wooden constructions. If this is the case, it means that sedentism was at least seasonal, if not permanent. The presence of large cache pits at Cohoe Creek more than 5,000 years ago suggests that the concept of storage may have developed. Data from the Skoglund's Landing site indicates that task groups were likely sent out from the home base to establish short-term specialized camps from which to acquire resources, which they would then take to consumers at the village. Some archaeologists believe, however, that Skoglund's Landing may be a remnant of a larger eroded base camp or village.

In addition to the presence of deep pits at Cohoe Creek, there are several other indicators that these people had food storage. First, they harvested and brought high numbers of large and small animals (salmon, fresh water fish, halibut, and sea mammals) to the village for consumption. Some form of storage must have been employed to avoid the wastage of meat. Second, house floors contain a variety of large pits. They perhaps served as some form of cache for the collection and (at minimum) short-term storage of food products. Finally, the middens contain multiple burials, some of which include significant grave goods, such as war clubs, placed in a sitting position within their interments. These items perhaps indicate the presence of status differentiation in the society. Most archaeologists working on the complex societies of the West Coast believe status inequality was predicated on the ability to acquire and store surpluses and use them in acts of generosity that demonstrated prowess. If this assumption is correct, the society would certainly need a food storage strategy.

It is hard to develop a complete reconstruction of early collector strategies in the Pacific Northwest because of an incomplete archaeological record (e.g., poor bone preservation in the Fraser Valley sites, or the lack of features at Namu) or incomplete archaeological reporting (e.g., limited reporting of key data sets from many sites). All things considered, however, we still find the Haida Gwaii data compelling. But we admit that further research is needed for the area and on the neighbouring coast to confirm this hypothesis.

If the development of storage facilities did happen first on Haida Gwaii, then the question becomes, why? There are several possibilities. First, the Haida Gwaii people were the most geographically isolated society in the region. If a group were to make a big break from the prevailing cultural model, it would have been here. Second, isolation might also have triggered the exploration of storage possibilities merely as an insurance policy. Finally, although marine resources are abundant around Haida Gwaii, its exposed location in the northeastern Pacific leaves it more vulnerable to severe winter storms than other, more protected, localities on the Mainland coast. As conditions got wetter and cooler, the population on Haida Gwaii experimented with sturdy house structures, more sedentary lifestyles, specialized resource targeting and, likely, food storage. The strategy, however conceived, apparently worked, because it was the only one that survived the cultural decimation that began just over 4,000 years ago.

Cultural Decimation

At least four basic approaches to hunting and gathering were practised 4,200 years ago in the Pacific Northwest: mobile foraging on the Canadian Plateau (Nesikep tradition); sedentary foraging on the Columbia Basin (Pithouse I) and possibly some portions of the Fraser Valley (Eayam phase); serial foraging on portions of the central Coast, especially near the Gulf of Georgia, Vancouver Island, and Puget Sound; and collecting on Haida Gwaii and possibly in some other scattered contexts (see Figure 2.9). All approaches were well adapted and apparently successful, for they left an abundant archaeological record. Although most had been around for only a short time, the mobile foragers of the Canadian Plateau had persisted, with little change, for nearly 4,000 years. Yet, nearly all of these adaptations began to fail about 4,100 years ago. The critical question is, why?

In some ways, we may view the period from 5,000 to 4,000 years ago as a honeymoon period, a good time followed by a growing awareness of a new reality. No hunter-gatherer at this point could know what we know now: that the increasing rainfall of the previous centuries was the beginnings of what scientists call the Neoglacial climatic period. The Neoglacial period marked a rapid yet temporary slide back toward the cold conditions of the previous ice age. Data from the Columbia Basin and the surrounding mountains suggest that it happened quickly. Colder water caused the growth of shellfish in the Columbia River to suddenly slow down. In contrast, salmon numbers grew under the optimal spawning conditions linked to clear and cool water. More frequent and intense frosts caused cave roofs and walls to fragment and sedimentation layers to rise. Forests expanded, closing off open meadows, and desert shrub lands declined.

The effect of these changes on human groups was intense and rapid. Possibly, over the period of a single human generation, people probably had to deal with much longer winters and far fewer opportunities for resource gathering. Things were particularly tough in the interiors of what are now British Columbia and Washington State. Salmon came in larger numbers each fall, but the runs probably lasted for a shorter period. Similarly, although the number of larger game animals probably remained relatively stable, winter access became problematic because of more extensive forests and more frequent winter snows. Wet meadows, which offered optimal growing conditions for camas, improved in the south, but dry meadow plants lost ground in the north.

Berry-producing plants often flourish in landscapes ravaged by fire. Visit a recently burned forest in the interior Pacific Northwest and you will struggle to pass through a nearly impenetrable thicket of wild rose, Oregon grape, Saskatoon, and snowberry bushes. Under wet conditions, fires are far less frequent, and berry bushes are less prominent in mature forests. Berry patches undoubtedly shrank during the Neoglacial period.

When cooling began, it was the Plateau societies in the Interior that were hit the hardest, perhaps because their foraging strategy, which was based on immediate returns, was not geared toward colder, wetter conditions. These foragers generally gather and consume their food daily and rarely preserve it for longer than a day or two. Daily foraging is a sensible adaptation when food is widely distributed in relatively reliable locations. Most of the hunting and gathering people of 4,000-5,000 years ago likely followed this pattern. In contrast, delayed return hunter-gatherers (e.g., collectors) anticipate future subsistence needs by gathering more than can be immediately eaten and storing it for later use in the year. This strategy is most effective when there is a true cold season that requires some foods to be collected under warmer conditions. Up until 3,600 years ago, only a few isolated groups, for instance, the Haida Gwaii food collectors, fit this model.

In the end, the mobile foragers of the Lochnore culture, who had successfully inhabited areas of central British Columbia for several thousand years, disappeared without a trace. There is no evidence of their descendants anywhere. It is possible that, as things got progressively worse, entire families starved to death during the long winters, their bodies consumed by scavengers the following spring. It is also possible that many people survived by moving in with groups outside the region, taking up the culture and tools of their hosts. Either way, the Lochnore culture disappeared nearly 4,000 years ago. Things were not much better down in the Columbia Basin. People who lived in the Pithouse I hamlets, those who focused on broad-spectrum food gathering, were apparently in no position to survive the colder conditions. Their lifeway disappeared in tandem with the Lochnore peoples. For the next five hundred years, the occasional individual or group moved rapidly across the Plateau, leaving a small hearth here or a few tools there. No one stayed in one place for long. Perhaps they were survivors of the disaster; perhaps they were visitors from afar who wondered about what had happened.

Things were not quite so stark on the Coast. It is clear that the Charles culture peoples were affected by climate change. Archaeologists are unclear about the process, but it appears that some groups began to stay for longer periods at the best fishing spots within the Gulf Islands of the Gulf of Georgia and around the mouth of the Fraser River. Some might have even developed and guarded territories. Experiments with large houses and dramatic public-cooking events peaked almost 3,800 years ago in the Fraser Valley, however, and came to an abrupt end between 3,500 and 3,000 years ago. The same period also saw a fluorescence of artwork, particularly work associated with burials in coastal contexts.

We can interpret this artwork in one of two ways. First, it is possible that the most successful groups demonstrated their power by burying their dead with great ceremony, sending elaborately carved horn spoons or hundreds of stone beads off with the deceased. Second, the artwork may be evidence of the revival of ritual practices, which often follow disasters and are expressed through elaborate graveside ceremonies. Whatever happened, it appears that this culture was ready for new ideas; it was one of the first to accept the new economic strategy, which likely came from the north.

The Expansion of the Collector Strategy

Although the forager societies apparently fell apart, those that possessed the collector strategy expanded (Figure 2.10). There was no apparent cultural change on Haida Gwaii around 4,000 years ago, suggesting that colder conditions caused no problems to an economy already organized to overcome seasonal shortages. Elsewhere, however, change was dramatic. In the Lower Fraser Valley, especially in the Fraser Delta region, evidence shows that people adopted new forms of collector behaviour about 3,600 years ago. The new Fraser Delta culture, termed the Locarno Beach phase (named by Charles Borden after a 3,000-year-old village located near the now popular bathing beach in Vancouver), exhibited many characteristics of the more ancient Haida Gwaii culture. Settlements were more stable, not permanent but certainly more sedentary than before. Task groups were sent out to harvest large quantities of salmon, rockfish, flatfish, and mussels. They processed salmon for storage. They removed the heads at the collection site, split the bodies open, likely smoked the flesh, and returned the fish to the village for later use. Locarno Beach shell middens are full of salmon vertebrae, ribs, and spines.

Locarno Beach people made leaf-shaped spear points, just like their ancient ancestors of the Old Cordilleran. But they also produced stemmed spear points and ground slate knives (Box 2.2). They still relied on a core and flake technology to produce basic short-term-use tools. Locarno Beach people also developed more sophisticated bone and antler technologies. Salmon fishing sometimes required specialized fish spears or Leister spears, which consisted of a tip with three points for spearing and holding a fish. As sea mammal hunting grew in importance, Locarno Beach hunters relied on a tool form called a toggling harpoon head. Archaeologists working in the Arctic note that northern people had two types of harpoon. The first, known as a non-toggling harpoon, had a single-shaft head with a line hole near the base and one or more barbs in the margin. It was designed to penetrate the prey and hold it with the barbs. The second, the toggling harpoon, had a more complex design that allowed the harpoon head to completely enter the animal's body. The hunter held the animal by pulling on a centrally attached line to twist the harpoon sideways under the animal's skin. Locarno Beach people designed their toggle harpoons with two halves or valves. When tied together in the centre, the valves left a slot on top for the attachment of a sharp blade. The two bases spread outward in sharp points. Once inside the prey, the harpoon would twist, catching the animal's flesh on its blade and on its basal barbs, effectively trapping the animal and allowing the hunter to retrieve it.

Locarno Beach bone and antler workers also produced thick antler wedges to split wood, presumably to make wooden salmon traps and house structures. Archaeologists do not know much about Locarno Beach houses. In some places, they consisted of small shallow pithouses; in others, they were more substantial wooden constructions. The people also made bone needles and awls for sewing and hooks and bipoints for fishing. The domestic economy included the production of small pieces of artwork, often in antler, such as beads and pendants. It was the beginnings of classic Northwest Coast culture.

BOX 2.2 THE LOCARNO BEACH PEOPLE AND GROUND-STONE KNIVES

Why did many Northwest Coast groups such as those of the Locarno Beach phase go to the trouble of making ground-stone knives, which are time-consuming to craft? Marine resources, especially salmon but also other fish and sea mammals such as harbour seals, were an essential part of the Locarno Beach economy. The people therefore developed or borrowed technological innovations from neighbouring groups up the Coast to help make harvesting these resources possible. Locarno Beach people expanded the Charles culture's ground slate industry by developing a wide range of knives, spears, and blades. To make these tools, the stoneworker must chip the object roughly into shape. Since slate breaks only along what geologists call cleavage plains,

the stoneworker has to grind the edges to make a sharp tool.

Why go to all that trouble? Would the old chipped-stone knives not have worked just as well? They would have, but chipped-stone tools dull relatively quickly, whereas ground-stone knives last much longer. If you have five hundred salmon to process, you don't have time to make new stone tools. Ground slate solves the problem. It holds a workable edge far longer and therefore requires less effort to resharpen. Fish (and other foods) can be processed more efficiently. Efficiency is not simply a modern Western concept: the Locarno Beach people recognized that it could mean the difference between life and death in the late winter.

The question remains, how did the collector strategy come to be the main approach employed by Fraser Delta people and their immediate neighbours? It is clear that the people of the Gulf of Georgia did not leave, and there is no evidence for an invasion by groups from other areas. The cultural similarities between the Charles culture and the Locarno Beach groups suggest that this shift could not have been the result of new people coming into the area. Two options remain: independent invention or cultural transmission (the imitation or borrowing of ideas). As noted earlier, the appearance of collecting in the Fraser Delta and Gulf Islands was not gradual but abrupt. This does not mean that collecting could not have been independently developed, but given the proximity of North Coast peoples and the regular trade networks that undoubtedly operated in the region, it is likely that central Coast folk were aware of interesting and innovative developments among their northern neighbours.

Archaeological evidence suggests that some members of the Locarno Beach culture did not stay put on the Coast. Almost as soon as the collector strategy appeared in the Lower Fraser Valley and the adjacent coast, it expanded to the Plateau. Just after 3,500 BP, a new culture appeared in the Columbia Basin, which archaeologists called Pithouse II. People of Pithouse II returned to living in communities along the Columbia and adjacent streams. Their small villages superficially resembled those of Pithouse I, but a closer examination reveals significant differences. Pithouse II settlements consist of clusters of smallish houses, and the houses contain storage pits and frequent-activity areas designated specially for processing foods. Animal bones suggest that Pithouse II subsistence strategies also differed from those followed by Pithouse I peoples. While Pithouse I sites contain equal numbers of many kinds of animals, Pithouse II sites contain fewer types of animals and indicate a greater reliance on one or two specific types, especially salmon. The lack of head bones at the houses suggests that the people probably processed salmon for storage at the initial fishing site.

It is tempting, if not logical, to conclude that Pithouse I simply evolved into Pithouse II. The facts, however, do not necessarily support this argument. First, it is now clear that the two cultures were separated by a 500-year period in which no pithouses were in use and few people lived in the Columbia Basin. Second, the artifacts recovered strongly resemble those of the central Northwest Coast rather than those of earlier local cultures. Pithouse II people made projectile points that were stemmed like those of the Locarno Beach people. They also had toggling and non-toggling harpoons much like those used on the Coast. Finally, Pithouse II peoples clearly had a collector economy much like that of the people at Locarno Beach, one that included the mass harvesting and storage of specific food resources such as salmon and camas.

The Pithouse II culture was successful and thrived for 1,000 years. If the coastal fishing culture could expand successfully into the dry Columbia Basin, it makes perfect sense that something like it could move into the less arid Canadian Plateau.

The Early Housepit Culture of the Mid-Fraser

The boy loves to hear stories about the salmon runs. His grandfather, face aglow in the firelight and shadow dancing on the wall behind him, recounts how the river had been so black with fish this spring that the children could almost walk across the water on their backs.

The boy had watched the fish leaping, their scales catching pieces of the sun. He had watched the older people hang their bodies on drying racks and had helped his mother pack the dried, oily fish, layer upon layer, in boxes and pits lined with bark. He thinks about the deer meat and berries, also snug and dry in their boxes, waiting for winter.

Grandfather finishes his story. The boy and his friends continue to play a pebble game in the shadows but grow still as they hear the other men's response.

The boy's uncle says, "True, there were many salmon this year, but there is little fat and not much beyond meat, aside from the berries. If the winter is cold, colder than usual, and long, will the berries give us enough energy to get us through the lean season?"

His mother asks, "What if our relatives nearby ask us to share our food with them? What then? We must travel to the meadows in the warmer areas to harvest roots. The patches here are too small."

The boy's uncle suggests that a small group of the strongest men and women should travel to the meadows. His mother says they can cook the roots at the site rather than carrying them all the way home raw. They can also collect toolstone cobbles and hunt for deer.

As the boy pushes a pebble into position, he wonders if his family will once again have to move.

The collector strategy came to the Mid-Fraser Canyon on the Canadian Plateau at about 3,500 years ago. Archaeological evidence suggests that early

FIGURE 2.11
Unexcavated small
pithouse along the Stein
River drainage, 1986.
Photograph by Ian Kuijt

FIGURE 2.12 Diagram
of a small Shuswap
horizon housepit village
at the Van Male site
near Kamloops. The
layout is typical of late
Shuswap horizon occu-
pations with relatively
few houses spaced
closely together.
Richards and Rousseau (1982)

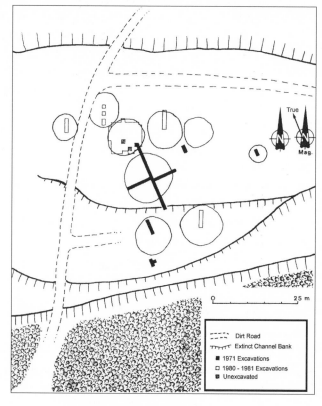

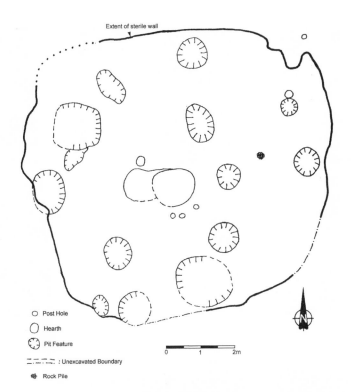

Extent of sterile wall

○ Post Hole
◖ Hearth
⚙ Pit Feature
⌐.⌐.⌐. : Unexcavated Boundary
❀ Rock Pile

0   1   2m

FIGURE 2.13 Diagram showing a Shuswap horizon housepit floor from the Van Male site. This is a typical late Shuswap horizon house floor with frequent cache pits for food storage.
Richards and Rousseau (1982)

groups were more mobile than those that came later. It is also possible that not all of the new groups persisted in the area for long time spans. Some might have suffered hardships associated with the long winters of the Neoglacial period.

Archaeologists first identified these early Mid-Fraser pithouse-using peoples during the 1960s. Beyond helping to define some of the earliest peoples on the Canadian Plateau, one of the major contributions of David Sanger's excavations was uncovering evidence for early pithouse users, now known as the people of the Shuswap horizon (see Figures 2.11 and 2.12). His research indicated that these people built their houses between about 2,500 and 3,500 years ago. The houses were circular and could be as large as 15 metres in diameter. Later research throughout the region suggested, however, that houses on average tended to be in the same size range as those of Pithouse II (Figures 2.10, 2.12, and 2.13). Some appear to have had side entrances, while evidence suggests that those without obvious side entrances had wooden ladders that stretched from a rooftop opening to the floor.

Stone tools from this early housepit culture were similar to those of the Coast, yet they also had some incredible similarities with those of the northern Great Plains, far to the east (Figure 2.14). Sanger found classic leaf-shaped and stemmed spear points that differed little from those of the Locarno Beach culture. Yet, he also found points with split-based stems that resembled those of the Oxbow and McKean cultures of Alberta and Montana to the east. The incredible range of variation in these points has never been explained fully. It could reflect a mixing of peoples, some coming in from the Coast and others moving west across the Rocky Mountains. But it more likely represents interaction between the new groups of the BC Interior and those of the Plains.

Beyond finely made spear points, Shuswap knappers frequently produced generalized flake tools. They also made triangular end scrapers for working hides, a phenomenon that is not surprising given their interior Plateau context, with its Neoglacial winters. Like the people of Pithouse II, Shuswap peoples employed an array of bone and antler tools, including antler wedges, non-toggling harpoons, spoons and other spatulate tools, and small bone points, which were possibly used as fish gorges (a form of fish hook). There is some evidence of trade with peoples on the Coast in the form of shell items, although this appears to have been rare.

Shuswap horizon foodways are not well known. Shuswap-era houses show few signs of storage pits until nearly 3,000 years ago, when they became standard. Various investigators have noted the appearance of salmon remains, but there are almost no systematic descriptions of Shuswap animal bone assemblages. Root roasting appears to have been extremely rare in this period, which is not surprising because dry meadows, which contained the greatest numbers of edible root-bearing plants, shrank during the Neoglacial period. Shuswap housepits contain thin floors and relatively little midden development, suggesting that the people stayed in place for only one or a few winters. The sites are also relatively rare. While this rarity may, in part, reflect fewer investigations compared to the Columbia Basin, it may also indicate that people did not always live in the same place across the Canadian Plateau. It also suggests that there were fewer people living in this area, especially during the Shuswap horizon's earlier period (circa 2,800 to 3,500 years ago).

What was life like for people who lived during the early Shuswap period? It is clear that they faced greater challenges than Columbia Basin pithouse users. Although both groups relied on salmon resources, their use of other key food sources differed. Shuswap and Lochnore peoples faced similar problems. Indeed, since the Neoglacial period peaked only about 3,000 years ago, conditions were likely even tougher. The time it took to search for deer and other large game probably remained high, limiting the numbers that could be predictably obtained.

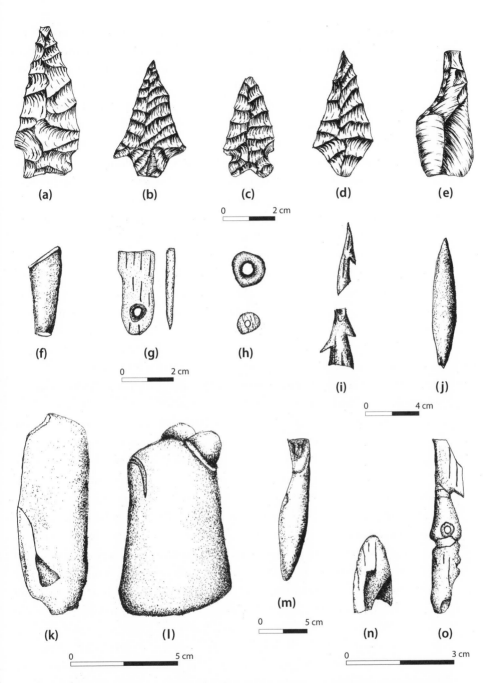

0   2 cm

0   2 cm

0   4 cm

0   5 cm

0   5 cm

0   3 cm

FIGURE 2.14 Artifacts associated with the Shuswap horizon and related cultures of the Plateau, ca. 3,500 to 2,400 years ago: *(a-d)* stemmed projectile points, *(e)* key-shaped uniface, *(f)* bone bead, *(g)* bone bracelet or pendant fragment, *(h)* bone disk beads, *(i)* non-toggling harpoon tip, *(j)* bone bipoint, *(k)* nephrite adze, *(l)* zoomorphic hand maul (Van Male site), *(m)* antler wedge, *(n)* portion of a toggling harpoon valve (Columbia Basin), *(o)* toggling harpoon tip (Columbia Basin).

Illustrations by Robert O'Boyle

Carbohydrate sources, particularly from edible root plants, might not have been easy to come by either. Because these people relied on a low-fat, high-protein diet focused on salmon, deer, and other mammals, reduced access to carbohydrates would have posed a serious problem. It is well known that people can starve to death on a high-protein diet. On the Great Plains, settlers called this phenomenon rabbit starvation. Perhaps it is not surprising that the number of people did not increase until the Neoglacial period peaked, when things started to warm up and carbohydrate resources expanded. Populations eventually increased and were reflected in larger villages in the northern Interior. We can imagine early Shuswap families collecting what they could and relying on salmon runs for protein and some fat. Tough times in winter perhaps caused some families to pick up and move multiple times in a never-ending search for food, especially food with some source of energy.

The origins of the Shuswap people are unclear. Oral histories hold few clues, and the question continues to be debated among archaeologists of the Canadian Plateau. During the early 1990s, a team of archaeologists led by Ian Wilson conducted an excavation of the Baker site, located in the South Thompson Valley east of Kamloops. The Baker site had several layers of occupations, including one (Layer 2) possibly associated with the Lochnore culture. But in Layer 3 the archaeologists uncovered something they had not expected, pithouses. The site contained three small houses, none larger than four metres in diameter. The sandy floors were dense with stone tools and debitage. The amount of this chipped-stone waste material was extraordinary: over 20,000 items in each house. The number of cache pits and the quantity of salmon were even more extraordinary. Many of the fish lacked heads, suggesting the possibility of storage processing.

The Baker site instantly became the subject of debate. Wilson, citing similarities in house construction and stone artifact styles, argued that the site had likely been occupied by a small group of Pithouse I peoples who temporarily explored a new drainage and fishery and tinkered with a collector-like economy. Other archaeologists, such as Arnoud Stryd and Mike Rousseau, suggested that Layer 3 at Baker was actually a Lochnore occupation. The site, they argued, was evidence for the development of collector strategies in the core area of the Canadian Plateau and was likely occupied by a culture ancestral to the Shuswap horizon.

There are, however, some serious problems with linking the Baker site to the Lochnore culture and suggesting that the culture was the ancestor of the Pithouse-using villagers of the late period in this region. First, there are no uniquely and unambiguously diagnostic Lochnore artifacts in the site's pithouse strata. The projectile point styles are much closer to those of Pithouse I than to

Lochnore. Second, the site dates to nearly 1,000 years before the appearance of the next pithouse users, the Shuswap horizon, in the region. Finally, the pits do not indicate the presence of a full-scale winter-village collector strategy. Fish- or root-storage pits from later periods are often as much as a metre deep and a metre wide. The Baker pits, by contrast, are shallow, rarely more than 30 centimetres in depth. They were likely used for something other than long-term storage and should not be called storage pits. Wilson was probably correct. The Baker site was likely a short-term experiment by people from outside the region, people who were not necessarily direct ancestors of later pithouse users on the Canadian Plateau.

If we stand back and look at the Shuswap horizon from a regional standpoint, we can see that it shares many artifacts and household features with the Pithouse II and Locarno Beach cultures. The subsistence pattern was likely the same, and the circular housepits were similar. Finally, all of these cultures relied on stemmed projectile points, generalized flake and core technologies, and a variety of specific bone or antler tools, including wedges, gorges, spoons, and harpoons. These combined data suggest a coastal origin for the Shuswap horizon; they suggest it was part of the larger Locarno Beach expansion. Times were probably tough in the northern Interior, especially during the long winters of the Neoglacial period. It would not be surprising, therefore, if the first settlers who moved in from the Coast were driven back. But the collector strategy as implemented by the Shuswap horizon peoples ultimately prevailed. A pithouse-using culture, one characterized by the storage of salmon and increased sedentism, was fully in place by 2,500 years ago. This culture became the dominant practice in the region and served as one of several social and economic foundations for the emergence of complex cultural lifeways.

3
The Early House Societies

Here it is. Between the trees and through the mist and rain, the people see
the place where the two great rivers meet. Just as grandmother had foretold,
the backs and tails of thousands of fish surge in the turbulent waters. A fish
leaps, drawing the people's attention to several bears prowling the shore.
Others feast in the shallows. Clouds of gulls spiral overhead, and an eagle
careens through their midst. The smell of fish hangs in the moist air.

They had never seen such bounty in one place. One man remarks that the
fish are like people gathering for a great meeting before a sacred duty. A boy
asks how long they will stay and smiles upon hearing the woman's reply. The
extra food, she says, will be shared with guests during winter dances and
feasts. Perhaps, she speculates, it is time to build a bigger house.

Nearly 4,000 years ago, people in the Northwest Coast began to face new
challenges brought about by the climatic changes of the Neoglacial period.
Winters were long and cold, but fishing and sea mammal hunting steadily
improved. Indeed, the people who occupied this region 3,000 years ago likely
enjoyed its most bountiful years. They had already developed the technology to
mass harvest wild foods and store them for long-term use. They had the tools
and the know-how to make large-scale wooden structures and monuments.
Increasing food resources allowed for population growth, and formal territorial

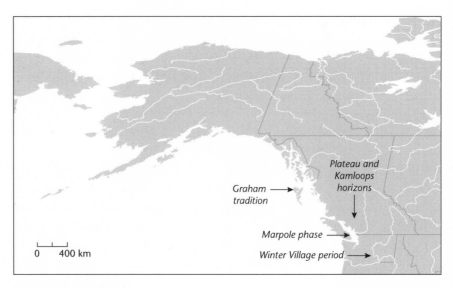

FIGURE 3.1 Major cultural patterns of the Pacific Northwest around 2,500 to 200 years ago.

boundaries likely developed between groups. Yet most people continued to live in small groups and in small houses. They gathered into larger groups during fishing season and likely dispersed during other parts of the year, as they had for centuries.

People who lived in the Interior experienced similar changes, but they were more extreme. In response, family groups in different regions at different points of the year were probably smaller and more flexible in terms of territory, marriage, residence rules, and lifeways. Yet, when food resources boomed, these people gathered in even greater numbers than those who lived on the Coast. Given that hunter-gatherers tend to live in conservative traditional societies, it makes perfect sense that this situation remained stable.

Yet dramatic cultural changes accompanied climatic change (see Box 3.1). In the forests of the Fraser Valley, near the modern-day towns of Chilliwack and Hope in particular, drastic changes to economic and social practices set the stage for the emergence of the complex cultures of the Late Period. Elements of this culture might have been at least partially ancestral to those of the Mid-Fraser Canyon. In this chapter, we explore aspects of the interior and Fraser Valley cultures (Figure 3.1) that predate the great Mid-Fraser villages to examine how and why significant changes occurred.

The Fraser Valley

Around 2,500 years ago, the long, cold winters of the Neoglacial period lost much of their edge. Indeed, on average, winters were milder and drier than those of the Neoglacial period. On the central Coast, forest fires became more frequent and changed the distribution of wild food resources used by hunter-gatherers. Warmer conditions meant rising stream and sea surface temperatures. Warm water is generally disastrous for marine ecosystems in the North Pacific and has a profound effect on spawning salmon. Archaeologist Dana Lepofsky and colleagues argue that many smaller spawning streams were closed off, leaving only larger rivers for spawning. The warm water, which contained increasing amounts of sediment from upland erosion, likely delayed spawning. Salmon would cluster around a few key places until they were given a biological signal to move upstream. Waiting too long at these spots resulted in too many fish and increased opportunities for the spread of disease. The creation of these resource hotspots led to what ecologists call a patchy environment. Salmon were available in enormous numbers at only a few places, usually the opening of river mouths.

BOX 3.1 THE EMERGENCE OF CULTURAL COMPLEXITY ON THE NORTHWEST COAST

The development of the first Northwest Coast villages is a subject of research and debate. Although collector settlements and subsistence behaviour existed almost everywhere 3,500 years ago, large permanent villages with plank houses appeared at different places at different times. It is possible that these structures were developed on Haida Gwaii over 5,000 years ago, and they were undoubtedly present in the Prince Rupert Harbour region between 4,500 and 4,000 years ago. Recent research in the area by archaeologist Andrew Martindale and colleagues suggests, however, that although these people had ethnographic-style row villages on beach fronts, their social relationships might have been quite different from those of later times.

The history of plank house villages on the central Coast is likely still incomplete. Drawing from current data presented by Dana Lepofsky and colleagues, we estimate that the Fraser Valley peoples experimented with these house forms off and on between 2,000 and 5,000 years ago, if not longer. Plank house settlements likely became widespread elsewhere in the Central and South Coast regions after 2,000 years ago. As Martindale and colleagues indicate, the appearance of plank house villages on beaches and river terraces does not necessarily mean that the communities were organized in the same manner as those existing at the time of European contact. They might have had different settlement and subsistence patterns, social relations, and rituals, and it is incumbent upon the region's archaeologists to avoid inappropriate reifications of the ethnographic record in their interpretations of the more ancient archaeological record.

This phenomenon likely reached its most intense level along the major stream choke points that emptied into the Fraser, such as the Harrison River. These places were a powerful magnet for humans. Indeed, control of these locations would offer major economic advantages to any group.

Salmon were not, however, the entire story. Although these fish offered a lot of lean protein and some fat, groups needed more than salmon to survive year round. Winter survival required other foods, particularly carbohydrates. Fires, whether from natural causes or purposefully generated by people, also created patchy environments in the mountains, where some places were burned completely while others ranged from being only partially burned to untouched. Because the burned landscapes regenerated quickly, the areas offered remarkable nutritional opportunities to human foragers. Many species of berry bushes flourished in the nutrient-rich land, as did a variety of other small shrubs, saplings, and grasses. Because plant growth draws animals, these foragers could also expect to find deer, elk, mountain sheep, bears, and other small mammals. For humans, berries and edible root-bearing plants, both fresh and dried, were a crucial source of carbohydrates. People hunted bears for meat and fat and ungulates (hoofed animals) for a major supplemental source of protein. These large animals also offered hides, antler, bone, and sinew, all of which were needed for producing clothing and tools.

Foraging in this patchy environment no longer entailed long journeys across vast marginally productive landscapes. Groups could instead target and pursue resources known to be in specific places. Ecologists tell us that when food resources come in clumps, so too do predators. Dana Lepofsky and colleagues suggest that there were definite islands of productivity 2,500 years ago, particularly at river mouths, surrounded by more extensive landscapes with lower production levels.

It is within this environment that late Locarno Beach phase collectors began to live in larger groups and in more substantial structures. They established villages and flourished in places such as at the mouth of the Harrison River near present-day Chilliwack or on the banks of the Fraser River near the base of the Lower Fraser Canyon near present-day Hope. Both offer excellent places for people to wait for salmon and for salmon to wait for the biological signal to move upstream. Both locations also provide access to the hemlock forests of the Coast Range. Although these areas were still in the coastal vegetative zone, they were 80 kilometers from the Coast, where the largest populations lived near present-day Vancouver and in the Gulf Islands. With no large local population to reinforce the rules of residence and intergroup relations, the people of the Fraser Valley had more opportunity to experiment. Unlike their coastal cousins, who relied more on marine foods scattered throughout the landscape, inland peoples began to focus on ecological hotspots. Evidence for this argument comes from the work of Dana Lepofsky and archaeologist Michael Blake, who initiated excavations at the Qithyil or Scowlitz site, an ancient village and cemetery near the mouth of the Harrison River (Figure 3.2). Lepofsky and Blake's teams found multiple house depressions and over two hundred small burial mounds. They concentrated on one large house, named Structure 3 (Figure 3.3).

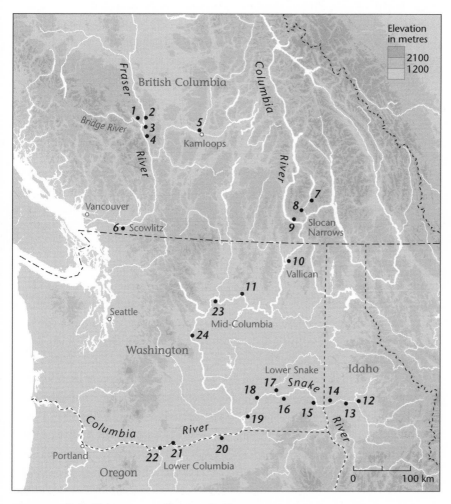

FIGURE 3.2 Major Plateau villages. The villages of the Middle Fraser Canyon include those near Bridge River, Keatley Creek, Bell, and Lochnore-Nesikep *(1-4)*; Kamloops *(5)*; and Scowlitz *(6)*. The map also identifies villages on the Upper Columbia, including Slocan Narrows and Vallican *(7-10)*; the Mid-Columbia villages *(11, 23-24)*; the Lower Snake River villages *(12-19)*; and the Lower Columbia villages *(20-22)*.

FIGURE 3.3 Excavation of
Structure 3, Scowlitz site,
1999. This is a large and early
dating house structure in the
Fraser Valley.
Photograph by Anna M. Prentiss

The team discovered that Structure 3 was nearly 17 metres in diameter. Its
interior included a series of large post-holes, presumably for a wooden roof.
Hearth features and clusters of artifacts sat adjacent to the posts and parallel to
each wall. This arrangement and European sources written at the time of contact
suggest that each family living in the large house had its own hearth. Charcoal
samples submitted for radiocarbon dating yielded another astounding discovery.
Structure 3 had been occupied somewhere between 2,700 and 2,000 years ago
and was only one of a series of unusually large houses that sat on the waterfront
at Qithyil. One other village, known as Sxwóxwiymlh or the Katz site, located
to the east, also featured rows of houses and dated to this period, but its houses
were smaller.

At some point, people in some parts of the Fraser Valley had stopped living
in the small houses associated with the Locarno Beach people and had begun

to live together in large houses composed of multiple families. Structure 3 at Qithyil might have had up to six families residing on its floor. If the families consisted of at least five people each (they were probably larger), the population of the house would have easily reached 30 people. Large numbers of people living in crowded conditions for long periods can lead to big trouble – interpersonal strife or simply the daily annoyances, such as noise and odours, associated with having others so close at hand. People must have had good reasons to live in such crowded conditions.

Like all predators, humans cluster around the locations of key or rich foods. If the environment is patchy, they may even defend their spatial position or territory. The people of these villages had both an opportunity and a problem. If they could hang on to their position at the mouth of the river, then they would have a guaranteed bonanza of food every fall in the form of salmon. Yet many of their other key food resources, located in the mountains, had to be harvested at the same time. Berries ripen in midsummer, when ungulates and bears are fattest. To guard their village, the people literally had to be in three places at once.

The people of the Fraser Valley apparently hit upon a strategy for managing this situation: they formed larger cooperative groups that were likely linked by kinship ties. This cooperation was probably the beginning of the classic Coast Salish house-based lineage system, a complex social arrangement that existed through to contact with European groups. The larger corporate groups could conduct simultaneous operations, ensuring control of the fishing site while sending smaller task groups into the mountains to get other valuable resources. Theoretically, by late fall each year, they would have harvested and stored a wide range of foods for winter use or exchange.

But even the best village could not provide access to everything; therefore, it was always good to have insurance policies in the form of arrangements with other groups. We can imagine that the excellent economic position of the Fraser Valley people and, later, others like them, permitted their household heads to negotiate beneficial exchanges, to establish permanent peaceful relations with neighbouring groups that were perhaps not quite so well off. Members of the more powerful group probably benefitted from arranged marriages, which cemented intergroup relations. But control of the most bountiful place in the landscape was the trump card. It permitted the holders of the place to always have a strong hand in sensitive negotiations. Holding this position, however, required a larger, more powerful group than was typical of the earlier Locarno Beach era.

The people of the Fraser Valley therefore developed a new strategy that archaeologists call complex collecting. The people were still collectors, just like the other peoples of the region, but they employed a whole new set of tactics that involved the operation of dense clusters of people based in large house groups. Archaeologists are not sure whether the complex collector strategy spread or groups in the coming centuries hit on the idea independently. It is clear, however, that the strategy did appear later, just after 2,000 BP (before the present), in the Fraser Delta area and in Puget Sound and on Vancouver Island (Box 3.2).

Occupation patterns at Qithyil and other Fraser Valley villages changed during an apparent regional population decline that occurred around 2,000 to 1,800 years ago. It is not clear why this decline occurred. Perhaps warmer temperatures caused salmon populations to fall. Perhaps the new, dense villages favoured the spread of disease. The Qithyil village was later used as a special place to gather plant resources, and it eventually became a cemetery so powerful and important that the Stó:lō still see it as a spiritual place. In its day, however, Qithyil and its sister villages such as Sxwóxwiymlh had the potential to exert a wide influence that may have extended up into the Mid-Fraser region.

On The Plateau

The Canadian Plateau

The families had been arriving at the gathering place for days. Men salvaged house timbers and dug dirt out of old pits. The man was covered with dust but happy. He could hear the elders giving instruction, the women singing songs. The families were reclaiming last year's fishing spot. Tomorrow, the younger men would set up camp at the fishing site. He would help build fish-drying racks while others worked to get the village ready.

Winter was in the air. The man thought a big harvest would be good for everyone. Catching and processing fish would bring them together. While the young men guarded the drying fish, he would lead the other men to the best hunting places and root-harvesting grounds. They would have enough food to survive for weeks, maybe months.

The man looked forward to the weddings and birthday celebrations, the gambling and trading. This year, his family would trade hides and finished leather goods for stone tools and rare items. Perhaps he would even have enough to trade for some obsidian or coastal shell.

BOX 3.2 THE MARPOLE PHASE OF THE CENTRAL NORTHWEST COAST

The Marpole phase of central Northwest Coast prehistory, generally dated to between 2,500 and 1,200 years ago, is often held up as the earliest fully developed Northwest Coast culture. This concept does mask significant spatiotemporal variation in late Holocene Northwest Coast cultures, but archaeologists widely recognize that the concept of a fully developed culture denotes the beginning of cultural patterns at least similar to those of the early colonial period. Marpole phase villages have been found in the lower Fraser River Valley, the Gulf Islands, and on the east side of Vancouver Island. During the phase's peak period, around 1,800 to 1,300 years ago, villages included multiple large plank houses positioned along beaches or river terraces. House size and position indicated rank within the village. Space within houses was also organized by rank. Archaeologists found clusters of beads, ground-stone bowls, and tools made from nonlocal raw materials such as nephrite jade and obsidian around the hearths of the most important families. Burials, placed outside the houses and best illustrated at Qithyil, also indicated status differentiation. The graves of elite individuals, including children, contained stone liners, occasionally with lime floors (as at Qithyil), and elaborate artifact displays that could include thousands of stone or shell beads. Elite children were marked for life by cranial deformation, the artificial flattening of the forehead.

Archaeologists have offered a variety of explanations for the emergence of the Marpole phase. Archaeologist David Burley argued that the complex collector people of the Marpole phase originated in, and spread from the Fraser Valley to the Coast. His argument, however, did not convince everyone. Archaeologists such as R.G. Matson have noted that artifacts from early Marpole middens looked like they could have evolved from the Locarno Beach phase. In Matson's view, the complex collectors of the Coast likely evolved slowly out of the Locarno Beach cultural phase. The actual process might have been more complex than either scenario implies, one shaped by population movement and the exchange of cultural ideas. More research will undoubtedly extend the debate well into the future.

The big question remains: why did inequality develop in the first place? Archaeologists have pondered this question for years and have offered a variety of hypotheses. Some suggest that opportunities for inequality evolved from ownership and control of resource collection places such as fishing sites. Others argue that status differentiation had more to do with control of trade and the advantages that came with it. Yet others propose that humans are hardwired to strive for power. This interpretation is based on the assumption that inequality simply needs to be let out; it is a proverbial Pandora's Box. One major problem in resolving this debate is that the archaeological record of the Northwest Coast does not provide a fine-grained picture of the events surrounding the shift to this form of social organization. It is rare to find a village that contains sealed evidence from individual houses that spans the transition from an egalitarian to a ranked society. Later developments in the Mid-Fraser Canyon offer a better understanding of the phenomenon.

FIGURE 3.4 A hillside filled with flowering balsamroot near Lytton.
Photograph by Ian Kuijt

The people of the Canadian Plateau drew a range of benefits from the environmental fluctuations of this period. As temperatures warmed, terrestrial animals such as deer and elk likely became more abundant. Dry meadows – populated by spring beauty, balsamroot, bitterroot, and other edible root plants – expanded rapidly (Figure 3.4). Access to deer in the higher elevations improved because of reduced snowfall and thinner forests. Many berry species also benefitted from drier conditions.

Environmental changes on the Canadian Plateau likely influenced socioeconomic change and population growth. As with earlier cultural periods, direct information on foodways is sparse for the period between 2,500 and 1,800 years ago. This period is known among archaeologists as the early Plateau horizon. We know from studies by archaeologists Sandra Peacock, David Pokotylo, and

Dana Lepofsky that root harvesting and roasting increased rapidly in importance during this period. Places such as Hat Creek Valley have dozens, maybe hundreds, of large dish-shaped roasting pits. Digging sticks for extracting roots also show up in the archaeological record during this period.

There is indirect evidence that hunters enjoyed greater success. It is well known among archaeologists that the more mobile and hunting-oriented peoples of northern latitudes tend to have the most carefully formed stone tools. Classic examples range from the Upper Paleolithic hunters of Eurasia, who had refined technologies based on carefully shaped blades, to pre-European Eskimos (in Alaska) and Inuit (in Canada), who are famous for their use of a wide range of tools, including specialized end blades for harpoons, spear points, arrow points, knives, and scrapers. The Middle Period on the Canadian Plateau offered another example. The Nesikep tradition featured specialized and finely made bifaces, unifaces, and microblades. When we examine early Plateau horizon technologies, we find significant refinements in tool making, including large and finely made corner-notched spear points, large and thin bifacial knives, ovoid to triangular hide scrapers, and a unique tool called a key-shape formed uniface, typically used to scrape wood to form atlatl, spear-thrower darts (Figure 3.5). The people focused on acquiring higher quality stone, presumably to make better tools. The number of small camps in upland areas, presumably devoted to hunting (among other things), might have increased. Overall, these data imply a focus on hunting midsize to larger game.

Hunting and root collecting were not the only facets of the economy. Although salmon became less reliable as a key food resource along the Coast, salmon numbers in the Plateau remained relatively high in key places such as the Six Mile Rapids of the Mid-Fraser Canyon. Fish congregated and rested in the rivers eddies before tackling places such as the Bridge River or heading farther up the Fraser. There might have been a similar bottleneck at the juncture of the North and South Thompson rivers to the east, in what is today Kamloops. Accessing salmon on a reliable basis required local knowledge and the ability to predict and relocate to the place of major runs. Interestingly, there is no evidence of intensive occupation of the Mid-Fraser region before about 1,900 to 1,800 years ago. This lack of evidence may be due to archaeological sampling. Occasional housepits have been dated to this period, but in general there are few well-dated occupations.

Large groups of people did, however, live in the Kamloops area (Figures 3.6 and 3.7) between 2,300 and 1,600 years ago. We know little about these occupations since most of the settlements were destroyed by urban development. Archaeologist Mike Rousseau suggests that these settlements were winter villages made up of dozens of small family-size houses (generally no larger than 8 metres

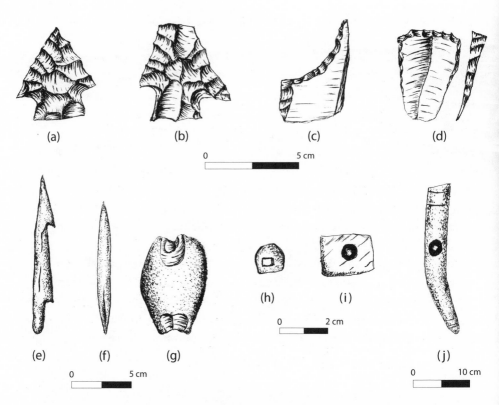

FIGURE 3.5 Stone tools of the Plateau horizon and related regional cultures: *(a-b)* corner-notched projectile points, *c)* key-shaped uniface, *(d)* end scraper, *(e)* harpoon (leister) tip, *(f)* bone bipoint, *(g)* net weight, *(h)* bone bead, *(i)* bone button (Keatley Creek site), and *(j)* digging-stick handle.

Illustrations by Robert O'Boyle

in diameter). Rousseau suggests that people occupied the settlements for long time spans. They made use of large storage pits and nearby field camps to collect animal and plant foods, including roots. Rousseau's theory makes sense because this location had major resource advantages. The villages would have been situated in a dry valley with a productive river and adjacent to high rolling grasslands and forests. The combination of resources available and the ability of groups to use logistical mobility to acquire foods from these patches likely made up for the remote location.

The evidence suggests that while many early Plateau horizon groups operated from small winter housepit hamlets, groups in the Kamloops area lived in larger villages, at least during the late summer and fall. One of the major questions is the permanence of the household occupations. Similar clusters of

3.6 A housepit along the Thompson River in Kamloops.

Photograph by Anna M. Prentiss at the Secwepemc Museum and Heritage Park

FIGURE 3.7
Archaeologist Nadine Gray directing the excavation of a housepit at the Secwepemc Museum and Heritage Park in Kamloops.

Photograph by Anna M. Prentiss

somewhat ephemeral housepits and mat lodges have been found around The Dalles in Washington and Oregon. The houses in this region more likely resulted from many groups gathering annually to take advantage of the fishing and to renew old ties, perform marriages, and trade goods. Once the activities ended, the families drifted off and continued their annual cycles on the land. Since the houses at the Kamloops area are small, possibly like those at The Dalles, it is possible that their occupants also lived in a more mobile settlement system.

Excavations at housepit sites around the Kamloops area support this hypothesis. Archaeologists discovered thin floors and little midden development. If people had lived in these houses for long spans of time, as did people in the Mid-Fraser Canyon, the archaeologists would have discovered thicker middens around the rims of the housepits and possibly thicker floors. Thick rims resulted from cleaning out hearths after countless cooking episodes and from rebuilding roofs multiple times. Ethnographies tell us that wooden roofs on pithouses needed to be replaced every 15 to 20 years because of wood rot and insect infestations. Rebuilding often meant burning down the old building and building a new one. The old roof materials were deposited on the outer rims of the new house as people refurbished the housepit. It appears, however, that around 2,000 years ago, this cycle of regular reroofing of old houses at Kamloops happened much less frequently than in the Mid-Fraser villages. These hypotheses should, ideally, be tested with more excavation, but verification may be impossible because of the tragic destruction of sites in the area.

Regardless of whether the Kamloops villages were permanent winter settlements, it is clear that their inhabitants were connected to a wider world in the Pacific Northwest. Early Plateau horizon peoples produced small art objects and jewellery in the form of beads and pendants. They likely traded beads and pendants, as well and other items, within wider networks on the Plateau and between the Plateau and the Coast. Archaeologists Brian Hayden and Rick Schulting argue that the rise of the Plateau trade network, which they call the Plateau Interaction Sphere, was driven by the demands of elite individuals seeking fancy items, ranging from stone sculptures to jewellery, which they could used in conspicuous displays during social events. To arrive at this conclusion, they draw upon the rich ethnographic literature of other places, such as New Guinea, where it is well known among anthropologists that "big men" used resource surplus (in their world, pigs and yams) to create debt via lavish competitive feasts. They argue that attendance at these feasts created social obligations: gifts had to be returned with interest. Those who amassed the largest surpluses and put on the biggest feasts became the highest-ranking people in the eyes of the community. Transporting this model to the Plateau, Hayden and Schulting believe this pattern developed around 2,000 years ago, perhaps earlier. They base their argument on the knowledge that large villages did exist and perhaps supported a social structure that permitted such behaviour.

If Mike Rousseau is correct, there was, indeed, a big village near Kamloops, and villages perhaps emerged on the lower Columbia River near The Dalles and closer to the Coast in the area around Portland, Oregon. Rousseau, however, offers a different interpretation of these early exchange systems. He suggests that it was not elite machinations that drove the exchange networks but rather demand for food and nonfood resources by ordinary people in the villages and smaller communities. He suggests that the people traded dried salmon and meat, roots, and key raw materials for specialized tools such as adzes, which were used for woodworking. He argues that demand had more to do with specific utilitarian needs than the desire for prestige. When people became tied to particular places such as villages with salmon-fishing sites, they not longer had access to all resources. They consequently established trade relations with their neighbours to get missing items and to foster amicable social relations for times of war or famine.

Rousseau's argument is understandable when we take a close look at the nature of the villages around 2,000 years ago. As will be pointed out in later chapters, new research suggests that the Mid-Fraser villages barely existed at this time. Dense aggregates of people were found in the Kamloops area, but it is still unclear how permanent these settlements were or whether they represent a different form of village. It is entirely possible that the people lived for most of the year in small, somewhat mobile communities, much as they had in previous centuries. We still have much to learn, but it is clear that human populations on the Canadian Plateau increased in size and sometimes lived in large aggregates, from which they conducted trade that spanned a much larger region.

The Columbia Plateau

The young man, covered in a wolf skin, dances within sight of the bison, then inches away as the beasts turn toward him. He yips and coughs and runs toward the cliff. Sagebrush snags at his clothes as he charges up the draw. He looks over his shoulder and sees the shaggy, lumbering animals in pursuit. Now the people of the village surround the bison on both sides. They shout and whip deerskin blankets, driving the beasts toward him. The young man leaps out of the way. He feels the ground tremble and chokes on dust and gravel as the animals surge past him into the ravine. He knows there is no place for them to run. In moments, atlatl darts will drop like rain.

The young man joins the others at the scene. A woman points to a bull that had stood his ground but now lies dead with the others. He, like many of his people, has never seen a bison but had heard stories of their massive size and thundering hooves. He had heard stories from people who had travelled far to the east to participate in other kills. His hands tremble from excitement and relief, but he realizes that the real work has not yet begun. After they eat the choicest parts to relieve their hunger, they will skin and dismember the carcasses, cut the meat, and crack and boil the bones for their marrow and their grease. There will be good times for a while.

Around 2,000 years ago, living conditions became much tougher in the Columbia Basin of present-day Washington State and Idaho. Unlike the Canadian Plateau, the environment of the Columbia Basin is more homogenous; it has limited ecological diversity. The region is characterized by low rolling hills, mesas, and buttes by grasslands and sagebrush steppes. In this context, warm and dry conditions can reduce access to a wider array of food resources than would be the case in the forested areas of the Canadian Plateau.

As in the north, salmon could be obtained reliably during this period at a few specific locations such as The Dalles. Drought probably caused reductions in the number of deer, though there is evidence that small populations of bison began to move into the area. Reduced precipitation brought drought and the expansion of desert areas. As the number of wet meadows decreased, so too did camas plants, a key carbohydrate source for people on the southern Plateau. There are few radiocarbon-dated sites in the Columbia Basin from this period, and the number does not rise again until about 1,800 years ago. The effects of warm and dry conditions appear to have been particularly pronounced in the middle to upper Columbia regions, where many villages were abandoned.

The Slocan Narrows village in the Slocan River Valley of southeastern British Columbia is an interesting example (Figure 3.8). The village is located to the north of the dry Columbia Basin, in a much wetter forest context associated with the upper Columbia drainage area. The Slocan Narrows village appears to have been an early experiment in which people built large houses (17 to 22 metres in diameter) that were occupied for only a limited period of time, around 2,800 years ago. Although the village contains large and deep housepits, excavations revealed that cultural materials in the form of artifacts and burned roof posts and beams were rare. The occupation, therefore, was likely temporary. We know little about why the community was so short-lived or why the people experimented with constructing houses so much larger than others in the Columbia

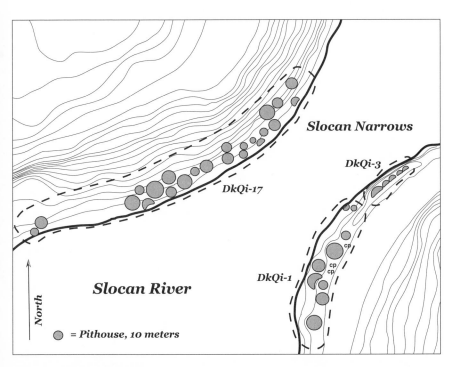

FIGURE 3.8 Spatial clustering of Slocan Narrows housepit villages on the east and west sides of the river.

region. Other villages likely cropped up near optimal fishing locations in and around the Slocan Valley during this period. Perhaps a process was underway that anticipated slightly later developments in the Fraser Valley. There was, however, no direct cultural relationship between the people of these two regions. Indeed, the massive houses of the early Slocan Narrows village had been abandoned for a thousand years before construction began on the first giant houses in the Mid-Fraser Canyon.

This does not mean that people abandoned all areas around 2,000 years ago. Larger clusters of small housepits have been found near The Dalles area, where salmon perhaps acted as a draw, much as they did at the junction of the North and South Thompson rivers. The overall pattern was, however, clusters of small groups of housepits. No sites from this period have houses greater than 14 metres in diameter, and most are considerably smaller. None of the housepits have extensive midden development. This evidence suggests that people used the housepits only for short periods, perhaps from one to a few years, and it reflects a situation of only limited stability. People did not reside in the same place for decades, as they would in the later Mid-Fraser villages.

People continued to use collector settlement and subsistence strategies. Archaeologists recognize an increasing array of specialized camps on the Columbia Plateau associated with task groups sent out to acquire such resources as fish, shellfish, roots, and larger game such as deer and sheep. Salmon and roots remained critical targets, but hunters did have some temporary success with bison. The question of bison numbers and access is a fascinating one. Why were bison not found throughout the Columbia Basin? Given the region's extensive grasslands, it would seem to be an obvious place for bison to thrive. Archaeologist Jim Chatters suggests that bison were highly desired. From an economic standpoint this makes sense. If we rank animals of the region by their caloric return per unit of processing time, bison represent double or triple the payoff of any other resource. People of the Plateau therefore should have preferred bison, if they could get it. Yet there is little evidence of people hunting and processing bison. Chatters argues that human predation might have kept bison numbers low. He notes that the only time that bison show up with any frequency in the inventories of animal bones from housepits or in game kill or processing sites is around 2,000 years ago, right when human populations dropped.

If times did get tough on the Columbia Plateau, people likely began to fight over food resources, territory, or any number of other issues. Chatters presents direct evidence of increased violence starting a little over 2,000 years ago. Settlement in large villages may reflect the availability of a desired food resource such as salmon; however, it can also result from the need for protection from raids. The best evidence in support of this hypothesis comes from the dry country east of the Columbia River, often called the Scablands, where local groups began constructing houses on buttes and mesas. Given the difficulty of accessing these places, defence can be only one reason for this phenomenon. The mortuary record of the Plateau is sparse, but there is some suggestion that the frequency of violent deaths began to increase about 2,000 years ago. Chatters argues that this increase reflects the appearance of the bow and arrow, which made lethal combat so much easier. He may be right, but food resource conditions and the reorganization of economic systems probably resulted in hardships at the regional level that fanned the flames of competition.

Into the Future

People on the Canadian Plateau continued their patterns of aggregation and dispersal while many in the Columbia Basin struggled to survive. Occupation patterns in the Fraser Valley were reorganized, and new more powerful communities emerged on the Coast. The stage was now set for the next big chapter in the ancient history of the Plateau, the emergence of the Mid-Fraser villages.

This was a phenomenon unlike anything seen in the region. During their day, these communities would eclipse in size and social complexity those elsewhere in the Interior or on the Coast. Nearly 2,000 years ago, however, things were just getting started.

4
The Rise of the Mid-Fraser Villages

Emerging from the forest on a high ridge top, the two visiting hunters watch in amazement. It would not be out of the ordinary to glimpse others moving across the landscape, but they are shocked by what they see. A large group of people is building three enormous new houses that are perched on a wide bench above the river. One of houses has been dug over a metre into the ground and is going to be so wide and deep that the roof will be held up by four tree trunks! A massive, partially hollowed-out trunk projects from the apex of the roof framework, marking what will apparently be an entrance. Heavy basket loads of clay are being hauled up the steep bluff to line the floors and roofs of the new residences. Hundreds of smaller timbers cut in the nearby forest are being worked further to create extensive indoor benches and storage racks.

Little do the hunters know that this is only the beginning. There will be more of these enormous houses, many more in this place and in others, and they will come to dominate this part of the Plateau. Down in the emerging village, several men work hard to fashion wooden posts and beams, using hafted stone adzes. A group of women is down inside the developing building working equally hard, finishing the floor and digging out the first storage pits. Children stay clear of the most dangerous activities and remain engaged in their own play-related activities. Young unmarried men and women seek to catch each other's eyes and work to gain respect from their parents through their participation.

Later, five families, most of them related, will take up residence in a single large house. Each will have their own section of the house floor in which to establish cooking and storage places. While individual families cook for themselves, it is clear that they are part of a larger group. At meals, household members share foods to underline their interconnections. Eventually, all will benefit from their group's ability to be in more than one place at a time. By late July and early August, many will be fishing in the nearby rapids. But this will not preclude other parties from seeking ripe berries or aggregated deer in another part of the landscape. Once the fish and berries have been stored, many will move up to higher elevations for deer hunting, root harvesting and processing, and quarrying of stone to make tools. Others will remain behind, guarding stored food and preparing for winter. It is an effective and flexible strategy, one that will permit these people to dominate this land for a millennium. But at first glance, the watching hunters can only gawk in amazement!

The Mid-Fraser villages were the product of improved environmental conditions, the development of key technologies, and greater cooperation among larger groups of people. After 1,800 years ago, the climate became cooler and wetter. On the Coast Range, the Lillooet Glacier came out of a thousand-year-long sleep and began to expand. It peaked in size about 1,200 years ago. Between 1,500 and 1,600 years ago, the Mid-Fraser region developed optimal conditions for intensive habitation by human groups. Salmon were highly predictable and abundant. Dry meadows had not yet begun to recede. Deer populations were probably stable, at least temporarily. Fires in previous decades had undoubtedly created vast thickets of berry bushes. Given these improved environmental conditions, it is not surprising that large villages, in some cases with 40 or more pithouses, emerged along the Mid-Fraser Canyon (Figure 4.1).

Housepits and Villages

The ethnographic record helps archaeologists understand how pithouses were constructed and used and, to some extent, what they meant to the people who lived in them (see Box 4.1). Today, abandoned large Mid-Fraser housepits tend to feature rings of debris that surround a floor and collapsed roof (Figure 4.2). They look like moon craters. Excavations reveal, however, that much like our own houses today, the interiors of pithouses were organized with spaces for cooking, sleeping, and other household tasks. Houses often had benches that

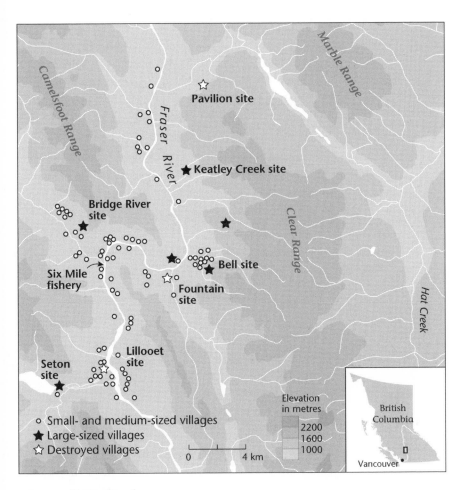

FIGURE 4.1 The location of major sites in the Mid-Fraser Canyon.

surrounded the floor and were used for sleeping and other activities. Baptiste Ritchie, a Mount Currie elder, described benches to ethnographers:

> Inside the pit which had been dug they constructed a platform about 1 foot [0.3 metre] high completely around the house, 5 feet [1.5 metres] in from the edges of the pit. This platform was called *ee-YAI-wash*. It was on this platform that the people slept, using boughs and pounded inner cedar bark as mattresses. Hides from mountain goats and other animals were used as blankets. Sometimes it was so crowded that the people had to sleep

FIGURE 4.2 **A burned pit-house during reconstruction. Workers are removing burned material to rebuild the house.**

Note the use of post-and-beam roof construction.
Illustration by Eric S. Carlson

with their heads at the sides of the pit and only the width of the platform in which to stretch out. The special hunters called *Tu-WEET,* shared their surplus animal hides with other people. [Bouchard and Kennedy 1977:64]

Cooking and storage features were often established on the floors of the houses. Ritchie (Bouchard and Kennedy 1977:64) described the creation and use of fireplaces: "A fire for cooking was made for an hour in the morning and an hour at night. The women placed hot rocks in water contained in water-tight baskets to cook each family's meal. Although only two fires were made each day, the underground house was always warm."

As was made clear by Ritchie, building a pithouse required a substantial labour commitment and could play a large role in defining house group membership:

In the old days, the people had to work together to be able to build an underground house. Only those people who helped build it would be allowed to live in it. Those people who would not work together with the others would have no choice but to spend the winter in shelters which had been constructed as summer lodges. [Bouchard and Kennedy 1977:63-64]

Community work was extremely important. If individuals didn't help, they would be excluded for the winter. There were often 20 to 30 people living in one underground house.

The results of archaeological excavations indicate that ethnographic descriptions are substantially accurate. Remains of burned roofs at the Keatley Creek and Bridge River sites indicate that roof beams were supported by several layers of timbers capped by mats made from grasses or pine needles. The mats were then covered with sediments, which vary from house to house, depending on the site and the time period. In general, roofs from later periods (about 1,200 to 1,300 years ago) are covered with loosely aggregated rocky sediment that often contains artifacts, bones, and fire-cracked rock. Many earlier roofs, particularly at Bridge River, are covered in clay-rich sediments that also contain similar cultural items. Archaeologists have concluded that the roofs were used as places for garbage disposal. But these rich sediment layers may also be a byproduct of activities conducted on the roof.

Entrances could be on the side of the house or on the roof. Roof entrances appear to have been preferred in the largest houses. According to some regional ethnographies, side entrances were constructed either to permit the elderly easier egress or as special entrances that would stop women from passing over the heads of men. Other ethnographic accounts point to side entrances as escape tunnels used during enemy attacks. Side entrances might also have enhanced ventilation and permitted material such as firewood to be more easily moved into the house.

Roof entrances required ladders, which were generally made from a single tree trunk. Notches for steps were cut into the trunk, and a household crest animal or guardian spirit was sometimes carved at the top. The underside of the log was sometimes grooved or hollowed out to provide handholds for climbers. The ladder, placed in a central position in the house, permitted people to come and go without disturbing family activity areas. Some ethnographers suggest that large houses featured two roof ladders to accommodate the movement of larger numbers of people.

Carved house ladders were the equivalent of the elaborately carved portal and crest poles of the Northwest Coast peoples. Rather than projecting from house interiors, poles on the Coast were attached to the fronts of houses and featured either zoomorphic or anthropomorphic designs of household crest figures, the mythical ancestors of the people. The yawning mouth of the lowest crest figure on a portal pole often offered entry into the house.

Benches such as those described by Ritchie are often found in ancient houses in the Mid-Fraser Canyon. Housepit 7 at Keatley Creek featured a bench on its east side. Excavations in several houses at Bridge River have also revealed either benches cut from surrounding sediment or arrangements of post-holes likely associated with a wooden bench.

The large multifamily group traditionally occupied the *s7ístken* (underground houses) during the winter. Smaller subsets of the groups, especially the elderly, remained year round. Elders who recalled life in the s7istken described it as a

BOX 4.1 ETHNOGRAPHIC ACCOUNTS OF PITHOUSE CONSTRUCTION

Pithouses were built in several major stages. The first stage involved excavating the area below the ground surface. The original houses were substantial buildings that featured a depression dug a metre or more into the ground and covered by a post-and-beam roof structure. By building the pithouse below the ground surface, the occupants protected themselves from the cold of winter and the heat of summer. Digging the depression with traditional tools must have been an arduous task. James Teit (1900:192), the famous 19th- and early 20th-century ethnographer, describes the construction process: "Then the women began to dig the soil with their digging sticks ... They also used wooden scrapers with sharp, flat blades. The loose earth was put into large baskets with the hands, and by means of small baskets."

The people then cut down trees of the required length and diameter for the frame. As Teit outlines, a large amount of wood had to be acquired using stone, bone, and antler tools:

Green timber was generally used for the heavy posts of the house ... This was measured with bark ropes, the length

being determined by eye, in accordance with the diameter of the hole. Then trees were cut, barked, and hauled to the building site with stout bark rope. Generally these timbers were not squared. They were worked with wedges, hammers, and stone adzes. The thin poles used for the roof of the house were also barked, except when dry wood was employed for this purpose. They were cut, tied into bundles, and carried to the building-site with ordinary packing-lines by men or women. [Teit 1900:192]

Four central posts created a square to rectangular frame to which dozens of beams were attached. There was some variation, however, in the number of posts used to support the roof. Smaller houses likely resembled conical mat lodges and had no central support posts at all. Exceptionally large houses perhaps had more than four support posts, which had to be placed carefully to support the roof. Teit notes,

After the wood was obtained and cut, the upright braces ... were erected. These were time for sleeping and making weapons but also as a time for gathering, feasting, and dancing. Winter was the only time of year when the people were not busy gathering food resources, trading or, on occasion, raiding the areas or camps of other groups.

Groups organized their activities based on the space available. Single families generally occupied small houses divided into specific activity rooms – for cooking, sleeping, tool making, and storage – by blankets or partitions. In contrast, the larger houses were typically arranged to accommodate multiple families. Ethnographies and oral accounts suggest that families likely had their own rooms positioned around the perimeter of the house. Within these family

placed about fifteen inches deep in the ground, which was firmly pressed down by stamping it with the feet and beating it with sticks. The tops of the braces were notched to support the rafters ... The butt-ends of these were placed about two feet deep in the ground, one at each of the four points marked when the circle was laid out. [Teit 1900:192-93]

Once the posts were in place, beams, or in Teit's words, rafters, were attached to provide a framework for the roof itself:

The braces and rafters were securely connected with willow withes. The rafters did not meet in the centre. The side-rafters (c) rested on the ground and on the outside of the main rafters, at the place where these were supported by the uprights. The rafters were either notched for the reception of the braces, or they were simply tied on, while their butt-ends were embedded in the ground. Horizontal poles (d) from one to two feet apart were tied to these rafters and side-rafters. They formed the support for the roof-covering. Above the place

where the side-rafters and main rafters join, the poles were placed much nearer together, often so that on the ends of the poles of two opposite sides rested the next pair of the other two sides. The ends of the rafters were connected by four heavy timbers (e), which formed the entrance. [1900:293]

The layers of timber provided a platform for woven mats made from pine needles and, at least in the later occupations, a layer of earth (in some villages, clay) was used as insulation. Again, Teit provides a clear description:

This structure was covered with poles or pieces of split wood, which ran from the ground to the entrance ... their ends resting on the rafters and side-rafters. They were not tied to the framework. They were covered with pine-needles or dry grass; and then the entire structure was covered with earth, which was beaten and stamped down firmly. [Teit 1900:293] zones, they designated specific areas for cooking, storage, sleeping, and tool making. In the large houses, the central space was left open and clean not only to allow people to move between family zones but also to create a space for large group gatherings such as winter dances and feasts.

These two different spatial arrangements are reflected in house features. In small houses, archaeologists typically find storage or cache pits in one area, hearths in another, and clusters of tool-making debris and discarded tools in yet another. In the large multifamily houses, archaeologists more typically uncover redundant activity areas around the housepit's perimeter. Each of these zones typically includes shallow hearths, storage pits, food debris, and a variety of discarded tools associated with food preparation and the manufacture of furniture, weapons, baskets, and other items. Analysis of the contents of these areas permits archaeologists to reconstruct variations in household economies and social relationships.

Evidence suggests that after many years the house posts would begin to rot, old food and human waste would attract more vermin, and the residents would decide it was time to burn the house down and build again. They salvaged usable timbers before the entire structure was brought down. In some cases, this event was followed by an intensive effort to clean up the house crater, including carrying out basket loads of old roof debris and perhaps even scraping out the old floor. They deposited the debris around the crater, thereby building up the rim. Over enough years, the outer rim midden would accumulate substantial depth. For archaeologists this is a major boon: if excavated correctly, rims can provide a life history of the house. The deposits contain, layer upon layer, not only roof and floor materials and sediments but also a substantial amount of human garbage in the form of plant and animal remains, fire-cracked rock, discarded tools and debitage, and other associated hearth debris such as charcoal.

The pithouse was not the only structure used by the St'át'imc people. During mild winters and often during the warm season, people made use of mat- or bark-covered conical lodges:

> In building circular lodges ... a dozen or more long poles were placed some distance apart, with their butts upon the ground, outside the cleared space, forming a complete circle from fifteen to twenty feet in diameter. The poles were placed with their small ends toward the centre of the space, where they met and supported one another without being fastened together ... At night and in bad weather the opening at the top was covered by a flap, which consisted of a mat or skin fastened to a long, slender pole. Sometimes the earth was banked up half a foot around the bottom of the lodge, and two or three layers of mats were used. [Teit 1900:196]

Although Teit describes large conical-shaped lodges, recent surveys, excavations, and ethnographic studies indicate that these structures could be much smaller, perhaps as small as two to three metres in diameter at the base. The St'át'imc probably also constructed conical-shaped lodges with side entrances over shallow pithouse depressions.

Archaeological and ethnographic records support the conclusion that large aggregations of people inhabited pithouses in many areas throughout the Mid-Fraser Canyon. Ethnographic accounts and oral histories suggest that some villages had two hundred or more adults and children, and the archaeological record indicates that some villages might have been substantially larger. At any given time, these communities would have included a range of different-sized pithouses, mat or bark lodges, external storage pits and structures, and cooking features located outside of buildings.

Although there is no physical evidence, it is possible that some communities had palisades for protection from attack, as described in the journals of Simon Fraser (1966:82): "The village is a fortification of 100 by 24 feet, surrounded with palisades eighteen feet high, slanting inwards, and lined with a shorter row that supports a shade, covered with bark, and which are the dwellings." Researchers remain unclear as to what, exactly, Fraser was describing. Dorothy Kennedy and Randy Bouchard argue that it is a summer village. This conclusion is reasonable given the small size of the enclosure and its location close to a salmon fishery. Archaeologists, however, have found no convincing evidence for fortifications in the Mid-Fraser area. Regardless, it is likely that they were used during periods when the threat of attack was likely, whether from other human groups or marauding bears.

Historical records, archaeological data, and oral histories suggest that the Mid-Fraser villages were busy places. It is not surprising that they left behind such abundant and obvious archaeological signatures.

Archaeological Research in the Mid-Fraser Canyon

Our knowledge of the history of the Mid-Fraser villages comes primarily from intensive research conducted at three villages: the Bell, Keatley Creek, and Bridge River sites (Figure 4.1). Although our ultimate goal is to gain a larger picture of the region's ancient history, our approach is premised on the understanding that building this history requires developing community-specific histories. Anthropologists and Aboriginal peoples alike have long known that the history of Pacific Northwest villages comprises the individual histories of many village households. As archaeologist Ken Ames has recently argued, Northwest Coast households waged a constant struggle not only to maintain their social standing within the greater community but also to have enough producing members to keep their house viable. Too few productive adults could mean economic disaster and the disintegration of the household. If households collapsed too frequently, then the entire community would fall apart. Given the deep economic and social interconnections between communities, the abandonment of a village would have had significant implications at the regional level. It is therefore necessary to develop an understanding of Mid-Fraser villages on a site-by-site basis. Where possible, we explore the histories of particular houses as a barometer of a community's scale, stability, and social and economic health. Yet we acknowledge that housepit deposits can often be complex and difficult to interpret. Problems of interpretation have led to a range of debates about the occupational histories of particular housepits and villages. To provide a more refined history of the Mid-Fraser villages, we offer some discussion of the histories of excavations and the debates associated with these places.

The Bell Site

During the early 1970s, archaeologist Arnoud Stryd began an intensive survey of housepit villages in the Mid-Fraser area. After recording many small and large sites, he settled on the Bell site, a large housepit village located on a high bench above the east side of the Fraser Canyon (Figure 4.3). Stryd documented 23 housepits of varying sizes that had been built between 1,700 and 1,000 years ago. Intensive excavations of several houses indicated that both large and small house groups had lived in the village. A child burial from a larger house contained highly elaborate grave goods: carved stone figurines, pipe fragments, an antler comb, a quartz crystal, red ochre, and 246 dentalium shell beads. The burial site dated to the final centuries of the village's occupation. Rich child burials on the Northwest Coast during the Late Period usually imply the presence of a hierarchy based on inherited status. Only children from important and powerful families were buried with such wealth. These remains suggest that inherited wealth and social positions could have emerged in the villages at some point in the late prehistory of the Mid-Fraser region. Confirmation, however, requires identifying similar burial practices for elite men and women.

The Keatley Creek Site

Intrigued by Arnoud Stryd's results at the Bell site, archaeologist Brian Hayden began excavating Keatley Creek village in 1986 (Figures 4.4 and 4.5). The site had been recorded but not excavated by Stryd in the 1970s. Hayden recognized that the Mid-Fraser villages were perfect for research into complex hunter-gatherer societies organized in household groups. Hayden, along with Aubrey Cannon, had previously published an important work on the archaeology of corporate groups, the basic socioeconomic unit in many societies. Corporate

FIGURE 4.3 Overgrown
pithouses at the Bell site.
Photograph by Ian Kuijt

groups usually consist of multifamily units that are often, but not necessarily, linked by kinship. The famous house groups of the Northwest Coast are an excellent example. These house groups were composed of sets of families that were normally members of a lineage group and sometimes tied to larger social units such as *numayms* among the Kwakwa̱ka̱'wakw or clans among the Tlingit and Haida. These groups conducted hunting, gathering, fishing, and trade operations for their own exclusive benefit, yet they also interacted with other groups within and beyond their villages. The term *corporate group* is apt, since these groups acted much like modern corporations: they pursued economic and social ventures and were responsible for their own success or failure, but they were also constrained and affected by the rules of society and the actions of the other social groups that surrounded them.

Based on ethnographic accounts and direct evidence of ranking among households, Hayden suspected that the large houses of Keatley Creek and other Mid-Fraser villages had been occupied by corporate groups. Perhaps smaller houses were outranked by the more powerful house groups? A few years before, archaeologists from Washington State University had excavated the famous Ozette site in northwest Washington State. The investigators discovered that house size could be used to identify lesser and greater households. The largest

FIGURE 4.4 Keatley Creek site as it looked in 1998. The image clearly shows the extent of the core village as indicated by large numbers of house depressions.

Photograph by Anna M. Prentiss

house at Ozette had more room for individual families. It also had a well-defined central area for social events and even a large, separate hearth area. The investigators found the greatest clusters of art objects and whaling gear at the far end of the house, the traditional position for the household chief among the Makah people. The largest house had by far the most whalebone, large amounts of salmon, and shellfish collected at a different beach from all the other houses.

Hayden pursued a research strategy analogous to the one at Ozette. He sought to excavate a series of entire house floors to gain an understanding of the complex social and economic relationships that existed among the ancient corporate groups of the village. Hayden's work was groundbreaking for Canadian Plateau archaeology. Most of the previous work had been exploratory and often

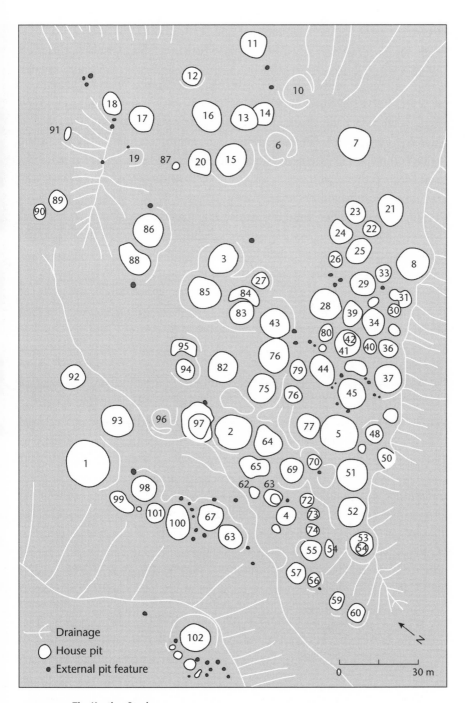

FIGURE 4.5 The Keatley Creek
housepit village.

oriented toward establishing basic culture history. It merely added, brick by brick, to the inventory of artifact characteristics associated with the region's cultures. Hayden, by contrast, sought to explain the social and economic dynamics of these ancient cultural systems and put forth scientific explanations for developments. To do this, he needed to collect new data. Plateau archaeologists generally like to dig fast; archaeologists call it moving dirt. Hayden's strategy required a lot of dirt to be moved, but in a much more painstaking manner. Artifacts and features such as hearths and cache pits had to be recorded in detail. In addition to the usual research into subsistence and stone technology via animal bone research, the researchers took samples of soil, charcoal, and wood (from former house posts and beams) for radiocarbon dating and to study soil chemistry and plant remains. Hayden wanted to reconstruct the architecture of the houses and the lifestyles of their inhabitants. He wanted to weave his evidence into a new portrait of life in a Plateau village.

Between 1986 and 1989, Hayden's teams excavated four major house floors and conducted limited test excavations of others. Major excavations focused on one large house (Housepit 7), a medium house (Housepit 3), and two smaller houses (Housepits 12 and 90). The deposits at Housepit 7 were the deepest (Figure 4.6).

Although the focus of Hayden's work was floors, the excavations sometimes moved into the rims. The small houses had almost no rim deposits, suggesting they had not been used for many seasons. As expected, the bigger houses had thick rims, nearly two metres deep in places. Archaeologists always want to know how old things are, and Hayden was no exception. His team collected charcoal samples from the floors and roof deposits of each house. Given its thick rim midden, Hayden determined that it was particularly important to date the history of Housepit 7. The team obtained samples from roof beams, which were burned and lying on the last floor, from bone within pits, and from the rim. Dating rims can be tricky because they contain charcoal and wood from all previous roofs and floors. Rims can also have materials from noncultural contexts such as forest fires. Aware of these issues, Hayden acquired a number of samples to complement other sources.

Hayden wanted to know how old the house was. The final floor was relatively recent. Arrow points recovered from the floor matched those of the Kamloops horizon, the Canadian Plateau cultural pattern of the last 1,200 years. But projectile points found in the deep rim deposits also ranged from the Lochnore phase to the Shuswap horizon. Could the house have been built in Lochnore times? Hayden didn't think so. He argued that there was a Lochnore component buried below parts of the rim at Housepit 7. Its materials likely got mixed up with early Housepit 7 debris. The Shuswap spear points posed a different,

FIGURE 4.6 Excavation of
Housepit 7, 1986. This image
shows the north-south trench
through rim.
Photograph by Ian Kuijt

and in some ways more challenging, problem. From the limited sampling
Hayden had done of the broader village, there was no evidence of an independent Shuswap occupation. Hayden therefore argued that the big house had first
been built during the Neoglacial climate period, during the Shuswap horizon,
perhaps more than 2,400 years ago. To test this theory, Hayden radiocarbon
dated samples from the rims. If old dates matched the points, then he could
conclude that Housepit 7 was an unusually long-lived house, one that spanned
1,500 or more years.

Hayden submitted his samples to the dating labs and waited for the results.
When they arrived, he recognized that they were wide-ranging. The floor dated
from around 1,000 years ago, while the rim had dates that extended back to
nearly 6,500 years ago: 1590, 2080, 2140, 2620, and 6470 BP (before the present).
Hayden threw out the final date as being too old but retained most of the others.
He also eliminated the 2140 date because it was in the same context as the 2620
date, and he felt that it should be in the older time range. He could now make

the argument that Housepit 7 and, by proxy, the aggregated village at Keatley Creek had been dated to at least 2,600 years ago, or well back into the Shuswap horizon.

But Housepit 7 was not the only house dated. Excavations in Housepits 3, 12, and 90 also focused on floors. Housepit 3, the medium-sized house, dated to the same time as Housepit 7's final floor. Housepits 12 and 90 had been built earlier, about 1,400 to 1,600 years ago. Although they were not dated by radiocarbon dating, limited testing at other housepits recovered a range of projectile points from different time periods. Collectively, these data created something of a conundrum for Hayden: he wanted to create a village portrait based on small, medium, and large houses from the same period, but it was clear that some pithouses had been occupied at different points of time. As with a slow-growing subdivision in any North American city, it appeared that the village was a patchwork quilt of houses that had been built next to one another (and at times on top of one another) and reused and rebuilt over hundreds of years and multiple generations. To overcome the discrepancy between his data and his model, Hayden assumed that Housepit 7 had been occupied in a similar manner throughout the life of the village. If the house's socioeconomic standing had not changed throughout time, then he could compare its last floor to the earlier floors of the other houses, assuming for heuristic purposes that they were of the same age. Archaeologists still actively debate his argument, but at the time it was the gospel of the Keatley Creek project.

During the excavations in 1989, Hayden's team found a small housepit floor beneath the northwest corner of Housepit 7. Given the frequent association of Lochnore and, occasionally, Shuswap projectile points in the lower Housepit 7 strata, it seemed reasonable to suspect that the small house would provide an early date. Anna Prentiss initiated a new round of excavations at Housepit 7 during the summers of 1999, 2001, and 2002. Her original goal was to develop a better understanding of the Shuswap horizon and Lochnore phase occupations of the Keatley Creek sites. The results were surprising. The investigators identified the small floor found in 1989 and called it Subhousepit 1 (or SHP1) because of its subterranean position. The excavators, however, began to expose additional layers below SHP1. Expanding the SHP1 area excavation revealed an even deeper and smaller house floor, which was eventually called Subhousepit 3 (SHP3). Subhousepit 3 is the deepest housepit stratum (or layer) at Housepit 7, and it lies directly beneath the floor of Housepit 7 (Figure 4.7). To fit the expected scenario, it should have dated to over 2,400 years ago. However, the radiocarbon date that came back was around 1600 BP. The implication was that Housepit 7 could not be nearly as old as everyone had assumed. In other words, its life history was different from what Hayden had presented.

FIGURE 4.7 Excavations of
Housepit 7, directed by Anna
Prentiss, in 2001.

Photograph by Anna M. Prentiss

Prentiss' excavations revealed a complex series of smaller housepit floors, living surfaces, and rim strata (Figure 4.8), some of which were underneath Housepit 7. Further radiocarbon dating confirmed that SHP3, which remained at the bottom of the entire sequence, dated to about 1,700 years ago. Following this short occupation, construction of Housepit 7 began, forming the first rim deposits. Two other small housepits (Subhousepits 1 and 4) were added onto Housepit 7's northwest margin between 1,350 and 1,200 years ago, suggesting that the big house could have had adjoining rooms. Rim accumulation during an intensive final occupation period that began nearly 1,200 years ago buried everything, forming a doughnut-shaped form that is still visible today. Re-examination of the dates for the final roof and floor suggested that the building had been abandoned at a slightly later date, about 800 to 1,000 years ago.

The data from Housepit 7 and other areas of Keatley Creek paint a dynamic and changing large village. It is likely that various areas of Keatley Creek were used by different generations. The result was a patchwork of settlements of various scales in the same location. Collective research also indicates that the most

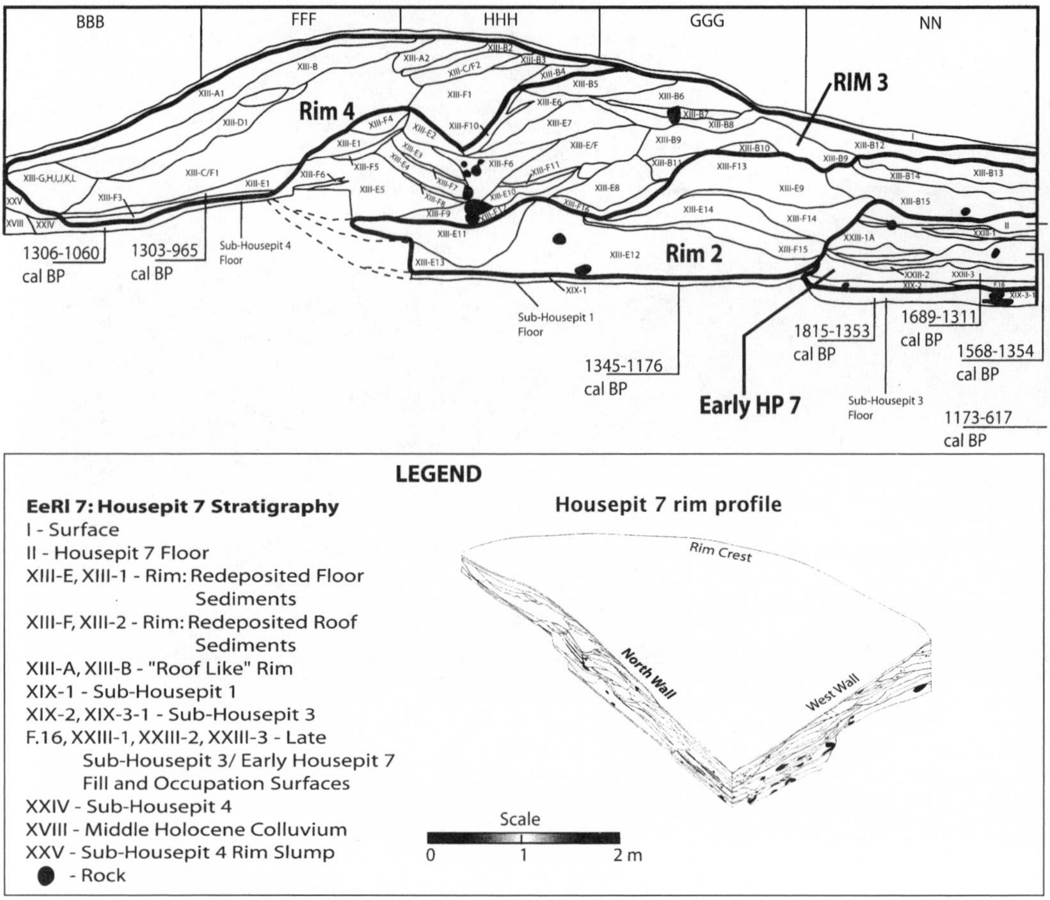
BBB
FFF
HHH
GGG
NN
Rim 4
RIM 3
Rim 2
Early HP 7
1306-1060 cal BP
1303-965 cal BP
Sub-Housepit 4 Floor
Sub-Housepit 1 Floor
1345-1176 cal BP
1815-1353 cal BP
1689-1311 cal BP
1568-1354 cal BP
Sub-Housepit 3 Floor
1173-617 cal BP
LEGEND
EeRl 7: Housepit 7 Stratigraphy
I - Surface
II - Housepit 7 Floor
XIII-E, XIII-1 - Rim: Redeposited Floor Sediments
XIII-F, XIII-2 - Rim: Redeposited Roof Sediments
XIII-A, XIII-B - "Roof Like" Rim
XIX-1 - Sub-Housepit 1
XIX-2, XIX-3-1 - Sub-Housepit 3
F.16, XXIII-1, XXIII-2, XXIII-3 - Late Sub-Housepit 3/ Early Housepit 7 Fill and Occupation Surfaces
XXIV - Sub-Housepit 4
XVIII - Middle Holocene Colluvium
XXV - Sub-Housepit 4 Rim Slump
- Rock
Housepit 7 rim profile
Rim Crest
North Wall
West Wall
Scale
0
1
2 m

FIGURE 4.8 Rim strata from Housepit 7 at the Keatley Creek site. Early housepit floors are defined as Subhousepits 1, 3, and 4.

intense occupation of Keatley Creek, reflected in the highest number of pithouses for the greatest number of people, did not occur until sometime after about 1600 BP, perhaps between 1200 and 1300 BP. Once present, houses such as Housepit 7 might have been reconstructed over several centuries and multiple generations. Without a detailed understanding of the dating of a range of different-sized housepits, there is no way to reconstruct how many pithouses of different sizes were occupied at different points of time. Just as important, it is also unclear whether the Keatley Creek chronology is exactly the same as those of other villages in the Mid-Fraser Canyon.

The Bridge River Site

The Bridge River site is another large village in the Mid-Fraser area (Figure 4.9). It is located about ten kilometres west of Keatley Creek, within the lower Bridge River Valley on the west side of the Fraser Canyon (Figure 4.10). Recognizing the site's importance in the 1970s, Arnoud Stryd opened up small test excavations in several housepits and obtained radiocarbon dates similar to those for the Keatley Creek houses. Anna Prentiss conducted detailed excavations at Bridge River between 2003 and 2009 to test the chronology of the Keatley Creek site and to explore a new approach to village-wide analysis. As part of this new approach, Guy Cross, a geophysicist from Vancouver, joined Prentiss's research group to begin a program of mapping and archaeological test excavations (Figures 4.11 and 4.12).

FIGURE 4.10 Aerial photograph
of the Bridge River site, facing
west.
Photographer unknown.

Prentiss wanted to look at the history of the entire village, not just the chronology of selected housepits. To do this, her teams used archaeological geophysics, more specifically, magnetometry (Box 4.2) studies, to predict the location of features containing datable materials. They then opened up relatively small excavation units (50 × 50 centimetres) to obtain dating material and to begin to explore the history of the Bridge River village. They eventually tested 67 housepits and 16 external pit features, ovens, and cache pits. Radiocarbon dating of 90 samples resulted in the dating of 13 external pit features and 55 housepits, some with multiple floors.

In a surprising contrast to the pattern at the Keatley Creek village, people who lived at the Bridge River village did not routinely remove their old floors when they refurbished their houses. At Keatley Creek, the excavation of housepits indicated that the people had routinely cleaned out floors and burned roof sediments before building the new roof. At Bridge River, they simply covered old floors with new flooring material (a fine clay-silt that contained tiny pieces of gravel). It was a bit like carpeting a modern home without removing the old

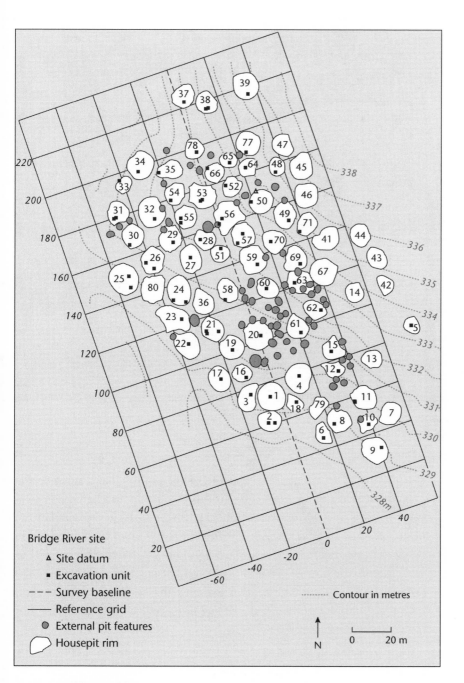

Bridge River site

△ Site datum
■ Excavation unit
--- Survey baseline
— Reference grid
● External pit features
⬭ Housepit rim

Contour in metres

N   0   20 m

FIGURE 4.11 This map of the
Bridge River site shows major
features, the excavation grid,
and small excavation units
from the 2003 and 2004 field
seasons.

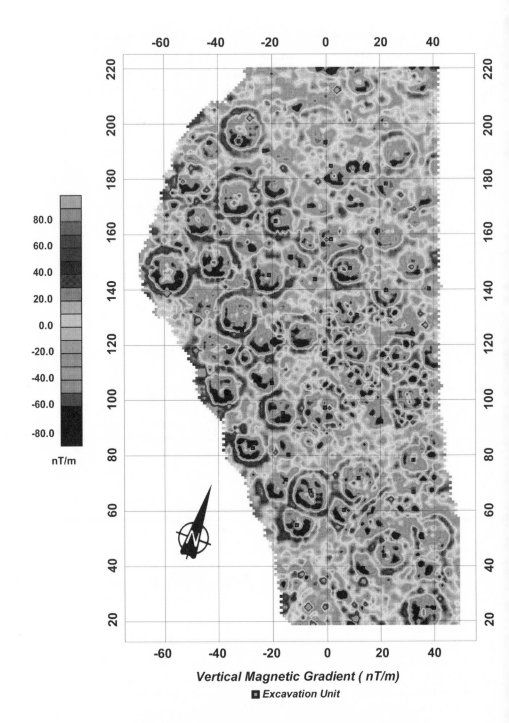

-60 **-40** **-20** **0** **20** **40**

80.0
60.0
40.0
20.0
0.0
-20.0
-40.0
-60.0
-80.0

nT/m

Vertical Magnetic Gradient (nT/m)

■ *Excavation Unit*

FIGURE 4.12 **Magnetometry map of the Bridge River site. This is a remote sensing map illustrating the locations of housepit floors,** rims, and subsurface features such as hearths and cache pits. Compare this map to that of 4.11.

Courtesy of Guy Cross

carpet. New floors were sometimes constructed on top of old roofs. Recent excavations at Bridge River confirm that some houses accumulated as many as 14 floors and 7 roofs, which were superimposed on one another like a complex layer cake.

The dating of Bridge River indicated that the village had been established slightly earlier than Keatley Creek, at some point between 1,900 and 1,800 years ago. The village had subsequently grown rapidly, from as few as 3 to 4 simultaneously occupied houses to perhaps 30, if not many more. It was abandoned just after 1200 BP (Figures 4.13 and 4.14). Like Keatley Creek, it was also reoccupied during the centuries before contact with Europeans. If Bridge River had, at one point, 30 or more simultaneously occupied houses, it is possible that it could have been inhabited by anywhere from 600 to over 1,000 people. If the larger houses at Keatley Creek are contemporary, then the community at its

BOX 4.2 GEOPHYSICAL METHODS IN ARCHAEOLOGY

Archaeologists can now look beneath the ground without digging. Over the last 30 years, they have developed new scientific methods to identify features and buildings hidden below the surface. These methods are referred to as geophysical research. During the 1990s, a team of archaeologists led by Ken Kvamme of the University of Arkansas initiated long-term studies of fortified villages in the upper Middle Missouri area of North Dakota. Drawing from earlier studies, particularly of the Old World, they began their research by conducting geophysical surveys of entire sites, using techniques such as magnetometry, conductivity, ground-penetrating radar, and aerial photography. The results were nothing short of astounding. Their maps delineated the outlines of ancient earth lodges, including the defensive ditches that surrounded villages.

Anna Prentiss recognized that this strategy and these techniques could pay off at the Bridge River site and spent several years working with Guy Cross. Two geophysical techniques provided the best results. Magnetometry

(specifically in this case, vertical magnetic gradiometry) measures interruptions to the earth's magnetic field. It is particularly useful for finding features that have altered the earth's magnetic structure through heat, such as hearths and roasting pits. Magnetometry also proved useful in identifying clusters of burned roof beams on floors and large cache pits in which the heat of rotting organic materials had created a magnetic impact on the surrounding sediments, somewhat like that of a hearth feature. Electric conductivity measures the ground's ability to conduct electricity. Dense sediments such as floors in Mid-Fraser housepits should, theoretically, hold moisture well and, consequently, conduct electricity better. In contrast, less compacted sediments, such as those from housepit rims, should not conduct electricity particularly well. Conductivity mapping confirmed the presence of housepit floors that matched the surface topography of the Bridge River site. We now know that the site consisted of 80 housepits in its core area.

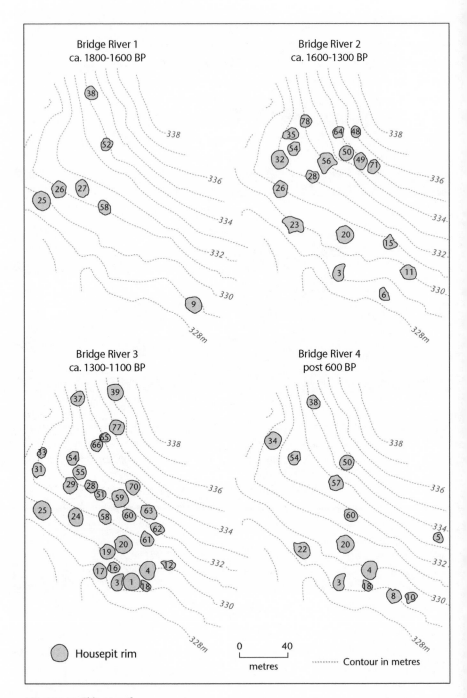

FIGURE 4.13 This map of the Bridge River village illustrates changes in the number and pattern of occupied housepits over time.

BRIDGE RIVER 1

BRIDGE RIVER 2

BRIDGE RIVER 3

FIGURE 4.14 The growth of the
Bridge River village between 1800
and 1100 BP. This artist's reconstruction was developed after
extensive radiocarbon dating of
floors in the housepits at Bridge
River. This permitted us to recognize the positions of occupied
houses during different times.

Illustration by Eric S. Carlson

peak could have had even more people, perhaps as many as 1,400, as Hayden suggested. We must be cautious with these estimates, however. Because we are relying on radiocarbon dates with error ranges of 25 to 40 years, it is possible that we are assuming a simultaneous occupation of the houses that, in fact, did not occur. The formal arrangements of houses at Bridge River during Periods 2 and 3 (see Figure 4.13) do suggest a strong likelihood of simultaneous occupation. We cannot be as confident about the occupational history of Keatley Creek, given the minimal number of dated houses.

Why Big Villages in the Mid-Fraser Canyon?

The Bell, Keatley Creek, and Bridge River sites were just a few of the many large villages that emerged up and down the Middle Fraser Canyon. If we combine the known housepit villages at Kelly, Leon, McKay, and Pavilion Creeks with the Lillooet, Lochnore-Nesikep Creeks, and Lytton area sites (which likely date to between 1,000 and 2,000 years ago, during what Brian Hayden and geologist June Ryder call the Classic Lillooet period), we can conclude that many thousands of people inhabited the Mid-Fraser area.

Something exciting happened in the region nearly 2,000 years ago, an event (or more likely a series of interconnected events) that brought about a period of substantial cultural growth. People began constructing and living in large aggregated villages permanently. Many of the houses were substantially larger than anything that had been seen in the region before this time. Did something trigger local people, used to living in smaller settlements composed of related families, to suddenly start living together with unrelated families in a new form of community? Had a group from outside the Mid-Fraser region simply recognized its value and moved in?

Life in densely packed villages during ancient times offered a variety of challenges. People ran the risk of depleting local food and non-food resources such as timber. The villages were usually placed in locations that provided optimal access to a limited number of critical resources such as salmon. The location of the Mid-Fraser villages, however, was a compromise. The villages were located near rivers that provided salmon, but other resources such as roots grew in upland areas. Local depletion combined with the suboptimal positioning of these foods could result in long journeys and higher transportation costs. Moreover, without modern waste disposal, these communities were likely to suffer a variety of health risks associated with the build-up of organic wastes. The close proximity of humans and vermin, for example, can both make life unpleasant and, more significantly, set the stage for the development of new infectious diseases.

So why would people want to live together in the first place? To answer this question, we must first consider the economic and otherwise practical reasons for such a transition. Ecologists interested in the spatial positioning of prey and predators predict that predators tend to concentrate on the most productive patches in their foraging efforts. We can even expect them to defend these spaces as territories if the surrounding landscape offers reduced opportunities in comparison. There is no reason that humans would not do the same thing; it makes basic economic sense to live near your food source and to protect your source of livelihood. People on the Northwest Coast followed this pattern in the Late Period. They situated major villages in places that offered protection from the elements and optimal access to food resources. The Ozette village, for example, was located next to one of the most productive reefs on the Northwest Coast, which attracted a wide range of fish, shellfish, and large mammals, including whales.

The Six Mile Rapids of the Mid-Fraser was another such place (Figure 4.15). Research by anthropologist Michael Kew suggests that during the weakest point of a four-year spawning cycle, the Mid-Fraser rapids could have 400 percent more salmon than any surrounding drainage system, including the Thompson River and Upper Fraser. Poor years are the make-or-break point for any hunter-gatherer group. It's easy to survive when resources are abundant: it's the tough times that define the viability of a people's economic strategy. Possession of a place such as the mouth of the Bridge River at the Six Mile Rapids would therefore offer incredible economic advantages during bad years.

Jim Chatters points out several other practical and economic advantages of living in larger groups. Larger groups derive some advantage from their greater ability to operate as units in the mass harvesting and processing of a resource such as salmon. Large groups offer more opportunities for craft specialization and the spread of innovations within the group. Chatters argues, however, that the fundamental advantage would come in the form of protection from attack. A large village could field a larger number of able-bodied warriors for defence purposes. This ability would be significant in a landscape where unfriendly neighbours routinely kill those outside of protected contexts. Reflecting on the past, contemporary elders at Bridge River noted recently that the village's position in the narrow Bridge River Valley allowed sentries, positioned on the higher ridges, to watch for incoming attackers, particularly in the late fall after the salmon harvest.

Living along the Mid-Fraser River offered significant economic advantages to human populations. Plateau people normally gathered at fishing grounds for short periods (no more than six to eight weeks) before dispersing into their

FIGURE 4.15 The confluence of
the Bridge and Fraser rivers,
known as the Six Mile Rapids.

Photograph by D. Backhouse-Prentiss

smaller winter encampments scattered about the region. Dense aggregates of small, briefly occupied housepits and mat lodges in The Dalles and Kamloops regions reflect this process. They mark only one part of a complex annual cycle of decision making and group movement that coincided with the availability of key food resources. It may even be that families gathered in the Mid-Fraser Canyon in a similar way during the late Shuswap and early Plateau horizons, leaving only ephemeral campsite materials behind on terraces near fishing places at Six Mile Rapids. The large and more permanent villages of the Mid-Fraser Canyon were a different thing altogether. These villages grew so large that some archaeologists, such as Brian Hayden, call them towns. Although this term is poorly defined, these settlements unquestionably featured houses big enough to hold 50 or more people. With enough big houses, these people might have had the opportunity to monopolize fishing sites and control regional trade relationships between the Coast and the Interior. To borrow terminology from Hayden and his colleagues, they were truly gateway communities. Something significant must have happened to trigger a change this drastic.

As we discuss in the previous chapter, archaeologists have thought a lot about why groups of otherwise egalitarian people would settle down and develop complex social organizations based on inequality. During the 1960s and '70s, researchers such as Mark Cohen looked at population pressure and suggested that growing populations led to packed villages and competition for control of food and other resources. The Mid-Fraser villages, however, appeared at a time of generally low population. There is no evidence for steady population growth in the region until after the villages came into existence. In an important counterargument, Brian Hayden suggests that aggregation followed the invention of tools to mass harvest and process resources such as salmon or grain. Hayden is correct in the sense that technological advances did precede the rise of the Mid-Fraser villages. Yet his argument is a major oversimplification. The process was more complex, and there might have been other, more proximate, factors at play. For example, if his argument is correct, then why is there no significant evidence for village development during the Shuswap horizon, when people used the same tools? Northwest Coast archaeologists such as R.G. Matson, as well as general ecologists, suggest that packing (crowding of people into particular spaces) and village formation would only follow the clustering of resources. Thus, once people shifted to a preference for salmon, they created larger and larger settlements along the most productive and advantageous locations on the Coast. This model seems to explain the economic underpinnings for nucleation in the Mid-Fraser Canyon, yet the question remains: why did the development not happen earlier?

One possible answer comes from evolutionary theory. In a series of articles, we, along with Jim Chatters, propose that early villagers of the Pacific Northwest, like cultures elsewhere, were locked into stable socioeconomic strategies. In other words, their annual cycle of movement and food gathering came to be so precisely scheduled that it might have been impossible for anyone to break out of the cycle. Anthropologists working elsewhere in the world have documented cases in which this happened, and the people caught in the cycle usually ended up not faring well. It is not surprising that in many parts of the world, the archaeological record supports the conclusion that long periods of cultural stability were typical of the ancient past.

One alternative explanation could be that at least one group undertook an incredibly risky venture – breaking loose from prevailing norms to establish a new pattern after the Neoglacial period. Change is not, however, always good for, at times, it comes with significant risk. Within a conservative learning environment, it would be hard to imagine that a radical new approach to scheduling and procuring resources would be readily accepted. At least initially, changes would have been gradual and based on minor shifts that perhaps involved only a limited number of villagers. It would be no surprise to learn that the early collector strategy employed by Shuswap and Plateau horizon hunter-gatherers locked the groups into cycles of movement, food gathering, and intergroup relations that were seriously compromised by the establishment of large, permanent villages. Perhaps the early Plateau horizon (pre-1800 BP) hunter-gatherers of the central Canadian Plateau were not even the primary ancestors of the Mid-Fraser village people.

Another possibility could be that another group developed a new, more complex strategy and brought it with them as they moved into the Mid-Fraser Canyon area, replacing the culturally locked groups of the early Plateau horizon. Recall that a form of socioeconomic organization that we call complex collector had already developed in and around the Lower Fraser Valley by 2500 BP and spread elsewhere on the Coast after 2000 BP. This strategy favoured aggregated settlements of unusually large houses that contained multiple families that probably acted as corporate groups. In other words, the Mid-Fraser strategy typical of the period after 1800 BP had already been employed by local groups for about a thousand years. When the people of the early Marpole culture of the central Coast became more widely distributed between about 1,800 and 2,000 years ago, it is possible that groups located in or around the Harrison and Lillooet rivers moved north into the Mid-Fraser area, bringing with them a fully developed complex collector strategy. This development would explain the sudden appearance of full-blown villages composed of large houses occupied by corporate groups. If this did happen, it is not hard to imagine the newcomers easily displacing the more dispersed hunter-gatherers.

A third possibility is that knowledge of complex collecting, available for so long in the Lower Fraser Valley, was somehow transmitted to people in the Mid-Fraser Valley. These people then overcame social prohibitions and successfully instituted corporate group-based living in what eventually became large villages.

Whatever their origins, the Mid-Fraser villages did appear suddenly. Over the centuries, they grew to surpass even the largest of the famous coastal villages. Their economy was based on the same resources used by earlier collectors in the region, but they processed massive quantities, stored the fruits of their harvests, and instituted new trade networks.

5
Hunting, Gathering, and Fishing

As long as she could remember, the salmon had always come. The first salmon of spring were a welcome relief from dried fish that had the texture and taste of wood. Midsummer runs brought different pleasures, thousands of fish and fruitful work. The women split the fish and hung them on racks to dry. Her wrinkled, spotted hands bear multiple scars from boiling the heads for oil. But it was worth it. People outside the region envied them their bounty, their stores of fish and fat for trade and the lean days of winter.

But this year, the run had nearly failed. Families from the big house still camp by the river. She can see younger men, on the rocks, swirling long dip nets through the churning waters in hopes that the run will come. Women stand by, waiting for the men to pass over the odd fish for processing. She knows that there are not enough to feed everyone for another winter. The people must look to other food sources, working harder to acquire deer, small game animals, roots, berries, and seeds. There are too many people on this land, she thinks. Trade obligations will certainly be broken. If things get bad enough, she will have to teach the young ones how to scrape and eat the inner bark from pines.

The rich, complex cultures of First Nations in the Fraser Canyon were built on a foundation of harvesting and processing abundant plant and animal food resources on a seasonal basis. The window of opportunity to collect and process these resources was small, at times only a few weeks, and was followed by long periods in which only secondary resources were available. Moreover, harvested foods were not always used simply for subsistence purposes. Everyone had social obligations within and beyond the village, and food was a critical trade item to fulfill these obligations. Oral accounts and historical records indicate that people routinely traded salmon, roots, and deer products to groups outside their immediate environment, and the success or failure of households and entire communities was linked to successful food gathering, processing and, at times, exchange.

Hunting, Gathering, and Fishing

People lived in Mid-Fraser villages because of salmon and wild root plants. Hunter-gatherers can be incredibly resourceful and are deeply knowledgeable about their environment. Some equatorial groups can, for example, make use of two hundred or more species of plants and animals in a given year. In contrast, groups that live in higher latitudes usually have a more restricted and specialized diet. Some Eskimo and Inuit people traditionally made use of no more than two dozen plants and animals during a yearly cycle. The people of the Mid-Fraser Canyon had a diet that was about midway between these two extremes.

Because hunter-gatherers in most parts of the world lived in small groups, difficulties in finding food could be overcome by simply moving to a new area. The peoples of the Mid-Fraser area, along with other more socially complex hunter-gatherers, such as those on the Northwest Coast or in some areas of the western Arctic, faced a different problem. By focusing on a specific resource, such as salmon, that was restricted to a specific time and place, they were bound to the seasons and tethered to the landscape and villages. Mobility was no longer a viable option, nor did it offer the same payoffs as it did to other hunter-gatherers. People in these regions were constrained by two fundamental factors. First, food resources tended to be clumped in time and space. In tropical and temperate environments, a wide variety of foods are accessible throughout the year. People simply need to move to where they can be found. Northern hunter-gatherers, by contrast, had access to food in short bursts, for instance, during salmon runs or caribou migrations. Survival was predicated on harvesting a lot of food from a single species and storing it for the lean seasons. As in many other contexts around the world, this situation creates a tether between people and their villages. When people are tied to particular places, they tend to use a more restricted territory.

The second constraint was a byproduct of the first. If survival is predicated on the mass harvest of foods that come only once or twice a year for short periods of time, then it is generally worthwhile to guard that location to prevent neighbours from stealing your fishing spot, the location where you get your winter food. Territorialism, therefore, emerged under these conditions. Moving into a neighbour's territory could result in death or slavery. Even groups who did not routinely keep slaves knew their value and traded captives to wealthier slave-holding groups in exchange for goods.

Because subsistence in the Mid-Fraser region was seasonally varied, survival meant constantly planning for the future. At almost any time of the year, people foraged for food to eat immediately and collected other items to store for later.

Traditional Foodways

Over the years, we have gained a remarkably detailed understanding of traditional foodways. The Mid-Fraser region is blessed with an excellent ethnographic and historical record of traditional subsistence practices. This rich understanding has emerged from two sources of data: the late 19th-century ethnographies, such as those by James Teit, and studies conducted since the 1970s by Michael Kew, Steven Romanoff, Nancy Turner, Diana Alexander, Dorothy Kennedy, and Randy Bouchard. Drawing on these impressive works, we provide an overview of the basics of traditional subsistence in the Mid-Fraser, focusing in particular on core foods: salmon, ungulates such as deer, and key plant foods.

Salmon

Interview anyone living in the Mid-Fraser Canyon today, and they will tell you the same thing: salmon is the top food. This is not to say that indigenous people only ate salmon, but salmon was king (Box 5.1). More realistically, salmon provided a critical link in the people's annual subsistence chain (Figure 5.1). Other important fish were trout, sucker, and sturgeon. Enormous numbers of fish concentrated in the region, particularly at the Six Mile Rapids, where they would rest in eddies before they charged up the river on the next leg of their journey (Figure 5.2). Some spawns headed up the Seton and Bridge rivers; many others continued up the Fraser. The number of migrating fish varied from year to year. Michael Kew suggests that the fish ran in cycles, which can be ranked from strongest to weakest. During the weakest year, the Mid-Fraser could still boast over four times more fish running through its waters than the Thompson River. Sockeye and spring salmon peaked in July and August. Even today, the air in August smells strongly of fish drying on racks. Little wonder that on the traditional St'át'imc calendar, these months were marked as fishing time. The salmon provided large amounts of food for immediate use; more importantly, salmon could be dried and stored for winter use.

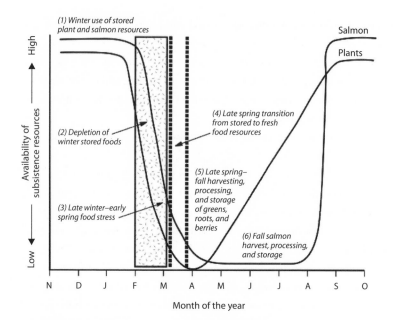

(1) Winter use of stored plant and salmon resources

High ← Availability of subsistence resources → Low

Salmon

Plants

(2) Depletion of winter stored foods

(3) Late winter–early spring food stress

(4) Late spring transition from stored to fresh food resources

(5) Late spring–fall harvesting, processing, and storage of greens, roots, and berries

(6) Fall salmon harvest, processing, and storage

N D J F M A M J J A S O

Month of the year

▲ FIGURE 5.1 Generalized ethnographic model of the seasonal round of traditional subsistence practices.

Illustration by Ian Kuijt

▼ FIGURE 5.2 The salmon fishing site at the Six Mile Rapids, located at the confluence of the Bridge and Fraser rivers.

Photograph by Duggan Backhouse-Prentiss

Sam Mitchell, a Fountain elder, described the Mid-Fraser fishing sites to ethnographers:

> When the salmon arrive here at Lillooet, the people come and camp over-night. This is during the summer and early fall. At the Bridge River rapids ... called *Sh-HIT-tl*, there is a drop in the river; the water is very swift. All summer people stay here and fish. There are enough fish-drying racks for everyone.

> Where the Bridge River meets the Fraser, there are names for the fishing spots. One of these fishing rocks, on the east shore of the Fraser River here, is called *Tlik-O-la-wh*, "a brace or prop in the land." Sometimes the water is so swift here that rocks get into the net. Another fishing place is *Min-MAN-alch*, "shade rock," and there is a spot called *Ho-shi-SHOOSH*, "foamy place," and another called *She-HAH*, the name of the person who owned the fishing rock. Another place named after a person is where the fish are found when the water is very low. As the water level at *Sh-HIT-tl* raises and lowers, different fishing rocks are used. [Bouchard and Kennedy 1977:64-66]

BOX 5.1 SALMON, SALMON EVERYWHERE, BUT WHICH SALMON TO USE?

Are all salmon created equal, or are some salmon species better suited for different uses? Although it is widely recognized that salmon are critical to First Nations in the Mid-Fraser Canyon, most people are unaware that the quality, size, and storage characteristics of different species vary. Several species of salmon spawn in the Fraser River: Chinook (known locally as spring salmon), sockeye, coho, pink, and chum. Chinook spawn throughout the watersheds of the Fraser River, well up through the Mid-Fraser area. They are the largest sal-mon, contain relatively high amounts of fat, and are highly sought after. Spawning begins in spring (hence the local name), peaks in July, and runs through early August. Sockeye are considerably smaller than Chinook, but both species contain significant fat. Appearing in enormous numbers, Sockeye spawn through-out the Fraser watershed from late July to mid-August. Sockeye were, and are, a subsistence mainstay to people in the region. Coho are intermediate in size but have less fat. They are far more common in the Lower Fraser Canyon and Thompson drainages and spawn in late summer to early fall. Pink salmon are small, low in fat, and tend to be restricted to the Lower Fraser Valley below Hell's Gate. But some have now colonized the Mid-Fraser area. Coho and pink salmon did not, apparently, play major roles in the people's subsistence patterns. Chum salmon, often referred to as dog salmon in Alaska, are large but low in fat. They never spawned higher than the town of Hope in the Lower Fraser Canyon and therefore played no role in Mid-Fraser subsistence.

People traditionally used a variety of nets to catch salmon. They connected the nets to large boulders and accessed the nets from wooden platforms built out over the river. Nets were made from bent wood and cordage derived from Indian hemp (sometimes described as milkweed). Mitchell described cordage manufacture to ethnographer Steven Romanoff:

> They sew reeds together with the only string they can get. In my language we call it *sp'ats'en*. That's the same weed they used to make fish twine. It's along the river ... When these weeds get dry, around in the fall, maybe in September or October ... they make lots of them, and they pound it up (to get bark off). I've seen my grandmother making them. They pound it up on wood to get the bark out of it. They weave it and make string out of it ... That's mostly for thread and it's also for fishnet ... But there are certain kinds of willows they call *nexwtin*. They make ropes out of it. They use that on the fishing racks they have ... They tie cross pieces with this ... They just twist it and make rope out of it. The full length of a bush may be 10 or 12 feet long ... They can also use it to anchor a net. [Romanoff 1992a:230]

Nets were set in deeper water to catch bottom-running spring salmon. The people also used set nets and dip nets (Figure 5.3). Set nets usually consisted of a large bag net placed on the end of a long pole that was anchored at its opposite end. The bag closed around the fish when they entered. Dip nets were smaller, unanchored versions of set nets. Fishermen stood on platforms or boulders adjacent to the rapids and swirled the nets in the water for hours. One informant told us that he once caught a dozen sockeye in one swirl. Even if there is some exaggeration in this claim, it illustrates the potential for major returns using these fishing methods.

Mitchell also provided detailed descriptions of fishing techniques:

> The spring salmon run deep in this part of the river. So [*bikol*] makes a platform way out from the rock; that's a big platform. That's where he sets his net. His net is four or five feet wide and it's about six feet in depth. He'll push it down so the top end of the net is about five feet below the surface. That will put the net all of ten feet down. And he's got his platform way out.
>
> The net was made of this milkweed or *sp'ats'en7ul.* They weave the net for one purpose, just for spring salmon. If there's any sockeye that go in, they'll go right through because the mesh on the net was wide enough for the sockeye to go right through. Only a spring salmon will be caught there ...

FIGURE 5.3 **Dip-net fishing along the Fraser River.**

Photograph by Eric S. Carlson.

That trip to the net – there's a trip that goes to the finger on the pole when he's sitting up there. That net is way down there ten feet. If a spring salmon hits, he knows it's a spring salmon, he lets the trip go. He pulls his pole up and the net falls down to the bottom of the bows. That holds whatever fish is in that net. [Romanoff 1992a:232]

Salmon-fishing sites were located along the Fraser River and its major tributaries. The best sites were generally large rocks perched along the river

▲ FIGURE 5.4 Fish-drying
rack, Fraser River, 2006.
Photograph by Eric S. Carlson

▼ FIGURE 5.5 Processed
salmon drying on racks,
Fraser River, 2006.
Photograph by Eric S. Carlson

adjacent to major eddies where the salmon tended to congregate. According to historical and oral accounts, particular villages claimed some sections of the rivers, while other areas were open for everyone's use. The most productive spots, however, tended to be owned and used exclusively by individuals or families. Because ownership of these places was inherited, a fishing site could remain in one family for generations and even acquire a name based upon that family's history of use. Owners typically built a scaffold and drying rack on the site. They claimed first use of the site but shared it with others once they were done.

With winter survival on the line, careful processing and storage was essential. Traditional racks, which were built along the Fraser, generally consisted of rows of horizontal poles (Romanoff describes eight) suspended on four posts. Some racks could be up to 15 × 25 feet, according to Romanoff. The butchered salmon were suspended over the poles and covered by fir boughs, which protected the fish from direct sunlight. Fish were traditionally prepared by splitting each fish up to the tail and drying the entire fish, along with the backbone. Some accounts suggest that fish heads in pre-modern times were left on during the drying process (Figure 5.4). Other accounts suggest that the people removed the heads and backbones prior to the drying process and then dried and stored them separately as backup food for the winter.

Salmon head bones are almost never found in archaeological contexts. One possibility is that the heads were removed at the fishing site and boiled down for their oil content (Box 5.2). Today, Aboriginal people process salmon by splitting each fish to the tail then often discarding the backbone and head. They score the meat on both sides to permit more efficient drying (Figure 5.5). Flies were always a problem and people traditionally dealt with it by scoring the meat finely so that it would harden up quickly, by keeping camps clean, and by picking the hottest and windiest places to dry the salmon. St'át'imc air-dried salmon was famous throughout the broader region for its good flavour and high quality. Coastal people, on the Lower Fraser River and elsewhere, are said to have grown tired of their smoked salmon and traded valuable goods to get Mid-Fraser salmon.

Ethnographers also recorded the occasional use of smoke drying among the St'át'imc. The filleted fish were placed flesh-side down on a drying rack built low over a smouldering fire. The fish could be eaten after it had been smoked for several days. Informants stated that this method worked best for the fattest fish. Fresh fish were sometimes also pit cooked, barbecued, or boiled for immediate consumption. Evidence for some of these procedures has been found at the Bridge River site, where outdoor ovens were used for roasting fish and ephemeral indoor hearths were likely used for barbecuing.

People buried salmon eggs in the ground within birch bark baskets for use in the late winter and early spring. William Samson described the use of salmon eggs to Steven Romanoff:

Salmon eggs taste kind of strong, but once you get the taste you'd like to have it to eat. You can't use it through the winter because it's frozen in the ground. When the ground thaws out, that's the time you can get it. You dig it out in the spring. After they get it out an hour, they invite their friends to come and get some. They come and help themselves to it. Then try some of the saskatoons. There is a special one that they dry. It is large and smooth. When it gets dry it tastes really sweet. When they start digging the salmon eggs, they'd have flour too. They boil the flour, put the

BOX 5.2 MAKING SALMON OIL

In the absence of domesticated animals, First Nations relied on salmon as a major source of fats and oils. It was a challenge to extract the oil from the fish. Boiling is one of the more effective means. Salmon were boiled in pit features or baskets at the fishing site or back at the pithouses. Elder Sam Mitchell describes the process:

The men make the oil because it's a big hole in the rock. On one end of the rock, it's kind of low, so he went and muddled it and made it even. That's where he built a fire and heated the rocks. He dumped the rocks there. When the rocks get hot, that's where he dumped everything, mostly salmon heads and guts and everything that's got oil in it. Mostly salmon heads. They save them. Then he poured water in it and it boiled there for one afternoon to the next afternoon before the whole thing kind of settle down and cooled down ... After this big hole ... cooled down, I noticed a yellowish layer on top. It looked like a sort of a cream on a milk pan. When

it did cool down ... he skims this yellow stuff off, then he starts on the oil itself. The oil on top of the water is maybe two or three inches thick, and it's kind of real brownish color. He skims from there and that's what he fills ... I don't think there was such thing as a funnel. But these salmon skin bottles, you can open it pretty wide. It will open out, stretch out. So the ladles that they use, they'll just skim the oil out and pour it in the bottle ... Whatever bones there are in there it just cooked like canned fish. It's cooked. You can just chew the bones. There's nothing to it ... We used to eat that when we were kids. A whole bunch of us go down and just grab them by the handful from that big hole. We ate until we couldn't eat anymore. [Romanoff 1992a:239]

As Mitchell outlines, boiling the leftover salmon parts provided a highly efficient means for extracting oil. When cooled, the oil and fats could be placed in a transportable container and stored for winter use.

FIGURE 5.6 Women adjacent to a cache pit in a pithouse in the Middle Fraser Canyon.
Illustration by Eric S. Carlson

saskatoons in with it, put the salmon eggs in with it. When you eat it you never go hungry. They do that every winter. [Romanoff 1992a:238-39]

Dried salmon was stored in underground cache pits (Figure 5.6) and above-ground facilities. Cache pits were dug both within and outside of houses. They were traditionally lined with grass and pine needles to repel mice and other vermin and to keep the fish clean. The above-ground facility consisted of a wooden structure raised up on four posts. Spaces between side timbers allowed wind to circulate, a necessity for keeping dried salmon for long periods. These box caches were kept in villages but could also be kept down by the river. As a rule, less oily fish lasted longer than oily fish. Therefore, if families were still eating last summer's salmon during late winter, it was normally leaner sockeye and coho salmon.

Deer, Elk, and Other Large Game
The Mid-Fraser area was historically rich with deer, elk, bighorn sheep, and mountain goat. Teit described hunting:

Animals hunted for their flesh, skins, sinew, antlers, horns, etc., were the mule-deer *(Cariacus macrois* and *Cariacus richardsonii)*, small black-tailed deer *(Cariacus columbianus lord)*, mountain-goat *(Aploceros monanus)*, bighorn sheep *(Ovis montana)*, and caribou *(Rangifer caribou Linn.)*. Goats and black-tailed deer are most common in the Lower Lillooet country, while mule deer and sheep are confined to the upper part of the country. Caribou were found in the extreme northwestern portion of the Lillooet hunting-grounds, but are now extinct there or have moved farther north. No white-tailed deer, prong-horn antelope, elk, moose, buffalo, badger, common or red marmot were ever known to exist in the present habitat of the Lillooet. Chief among other animals hunted for their flesh and skins were the hoary marmot and black bear, both of which were plentiful throughout all the mountains of the country. Besides these, were the beaver, rabbit, rock-rabbit, squirrel, seal, and raccoon. The last named was confined to some parts of the Lower Lillooet country, and seals were only found on Harrison Lake and in some of the coast inlets where the Lillooet sometimes hunted. Porcupines were killed for their flesh and quills, and grisly bears and panthers for their skins and claws. In times of scarcity the flesh of lynx, coyote, and other animals was eaten. [Teit 1900:225]

According to ethnographers, deer hunting has historically been a significant focus for Aboriginal peoples in this area. Deer populations move with the seasons: they congregate in valleys in the cold season to avoid deep snow and move into the mountains in the warm season to find better forage. People employed a variety of strategies to hunt the animals throughout the year. Chance encounters made it possible for individual hunters to obtain deer at any time, but they were most easily obtained in the late summer and fall, when they were fattest and preoccupied with the rut. People also built fences across migration routes to trap deer. An occasional hole in the fence contained some form of trap to hold the animal until the hunter came. Groups of hunters would also hold deer drives in the mountains, sometimes funnelling the animals into a narrow place where they could be dispatched. Modern Mid-Fraser deer populations fluctuate enormously. In the area between Fountain Valley and Pavilion Mountain, for example, archaeologist Diana Alexander estimates that deer populations today can range from 25 to 600 animals. As in the present, herd sizes in the past would have fluctuated depending on forage conditions and snowfall. Significant levels of snow would have led to winter die offs and human predation.

Elder Sam Mitchell described deer hunting:

FIGURE 5.7 Food preparation activities at Keatley Creek housepit village around 1,300 years ago. The image depicts what could be a spring day when people are engaged in a variety of food-related pursuits including butchering, transport of fish and fishing gear, and deer processing.

Illustration by Eric S. Carlson

A long time ago, our people shot deer with a bow and arrow. Deer were also caught by means of snares and deadfall traps. Hunting dogs were trained to track deer and herd them down to the water where they could be shot or clubbed. Some of the dogs were so fast they could outrun the deer. When the dog was a young pup, the hunter put the stomach of a freshly killed deer over the dog's head. This made it a good hunting dog. [Bouchard and Kennedy 1977:70-71]

Access to deer was important for people in the Mid-Fraser region. Deer supplemented salmon in their diet. When salmon numbers were low, deer could provide enough meat to survive the winter. Deer fat was also necessary for winter survival. To make the most effective use of deer or other ungulates, the people had to preserve the animals for storage (Figure 5.7). Deer acquired close to a winter village could be hauled whole into the village for processing. More typically, animals were acquired at some distance from the permanent residence and required some field butchery. Short hauls meant sectioning the animals. When distances were substantial, however, the people would strip meat from the animal and haul it back to the village in the hide. They usually smoked the meat in the field. Smoking helped prepare the meat for storage and lightened the load by reducing moisture. According to Mitchell, "After the hunter killed some animals he told the other people where they were so that they could pack them back to camp" (Bouchard and Kennedy 1977:71).

Storing meat in the village likely required some above-ground facilities. There are no historical or ethnographic accounts of the use of pits for meat storage. Above-ground wooden caches, much like those used for salmon, likely held substantial amounts of smoked and dried deer meat. Hides were generally processed in the village, as were other products of the hunt such as antler and sinew. Ethnographic accounts indicate that hides were tanned using a combination of urine and brains. They were then scraped to remove tissue and to soften the leather. Since successful hunters were not always common in the ancient villages and since deer numbers fluctuated a lot, ownership of deer-hide clothing was not possible for everyone. Many had to rely on clothing made from woven fibres and other materials such as salmon skin. Mitchell described the characteristics of and payoffs for the successful hunter:

> They say that the person that don't sleep, gets up early in the morning, goes around hunting, he always has a lot of wives. They say he'll have plenty of food all the time, plenty of meat. So he'll have plenty of wives too, in them days. Some of them have ten. That's the guy who goes out and hunts. Never gets lazy, never stays at home. But the lazy guys have a little breech clout nothing else. Kind of a buckskin here to hide his private parts. [Romanoff 1992b:479]

Berries and Roots

Berries and roots provided the final critical dietary component for people in the Mid-Fraser region. Most protein consumed in the region was lean; while this is good in today's world, it could be problematic in ancient times. Processing protein within our bodies consumes a lot of energy. Consequently, we require a matching energy source to fuel the process. People from the Arctic solve the problem by eating copious amounts of fat from seals, walrus, and whales. In the Mid-Fraser region, people had only limited, seasonal, access to fat from salmon and some mammals. Salmon fat is unsaturated and does not store well. Deer fat is saturated and stores well but was rarely available in high quantities.

Trade with coastal peoples sometimes generated eulachon oil, which stored well, but this source could not be relied upon. Without a stable or substantial source of fat, carbohydrates were critical.

Berries and roots are a rich source of carbohydrates. Essential root foods included spring beauty or Indian potato, balsamroot, yellow avalanche lily, and wild onions. Most of the root foods were obtained from open meadows at intermediate or higher elevations. The productivity of the meadows depended upon climatic regimes. Many of the region's root food plants or geophytes required open and relatively dry meadows. Wet conditions could result in reduced habitats for these plants. It is not clear how human predation of geophytes affected local populations. There is some evidence to suggest that people disturbed the ground and replanted smaller bulbs and corms to increase the geophyte harvest. Was there ever a point, however, when people overharvested these plants? This question cannot be answered at the present time. However, ethnobotanist Nancy Turner speculates that reductions in populations of yellow avalanche lily could have been due to intensive harvesting in ancient times. Root harvesting took place at varying times during the warm season: spring beauty in the spring, yellow avalanche lily in the summer, and balsamroot in the early fall.

Root foods generally required intensive processing after harvest. Ethnographic accounts describe parties of women carrying digging sticks and returning with baskets of roots. The women cleaned most species and then roasted or steamed them in heated earthen pits located away from the village. This process rendered them edible by converting inulin to fructose through exposure to intense heat. Once they were cooked and dried, the roots could be stored in pits or strung on sticks. Roots were reconstituted in water before consumption and are said to have been sweet in flavour. Roots were undoubtedly an important winter food, and dried geophytes were valued as a trade item.

Important berries included Saskatoon berries, huckleberries, chokecherries, soapberries, and thimble berries. Depending on the species, berries were harvested in dry contexts at lower elevations (Saskatoons) or in wetter places at higher elevations (huckleberries). Edith O'Donaghy described berry (and other resource) harvesting to ethnobotanist Nancy Turner:

> We used to go (in mid-July) up the Bridge River valley (from Shalalth) to get soapberries, or across Seton lake ... We used to dry them and store them in great sacks. They had special buckets for soapberries and other kinds of berries, ones that won't leak ... woven of cedar roots.
>
> There used to be lots of gooseberries [at a place near Shalalth called White Slide]. We used to pick them when they were green and put them

in flour sacks. We would go there to pick them for a whole day ... They used to pick lots and lots of those Oregon-grapes [around Shalalth].

(In mid-August) a whole bunch of (many families ...) would go up ... on top of the mountain, way up high, close to the snow line (to Mission Ridge, above Shalalth) ... for a few days, three or four days or a week, mainly to pick (black) huckleberries. These berries are ripe in August, and that's when people would go up ... We got huckleberries, and dug roots while we were up there, wild potatoes (spring beauty corms), wild onions, whatever we could find up on the mountain ... They'd gather (avalanche lily corms), a whole bunch of tiger lily bulbs ... that black moss (black tree lichen) ... We'd bring down six or eight (large coiled cedar root baskets) baskets ... baskets and sacks of mountain potatoes. [Turner 1992:417-18]

Berries were harvested from June (Saskatoons) through early fall (choke-cherries) and were either eaten fresh or, more importantly, dried and saved for long-term survival and winter consumption. Dried berries could be reconstituted, cooked, and consumed with fish and meat. They added flavour and contributed a wide array of nutritional benefits. Dried berries were a typical trade item, particularly with the Lower Lillooet people.

Charlie Mack, a Mount Currie elder, described the collection and preparation of berry foods to ethnographers:

In July, our people pick *sh-Ho-shome*, soapberries. The berries are whipped with an instrument called *tsath-ee-Mam*, which is made out of *TLA-qua-maz*, bunchgrass. This causes the berries to foam up, hence the name "Indian ice cream." Other berries can be added to this. "Indian ice cream" is very rich, so you can't eat too much of it.

In the old days, our people also made the soapberries into "loaves." After the berries were boiled, the juice was extracted and the pulp was dried between layers of bunch grass. The finished "loaves" were about 10 inches (25 centimetres) wide and about 2 inches (5 centimetres) thick. The soap-berry juice was then poured on to the "loaves"; it soaked into them. When the people wanted some "Indian ice cream," they cut off a slice of this and whipped it up.

Also in July, our people picked *im-HAZ*, black huckleberries, which were plentiful in the mountains around Mount Currie. As the summer progressed the women had to go further up the mountain to find *im-HAZ*. These berries were one of the major foods of our people because they keep very well and are sweet. After they are picked, the berries are spread on a mat to dry in the sun. Sometimes they are put on a 5 foot (1.5 metre) high cedar plank rack. A fire was made below the rack and the berries were smoke dried. This was what they had to do when the weather was bad. Blackcap berries, called *chah-O-sha,* were also picked. They were prepared in the same way as black huckleberries.

In July the salmonberries were ripe, but they were never very plentiful. These berries are called *to-WAN.* Very few of our people bothered to dry them as they were never able to find enough. Wild raspberries, *EYE-chuck,* grow in this country. My mother used to pick them and put them on the roof to dry. A cover had to be put over them so that the birds would not eat them.

Also in July, thimbleberries, *THLEE-kak,* are ripe, although there never were enough to store for winter. They were one of our favourite berries. [Bouchard and Kennedy 1977:74].

The Seasonal Round

How did people who lived in the Mid-Fraser region organize the complex tasks of finding, harvesting, and storing wild foods? The St'át'imc used a collector strategy, which required them to anticipate future needs by harvesting and storing surplus food and other items. Food-related activities in any season included acquiring fresh food for immediate use and harvesting additional food for the following month or even year. Much like when people go to the store today, people in the past would have preferred fresh food for dinner, but they often relied on stored food.

Diana Alexander, ethnographer and archaeologist, notes that the new year started in November, when people moved into winter residences. During this time, people lived on a variety of foods, particularly dried salmon, deer, roots, and berries. This diet was supplemented occasionally by fresh meat provided by men hunting near the village. After eating the same foods each day for at least three months, and with few ways to flavour their food, people moved out of the winter houses in late January or February. Not surprisingly, St'át'imc people say that the people were ready by this time to move to the summer lodges and start the warm season cycle of fishing, hunting, and gathering.

During early spring, people foraged widely not only in the lower elevations, including river bottoms and terraces, but also in the higher grasslands. They sought fresh greens and animals such as deer. The deer, however, were in poor condition after a long winter and hard to come by. Some people sought the first spring salmon on the fishing rocks. In late spring, families moved into slightly higher elevations. They camped in and around lakes and grasslands and foraged for spawning trout, geophytes, and deer. They processed deer and roots for use later in the summer during fishing season or for the winter.

June and July brought intensive berry harvesting and processing. Ethnographic accounts tell us that these were primarily women's activities. From mid-July to mid-August, all activities focused on salmon fishing and processing. By the end of this period, people would have acquired stores of roots, berries, and sockeye and spring salmon.

The close of salmon-fishing season marked the beginning of the fall cycle. Families moved away from fishing camps and focused on higher elevations, the montane parklands above grasslands and lakes. Men hunted intensively for deer, elk, and sheep; women either accompanied them or searched for mid- to lower-elevation plant foods. All of the food they accumulated and processed was hauled back to the winter villages. Given the absence of large domestic pack animals, transporting the food required many trips over many miles. In November, the scattered families moved back into the winter villages, and the annual cycle began again.

Subsistence Technology

Gathering and processing food in the Mid-Fraser region required sophisticated technologies and tools (Figures 5.8 and 5.9). Salmon fishing required large dip nets, often hung on the end of long wooden poles or Leister spears (Figure 5.10). The people used a variety of heavy-duty scrapers to manufacture these poles and digging sticks for root collecting, hunting gear such as atlatls and darts, and bows and arrows. Chipped-stone knives were required for fish processing and for butchering larger mammals such as deer. The people used stone scrapers to remove flesh from and soften hides, and they used a wide range of small flake tools and larger ground-stone hammers, mauls, and grinding stones in day-to-day household activities such as food preparation (Figures 5.11 to 5.16; see also Box 5.3).

▶ FIGURE 5.8 Tools typical of the Mid-Fraser villages around 1,800 to 1,200 years ago: *(a-b)* corner-notched projectile points, *(c)* basal-notched projectile point, *(d)* thin-stemmed projectile point (more typical of the Columbia Plateau), *(e)* nephrite adze (Bridge River site), *(f)* pipe fragment (Keatley Creek site), *(g)* biface, *(h)* ground slate knife with drilled hole (Bridge River site), *(i)* atlatl dart forshaft (Bridge River site), *(j)* bone awl, *(k)* stemmed bone projectile point (Bridge River site), *(l)* dentalium shell bead, *(m)* end scraper, *(n)* bone needle, and *(o)* hand maul.
Illustrations by Robert O'Boyle

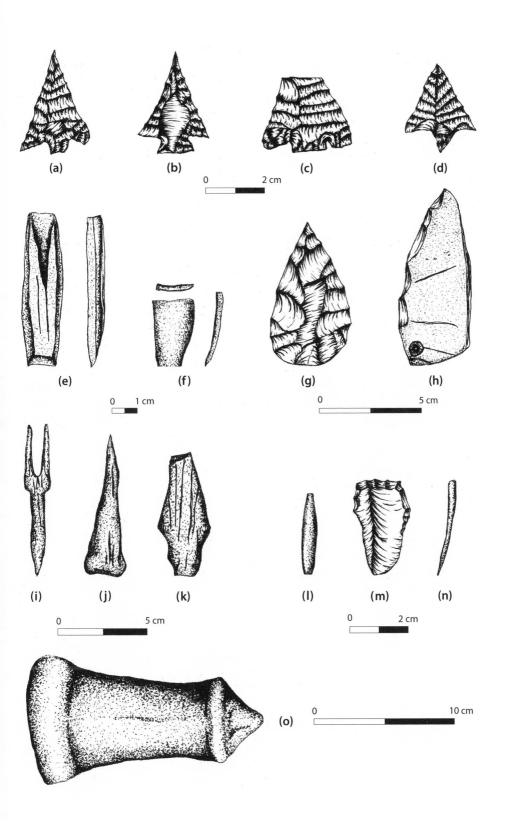

(a)

(b)

(c)

(d)

0   2 cm

(e)

(f)

(g)

(h)

0   1 cm

0   5 cm

(i)   (j)   (k)   (l)   (m)   (n)

0   5 cm

0   2 cm

(o)

0   10 cm

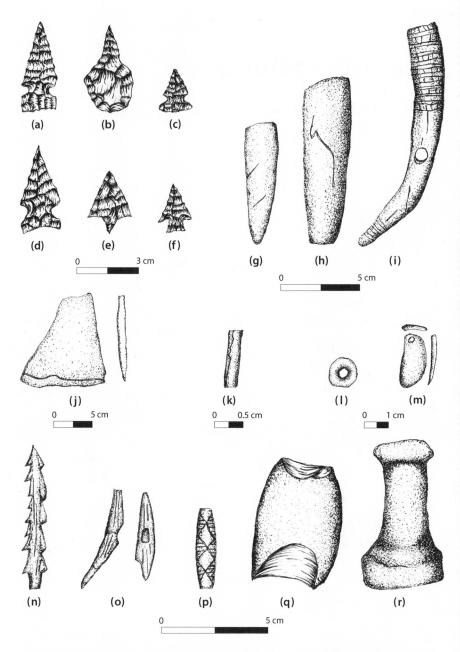

▶ FIGURE 5.9 Tools typical of the Mid-Fraser villages around 1,200 to 700 years ago: *(a,c, and d)* Kamloops side-notched projectile points, *(b)* chipped-stone drill, *(e)* small thin-stemmed projectile point (more typical of the Columbia Plateau), *(f)* small corner-notched projectile point, *(g)* pestle; *(h)* nephrite adze, *(i)* digging-stick handle, *(j)* sandstone saw (Keatley Creek site), *(k)* copper bead, *(l)* steatite bead, *(m)* polished steatite pipe fragment with hole drilled for use as a pendant (Keatley Creek site), *(n)* harpoon (Leister) tip, *(o)* toggling harpoon valve, *(p)* bone gaming piece, *(q)* net sinker, and *(r)* hand maul.

Illustrations by Robert O'Boyle

Fishing Techniques

Mid-Fraser Canyon, British Columbia

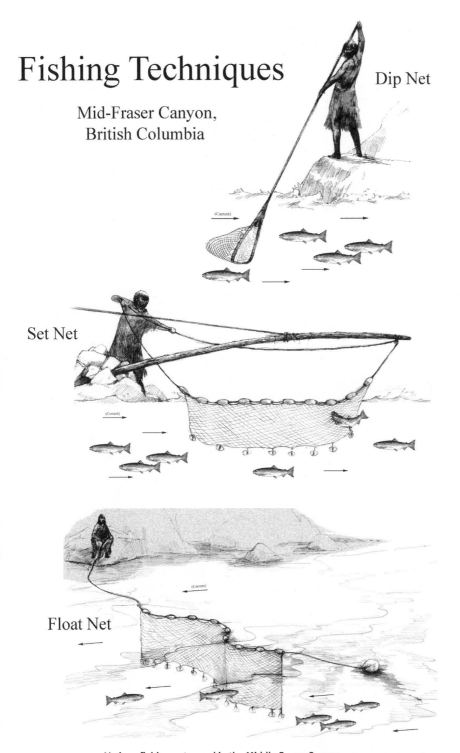

Dip Net

Set Net

Float Net

FIGURE 5.10 **Various fishing nets used in the Middle Fraser Canyon.** *Illustration by Eric S. Carlson*

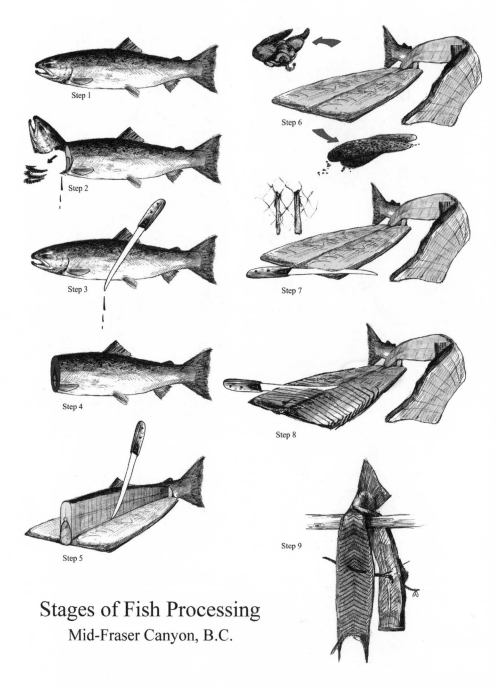

Stages of Fish Processing
Mid-Fraser Canyon, B.C.

Step 1

Step 2

Step 3

Step 4

Step 5

Step 6

Step 7

Step 8

Step 9

FIGURE 5.11 **The various stages of salmon processing.**
Illustration by Eric S. Carlson

FIGURE 5.12 An image of traditional dip-net fishing illustrating relationships between fishing people, net technology, and prey (salmon).

Illustration by Eric S. Carlson

FIGURE 5.13 The initial stage of fish processing, where fish are filleted and prepared for drying.

Illustration by Eric S. Carlson

FIGURE 5.14 Fish processing, where final details of splitting and scoring occur before fish is placed on drying racks.

Illustration by Eric S. Carlson

FIGURE 5.15 A large traditional salmon drying rack. Large numbers of fish would be hung on these racks under hot and windy conditions, but still protected from direct sunlight.

Illustration by Eric S. Carlson

FIGURE 5.16 Traditional drying racks showing the variation in technologies employed to prepare salmon for later consumption.

Illustration by Eric S. Carlson

James Teit described a variety of stone weapons:

> Another weapon was made of polished greenish stone. Its blade, sharpened
> on each edge, was from three inches to three inches and a half wide, ter-
> minating at one end in a three inch long point for stabbing. The other end
> was small, and finished with a knob for grasping with the hand.
>
> To this class of weapon belongs the copper club found at Spuzzumn.
> Still another kind had a broad, thin head ending in a spike in front. Into
> a wooden handle a foot and a half in length, stone heads, often axe or
> tomahawk shaped, or V or spike shaped, were fastened with thongs. Some
> of these had back spikes. Sometimes horn or bone was substituted for
> stone. [Teit 1900:264]

He also described various wood- and hide-working tools made of stone:

BOX 5.3 BEFORE IRON: STONE TOOLS IN THE MID-FRASER CANYON

How and why did Aboriginal people make stone tools? Before iron was introduced in the 17th century, people relied on stone tools for all their chopping, cutting, and food-processing tasks. Tool making was an important skill within villages, one that had major economic importance. Unlike many parts of North America, there are ethnographic descriptions of stone tool making from the Mid-Fraser area. When James Teit travelled through the Interior in the 19th century, some people still made stone tools while others carried the knowledge of how it had been done. Teit described how the Thompson people manufactured tools:

"Stones were battered into shape, cut, and flaked. Jade and serpentine boulders were cut by means of gritstones or beaver-teeth. But few polished implements are found. Steatite pipes were polished with stems of Equiselum and a mixture of grease and pitch of the black pine. Stone skin-scrapers and hand-hammers are used up to this day." [Teit 1900:182].

According to Teit, stone tools were used for an extraordinary range of tasks:

Adze-shaped implements were made of jade, serpentine, and a dark gray or black variety of stone, which was also used for making polished knives and spear-heads. These implements were used as adzes, chisels, skin-scrapers, and tomahawk-heads. Glassy basalt was the stone most commonly used for chipping and flaking, and for making arrow-heads, spear-heads, and knives. Skin-scrapers and adzes were frequently made of the same material; and jasper, obsidian, and other stones occasionally served the same purposes. Most skin-scrapers were simply thin pieces flaked off from pebbles of various kinds, and were slightly chipped on one edge

Adzes and axes of jade – and serpentine were in common use. Stone chisels were fastened into handles with sockets, in which the stone was inserted. These tools were also used for building canoes. For cutting and carving, chipped-stone knives or beaver-tooth knives were used. The former were similar to the crooked knives of the Coast Indians ... Buckskin for shirts, leggings, etc., is first scraped by means of a stone scraper or a bone or horn chisel of the same form as that used in woodwork. [Teit 1900:182-83]

The people likely acquired the stone to make the tools through an embedded strategy. Groups would visit remote stone quarries during their hunting and gathering trips in the grasslands and mountains. Some of these quarries were owned by certain groups. Early ethnographer A.G. Morice noted:

The material chosen in preference to fashion arrow or spear heads with was loose, broken pieces of rock such as were found on the surface. Of course,

only. Arrow-smoothers were made of sandstone of a fine grain; and files for cutting and smoothing stone implements, of coarse-grained sandstone and also of a dark-colored stone. Steatite and other soft stones and copper were cut with beaver-tooth knives. Some of the hard stones were cut with crystals of quartz and with agate. [Teit 1900:182]

Teit also described how to make arrowheads:

The Indians are still familiar with the art of making arrow-heads. When these were to be made from a boulder, the following method was employed. The boulder was split by being laid on a stone and struck with a hand-hammer, generally a pebble of handy size. When a suitable piece had been obtained, its edges were trimmed off with a hard stone. Then it was wrapped in grass or hay, placed on edge on a stone, and large flakes were split off with a hand-hammer. After a suitable piece had been obtained, it was placed on a pad in the left hand and held in position with the fingers. It was given its final shape by means of a flaker made of antler, which was used with a forward and downward pressure. The blunt point served for flaking off larger chips, while the smaller one was used for the final stages of the work. In later times iron flakers were often used. The method of holding the flake was the same as that of the Carriers of northern British Columbia. [Teit 1900:182]

This account highlights the extraordinary amount of work required to get a sharp cutting edge, let alone a finished projectile point. It is no wonder that the introduction of iron for knives and projectile points had such a far-reaching impact in the Interior.

these were confined to a few localities only wherein were situated sorts of quarries which were jealously guarded against any person, even of the same tribe, whose right to share in their contents was not fully established. A violation of this traditional law was often considered *casus belli* between the co-clansmen of the trespassers and those of the proprietors of the quarry. [Morice 1893:65]

Smaller blocks of material were transported to the villages, particularly in the fall, to be stockpiled for winter use. When raw materials ran low during late winter, many tools and exhausted nodules or cores were recycled using the bipolar or block-on-block technique. The toolmaker placed the item on some form of anvil and struck it with a hammer stone, causing it to split. Even the smallest items could be exploited in this way.

As described by elder Sam Mitchell, deer products were used to create a variety of tools:

Deer had many uses. The meat was eaten fresh and smoke-dried. The heads were barbecued and the brains were used for tanning deerhides to make buckskin (the flesh on the hides was removed with a deer-rib scraper). Root-digging sticks were made from the deer's antlers. Awls, made from the deer's shin bone, were used by women when they were weaving baskets. [Bouchard and Kennedy 1977:71]

The St'át'imc maintained a highly developed tradition of basketry manufacture, described in detail by James Teit:

Birch-bark baskets were made and used a great deal, especially by the Upper Lillooet. They were of the same sizes and shapes as those of the Shuswap and Thompson. Baskets of sprucebark, white-pine bark, and cottonwood-bark were occasionally made. The most common baskets, however, are those of coiled and imbricated basketry. They are made of cedar-root. When cedar-root is not obtainable, some of the Upper Lillooet use spruce-root instead. In the best baskets the coils are made of bundles of finely split cedar-root, while in the poorest class of baskets they consisted of thin and wide strips of cedar-sap of equal width, placed in layers. The Lillooet claim that formerly roots were picked with great care, the coils were smaller, the stitches finer, and the baskets more durable and pliable. In many cases the rim of the basket consists of one coil, which is fastened to the preceding coil at regular intervals, forming stiff loops between the points of attachment. In these loops the coil is wrapped with the same kind of material that serves to hold the coils together, and also to stitch the loops to the last coil. In modern baskets, open-work is produced in the same manner, by introducing loops into the body of the basket. Ornamentation in basketry is produced with the bark of bird-cherry *(Prunus demissa walpers)*, which is dyed black, or used in its natural brown color. [Teit 1900:205]

Mats were also manufactured for a variety of surfaces, including floors and benches, and for roof and tent covers.

Weaving was used in a variety of ways in St'át'imc houses:

The household utensils of the Lillooet were very similar to those of the Thompson Indians, and consisted principally of baskets, bags, mats, etc. Plaited cedar-bark were used by the Lower Lillooet for covering the walls and floors of houses, for sitting on in canoes, and for other purposes. The Upper Lillooet used tule mats for covering lodges, and rush mats for bedding and seats. Other rush mats were used for spreading food on at meal-times. Rush mats were also much used by the Pemberton band. Bedding consisted also of goat-hair blankets and bear-skins. Coiled cedar-root baskets were used throughout the entire tribe for purposes of carrying and storage. They were of many sizes and shapes, – round, oblong, conical, and flat-backed, – covered and open. Large round open baskets were used for boiling food in and for holding water. Nut-shaped baskets were principally used for holding dried berries, and occasionally: for holding water. Large and medium-sized baskets of birch, poplar, or spruce bark were used as buckets for carrying water. Some of them were funnel-shaped. The Lillooet River band used for this purpose square-shaped buckets of bent cedar wood which they are said to have copied from the Lower Fraser Indians. Girls used small birch-bark baskets for berry picking. Open-work baskets were used by the Lower Lillooet and the Lake band for carrying fish, etc. Food at meal-times was spread on 31 cm. table-mats, or served in baskets and in trays made of birch bark or of basketry. These were round, like baskets for boiling, but smaller, and provided with loops around the rim. Fish was generally served in wooden dishes, square or oblong in shape. They were of various sizes, and hollowed out of birch or maple wood. Cups were of birch-bark or of basketry, and spoons were made of birch-wood and of horn. Wallets, bags, pouches, etc., were much used, and were woven of grass, rushes, fibre of *Verarum californicum,* bark thread, and cedar-bark. Those of cedar-bark were used by the Lower Lillooet only. Women's work-baskets were made of coiled basketry, and were rectangular in form and provided with lids. Bags woven of bark thread were manufactured by the Upper

Lillooet only, and were of the same styles as obtained among the Thompson Indians. [Teit 1900:215-17]

These items are, unfortunately, rarely preserved in the archaeological record. These descriptions therefore provide us with essential insight into a range of technologies not accessible to archaeologists.

Foodways in the Ancient Villages

People started building and living in larger villages along the Mid-Fraser Valley around 1,800 years ago. Some villages, such as Keatley Creek and Bell, persisted for a thousand years. Others, such as Bridge River, were abandoned a little earlier, around 1,100 years ago. The reasons for these variations are not clear. Consideration of the subsistence economies of the Early and Late Period villages does, however, offer some preliminary ideas. It is important to reconstruct foodways to understand life in these communities. As is illustrated in ethnographic accounts, people spent much of their time searching for, processing, and storing food during the annual cycle. Food also played a major role in social relationships: it could be used to cement relationships, demonstrate generosity, and even create debt obligations. At the moment, the most detailed evidence comes from Keatley Creek and, to a lesser extent, from the Bridge River site.

Keatley Creek

One of the many major contributions of Brian Hayden's research program at Keatley Creek was the impetus it gave to the study of foodways. Hayden drew important links between food production and social relationships, particularly at Keatley Creek during its peak occupation. Building on the innovative work of Hayden and his colleagues, other researchers have sought to better understand the dynamic history of subsistence at Keatley Creek, Bridge River, and elsewhere.

When people started to move into the Keatley Creek village between 1,600 and 1,700 years ago, they enjoyed a varied diet dominated by sockeye salmon (Figure 5.17). Early layers from Housepit 7 contained abundant salmon bones without head parts. This implies that the salmon were processed elsewhere, possibly in fish camps. There is also evidence that the people collected shellfish and hunted birds, beaver, marmots, and deer. Deer were apparently hunted relatively close to the village, for the skeletons are nearly complete. Had deer been acquired at much greater distances, the remains would consist largely of limb bones. Based upon the presence of bones with modifications such as cut marks and burning, dogs were apparently also on the menu, though not in large

FIGURE 5.17 Women hauling
fish in baskets to the Keatley
Creek village around 1,300
years ago.
Illustration by Eric S. Carlson

numbers. Plant remains include large numbers of blue elderberries, along with
limited amounts of heather berries, Saskatoon berries, and prickly pear cactus
seeds. Archaeologists have only recently begun to identify plant varieties from
burned tissues, and this technique has not yet been applied to the Mid-Fraser
Canyon. It is therefore unclear what greens or root foods were brought into the
housepits. Indirect evidence suggests, however, that root foods were roasted in
the village in what might have been communal roasting pits.

Hayden excavated two small house floors that appear to date to early in the
life of the village. Housepit 12, located close to Housepit 7 on the east side of
the village, contained a similar profile of animal bones, dominated heavily by
salmon. The presence of a cache pit that contained dozens of intact salmon
skeletons (minus heads) was particularly notable. These bones might have been
saved for late winter soup making. Housepit 90 was extremely small and shallow.
It probably consisted of not much more than a shallow subterranean floor and
a mat lodge, a teepee-like lodge walled with timbers and woven mats. The animal
remains included a disproportionately high number of medium to large mammal bones (especially deer). Evidence for plant consumption was limited at these
housepits to rare blueberries, huckleberries, and rose hips.

The food remains from early Keatley Creek are similar to those mentioned in oral accounts and historical records. Larger housepits were undoubtedly winter residences. The plant and animal remains found in them were normally harvested for storage in late summer and fall. The people's diet was clearly salmon-focused and supplemented by a range of mammals, especially deer, likely hunted within a day's walk of the village. Important carbohydrate sources included root foods and berries. Most of the berries likewise came from plants that grew in dry habitats located close to the village. Evidence that the people cooked root foods in the village also suggests that they travelled short distances to obtain baskets of at least some root species, which they then processed at home. Housepit 90 might have been a warm season household in which hunting was an important subsistence activity.

Nearly 1,200 years ago, subsistence tactics changed at Keatley Creek. While further study is required, current evidence suggests that smaller housepits were abandoned at this time. Drawing from 2001 and 2002 excavation data, the rim strata of Housepit 7 indicate a major reduction in the number of salmon bones until the final floor, when they once again become abundant. In contrast, there is a jump in the number of larger mammal bones, especially deer, but also sheep and mountain goats. After this period, deer bones consist mostly of lower limb parts, which suggests that human hunters had to travel farther for their quarry and engaged in more extensive field processing. Smaller mammals, especially beaver, are less common. Berries are common, but species more typical of wetter mountain contexts, such as heather and blueberries and huckleberries, dominate. There is no evidence for root processing in the village after about 1,200 to 1,300 years ago. Large numbers of prickly pear cactus seeds and pine nuts appear in the rim deposits, and it is possible that at least some of these seeds were the result of human predation.

As access to salmon declined, the people of Keatley Creek began to rely to a greater degree on meat from medium to large mammals (see Figure 5.7). It is entirely possible that local game populations were so reduced that hunters had to make more frequent and longer-distance trips to find and kill large mammals. The same goes for plants, but the evidence is not clear. Evidence of more berries acquired in wetter habitats supports the assumption that people began to travel longer distances during foraging trips. Likewise, the absence of evidence for in-village roasting also suggests reductions in local root resources. Indeed, if the cactus seeds and pine nuts were becoming regular food sources, it is likely that favoured carbohydrate sources were in short supply. We can draw this conclusion because research has shown that the caloric payoff per hour of processing time is far higher for roots than for any kind of seed.

So what happened at Keatley Creek? The people had founded this village on the basis of a salmon-based economy, supplemented by deer, roots, berries, and other carbohydrate resources. Salmon remained important to the diet, but the use of deer increased and root processing became less frequent. Some rather marginal plant foods might have been added to the diet as well. Examining the overall pattern (again, relying on somewhat limited excavation data), it is apparent that the total range of resources increased over time. Archaeologists call this subsistence diversification. Diversification usually happens as the most favoured resources become harder to get or, at least, less predictable. As the favoured item declines, it makes sense to incorporate other species, which have different growing or habitat conditions, as a safety net. Diversity generally reduces the costs of searching because the forager is less picky, but it may increase processing time and result in less food being available. However, if the favoured resource came in large numbers in one place (salmon) and the next favoured resource was more dispersed (deer), then it would take more time and energy to search for less-favoured resources. The hunter-gatherers paid double: they searched for longer and worked harder once they had their quarry. Beginning at about 1,200 years ago, the people at Keatley Creek appear to have faced increasingly disappointing salmon runs and longer searches for deer, roots, and berries. Sometimes, these trips failed, and they had to accept less desirable substitutes such as seeds. Everyone was probably working harder during the final stanza in the life of the village.

Bridge River

The Bridge River village was likely established earlier than Keatley Creek, perhaps around 1,800 years ago. By excavating small sections of multiple houses throughout the village, Anna Prentiss and her team gained insight into foods eaten throughout the entire village. Recent excavations have also begun to examine the histories of individual houses.

The lifespan of the Bridge River village falls almost entirely within the Early Period (around 1,800 to 1,200 years ago) at Keatley Creek. Not surprisingly, the diet was heavily dominated by salmon protein. Typical of Mid-Fraser villages, recovered salmon remains at the site for the most part lack head parts. Mammal bones are common but are often broken into so many small pieces that it is difficult to identify the species. Archaeologists have, nevertheless, identified deer, elk, beaver, lynx, rabbit, squirrel, marten, and dog bones.

Preliminary results from excavations in 2008 and 2009 indicate that the people who lived at Bridge River, like those at Keatley Creek, changed how they hunted over time. Faunal assemblages from smaller houses (e.g., Housepit 54) and larger houses (e.g., Housepit 20) contained deer bone assemblages with representations of all body parts (limbs, backbones, ribs, and heads) that dated to about 1,500 years ago. Later material from about 1,200 to 1,300 years ago include more frequent lower limb bones. Here, again, is potential evidence that reductions in local deer populations required hunters to travel farther to find game and to conduct more extensive butchery while in the field.

There is a large assemblage of berry seeds from Bridge River that appears to include blueberries and huckleberries, kinnikinnick, and Saskatoon berries. It is not surprising that the berry assemblage includes moist soil and montane species since the village is deeper in the mountains than villages such as the Keatley Creek and Bell sites, which are located on the drier east side of the Fraser River. There is no significant evidence for change in the number of berry species used in the village. Interestingly, Saskatoon berries are rare in early deposits from Bridge River. This suggests that either the plants were not common during the early occupation of the village or that the berries were processed or discarded in a different way compared to later times. Additional evidence for limited use of Saskatoon berries is provided by the work of archaeologist Ali Dietz, who studied outdoor roasting pits at Bridge River. Saskatoon berries are present only in pits dated to the most recent centuries.

By the final centuries of occupation at Bridge River, people had begun to cook significant amounts of food in outdoor ovens located within the village (Figure 5.18). Dietz's study indicates, however, that the ovens were not used to roast roots but, rather, meat or fish. This means that berries and some greens were probably also cooked in these features. Roots were undoubtedly important to the Bridge River people, but there is, at present, no evidence that they were cooked in the village. We have to assume that people processed roots at some distance from the village or even traded them in from elsewhere. Thus, the Bridge River site was optimally positioned for salmon but not as well set for obtaining root foods.

The Bridge River village was abandoned around 1,100 years ago (it was re-occupied again around 500 years ago). Current research indicates that access to food resources might have played a significant role in the village's history.

Food and the Growth of the Mid-Fraser Villages

Paleoecologists – that is, scientists who study ancient environments – tell us that climatic conditions were good for marine and anadromous (salmon, for example) fish between about 1,600 and 1,200 years ago. The climate apparently got steadily cooler and wetter throughout the region, favouring abundant marine life. Cooler waters also favoured highly abundant salmon in the rivers. The early occupations of Keatley Creek and Bridge River represent adaptations to this

FIGURE 5.18 Women roasting meat and fish at the Bridge River village around 1,200 years ago.

Illustration by Eric S. Carlson

optimal period. Many of the subsistence practices documented in the ethnographic record and practised today were developed during this time.

Paleoclimatic conditions appear, however, to have been suboptimal for peoples elsewhere on the Canadian Plateau. Interestingly, the intense occupations at the confluence of the South and North Thompson rivers might have been reduced as cooler temperatures set in. Data from around the region suggest that peoples outside of the Mid-Fraser region continued to live in smaller family groups, cycling between dispersed summer and more sedentary winter residences. The persistence of this pattern is curious and unexplained since the salmon populations appear to have been on the rise. It is possible that cooler climatic conditions reduced geophyte-bearing meadows and increased search times for deer. If salmon were available in at least moderate numbers throughout the

Thompson system, and if the other resources were more dispersed, then it would make sense that people on the interior Plateau had to live within a more dispersed settlement pattern. Alternatively, it is also possible that many Canadian Plateau groups chose to participate in the Mid-Fraser phenomenon by moving into established villages or creating new ones.

In the Mid-Fraser region between 1,600 and 1,200 years ago, salmon were probably available in extremely high numbers. Located at the interface between the Coast Range and the more arid Interior, the region probably also offered the greatest range of other terrestrial resources, including a diversity of mammals and root and berry crops. As noted in the previous chapter, there are good economic reasons that the large villages developed in these locations. If salmon numbers increased, then people could take advantage of their location to generate a food surplus. This surplus could, in turn, be traded for rare resources, including meat and roots from the east and marine products such as fish oil and dentalium shells from the Coast. To make things even better, western valleys such as Bridge River contain abundant quantities of highly valuable tool stone such as nephrite jade and soapstone. These raw materials could be used to fashion an array of highly valued tools and ornaments to be given as gifts or traded for other valuable goods. As long as the positive climatic conditions persisted, the villages could grow. Current evidence suggests that the Bridge River village grew over 300 percent during this period, and it is possible that populations at Keatley Creek increased in a similar fashion. Additional archaeological evidence indicates that there were many other major villages such as these in the past, as well as a host of smaller communities. Thus, it is possible that the Mid-Fraser Canyon around Lillooet could have been home to thousands of permanent residents.

At the height of their occupation, the Mid-Fraser villages were a powerful force in the Pacific Northwest. Brian Hayden suggests that the leaders of these gateway communities controlled the movement of goods through their communities before their ultimate deposition east or west. Food was the basis for affluence. Without salmon, people who lived along the Mid-Fraser Valley would have had no advantage over Plateau dwellers to the east. But they were different, so different that many researchers now regard the villages as reflective of a complex social phenomenon that is similar to that of agricultural communities located in other areas of the world.

6
Living Together
Social Organization

The chief leaned closer to hear the visiting hunter. The man brought news about their neighbours. The village at Bridge River had been abandoned, and the hunter had heard that other villages, the ones to the south and farther back in the mountains west of the big river, had also fallen.

The chief could not believe it. The Bridge River village had been one of the largest and strongest. Its people had enjoyed booming salmon runs and access to surplus quantities of copper, nephrite jade, and soapstone. Their craftsmen were renowned throughout the Interior and up and down the Coast for their jade adzes and personal ornaments. The village had held nearly a thousand people during the winter and took direction from a formidable, wily chief.

The first time the salmon had failed to come, the chief had foreseen a similar fate for his own village at Keatley Creek and had taken measures to preserve and protect his house. He sent special teams fanning throughout the hills to the east in search of a wider range of foods. The great houses had held on, but they had paid a price. The chief looked at his people as they sat and listened to the hunters' tales and saw the stress of those first few years without salmon inscribed on their faces, in deep lines and loose flesh, in features that betrayed the sadness brought on by loved ones who had either died of hunger, moved away, or been killed during skirmishes with neighbouring villages. Some of these people had joined his house from smaller houses on the point of collapse, houses that could no longer convince younger members from neighbouring communities to marry in.

The chief knew he could preserve his house and carry it on for future generations. He had decided to host a public feast and sent his best hunters high into the mountains for bighorn sheep and mountain goats. They had also collected a young, plump dog. People came to eat sheep, goat, and dog, salmon and beaver, and an abundance of berries. The residents donned their finest clothing and offered gifts. The big house, the chief had vowed, would be a force to be reckoned with, even in bad times. Now that entire villages were falling apart, more people like the hunter would appear. He would take in and recruit only the best.

The chief vowed to grant them safety and sustenance but not the right to crests, stories, property, or land. He had seen bad times and would never let his family suffer again. Only direct members of his line would inherit household property and control access to fishing stations and the trade items associated with them. New residents would benefit from membership in the group, but they would remain poor. It was better, he thought, than starving to death or being killed by unfriendly neighbours.

W hy did social inequality eventually become part of the social systems of the Mid-Fraser villages? Current archaeological investigations indicate that a social system in which only some people had significant rights to the use of property and cultural traditions was not part of life in the early Mid-Fraser villages. Yet, at some point, all villages became nonegalitarian (Box 6.1). How do researchers explain this fundamental shift?

Archaeologists have long been interested in social change in ancient societies and the factors behind the rise of complex societies. During the 1980s, a group of archaeologists began to recognize that the earliest forms of social complexity probably emerged within hunting and gathering societies. These early complex societies represent the first social systems organized around something other than obligatory generosity, which was based on food sharing and other practices typical of generalized hunter-gatherers. They emerged at a point at which a group's size increased, people started living together, and a few individuals started hoarding and controlling food surpluses. These surpluses were sometimes used to acquire rare trade items not normally available within band territory. The people probably also changed the way they perceived the landscape and developed new strategies to better define and guard their local resources.

A basic egalitarian hunter-gatherer pattern characterized nearly all human groups for tens of thousands of years. Everyone was equal and shared what was available. Given that humans had maintained this cultural adaptation for so long, what forces brought about the emergence of complex societies? Some archaeologists argue that these societies emerged in response to population pressure. Others suggest that it was not only population pressure but also ecological imbalances between human groups and food sources that triggered more competitive behaviour. A number of archaeologists argue that self-interested individuals stimulated the formation of these groups once they could get away with manipulating food surpluses for their own advantage.

Whatever the trigger, we know that this transition to complex hunter-gatherer societies occurred many times in many regions of the world. In North America, for example, it occurred on both coasts. In the western Arctic, people began to recognize elite boat owners or *umialit* as individuals who had the capacity to organize and direct the whale hunt and its material byproducts. These individuals consequently enjoyed great respect and status in their villages. Members of Northwest Coast societies were ranked as individuals and by membership in houses, lineages, and sometimes clans. Status was inherited at birth and maintained via successful economic ventures and competitive actions, such as hosting a potlatch or holding communal feasts. The Chumash people of coastal southern California also lived within a society that featured an inherited ranking system and hereditary village chiefs. Groups of villages acted as sociopolitical units or polities administered by a head chief from a larger or more powerful village. One of the most complex hunter-gatherer societies was the Calusa of southwestern Florida. The Calusa operated what anthropologists call a paramount chiefdom, in which a God-like paramount chief had complete authority over hundreds of smaller communities and could enforce his will with a police force or a small army.

The great villages of the Mid-Fraser Canyon were likely complex and marked by social differentiation. The ethnographic record clearly demonstrates that the post-17th-century societies of the Lillooet area were complex hunter-gatherers. This chapter explores the social organization of the Mid-Fraser peoples and then steps back in time to examine changes in the organization of these past societies.

Social Life within the Mid-Fraser Villages

Anthropologists generally conceive of human social relations as being organized along horizontal and vertical dimensions. Along the horizontal dimension, anthropologists recognize an array of family-based social units such as clans and other organizations such as clubs and secret societies. Truly complex societies have many organizations in this dimension. Along the vertical dimension – in contemporary society at the state level, for example – political organizations range from the municipal, county, district, and state or provincial levels to national and international organizations. Power and influence increase as individuals move up the ladder. Anthropologists also recognize vertical social structures in smaller-scale societies, which are often expressed through differential access to food, material goods, the right to use or own noncorporeal property such as songs, and even marriage. More egalitarian hunter-gatherers usually have only one level on the vertical scale. More complex societies, such as those of the Northwest Coast, featured inequalities between high-ranked persons such as chiefs and nobles, less well-off commoners and, at the bottom of the system, human slaves, who existed as property.

Ethnographic documentation and, more importantly, interviews with living St'át'imc people, highlight that in the past, as in the present, St'át'imc society was organized around the family. Kinship was bilateral: there was no significant

BOX 6.1 EQUALITY AND INEQUALITY AMONG HUNTING AND GATHERING PEOPLES

For decades, archaeologists assumed that hunting and gathering peoples around the world were organized primarily in small-scale egalitarian groups. Material wealth accumulation was not possible and, outside of some minor age- and gender-based distinctions, everyone was equally well off. This model was supported by classic ethnographic studies of the Kalahari San peoples of Africa. In one particularly telling account, ethnographer Richard Lee described how he had sought to reward his informants by providing them with a large ox for a feast. Despite the obvious size of the animal, the people teased him for his poor choice. He eventually learned that no hunter could turn his prowess into an opportunity for aggrandizing, because the community was hostile to such behaviour. Other studies supported Lee's conclusions by revealing a pattern of mandatory sharing among the San. Lee's data, combined with similar results from studies of foragers elsewhere (Australia, western North America, and Africa), led archaeologists to construct a standard cultural type, termed generalized or egalitarian hunter-gatherers.

By the 1980s, archaeologists were contrasting the generalized hunter-gatherer type with a new type, known as complex hunter-gatherers, people characterized by a greater degree of sedentism, social ranking, and material wealth accumulation in households.

Recent research in cultural anthropology suggests that we need to be careful about using simplistic cultural categories. There might have been greater variation among small-scale hunter-gatherers than archaeologists originally credited. For example, even among Kalahari peoples, opportunities for enhanced social networking and better nutrition were inherited within specific families. These advantages were not, however, manifested as material wealth. The development of inherited material wealth likely required larger-scale populations, greater group sedentism, and unequal access to resources. Studies of social change in the Mid-Fraser villages provide opportunities to develop a better understanding of the processes behind the evolution of social inequality.

distinction between the mother's and the father's side when it came to relatives and inheritance. Kinship organization did not distinguish between siblings and first cousins. Families were organized into larger multifamily units, termed clans by the ethnographer James Teit. Teit documented a range of St'át'imc clans, many of which still exist today. For example, Bridge River or Xwisten people are members of the Bear clan; Lillooet or Tit'qet people are of the Frog clan, and so on. Members of clan groups interviewed by Teit believed they had descended from ancient human or animal beings. Group members could wear masks representing that being during dances. It is not clear whether villages could include more than one clan. Ethnographers Dorothy Kennedy and Randy Bouchard suggest that the earliest villages might have housed only one clan but that this situation perhaps changed with population growth and the expansion and formation of new villages.

According to ethnographers, clan or family groups were organized around hereditary chiefs, and their immediate families and select relatives garnered greater respect within their communities. Drawing on interviews he conducted at the turn of the century, Teit (1906:253) described the position of hereditary chief:

> Each clan – and in early times, therefore, each village community – had a hereditary chief. Children and grandchildren of these chiefs were called "chiefs children." They formed an aristocracy of descent, but had no privileges of any kind. The hereditary chief was the chief of the families composing a village. [Teit 1906:253]

It is also possible that some village chiefs held some degree of power that extended beyond a single village. At times, groups separated from older established communities and established new villages. The new group often retained its original chief, who continued to live in the original village. Teit offered this description:

> The hereditary chief was the chief of the families composing a village. When a clan spread over several villages, the branches still had one chief in common. He resided at the original home of the clan. In a village that contained several clans, the chief of the original clan was the head chief. [Teit 1906:254]

More recent research by archaeologist David Schaepe in the Lower Fraser Canyon area indicates that the Halkomelem (Salish)-speaking Stó:lō had chiefs who presided over multiple villages. The duties of these chiefs probably included the maintenance of economic ventures and, more importantly, the coordination of defence from attacking coastal warriors. It is not unreasonable to suspect that similarly complex village systems also existed in the Mid-Fraser Canyon.

Teit's ethnographic research also makes it clear that a person could achieve the rank of chief through personal actions and oratory.

> The term "chief" was also applied to men who had gained influence, although they did not belong to the chief's family. Such men acquired influence through their wealth, wisdom, oratory, liberality – shown, for instance, by giving feasts and presents without receiving an equivalent in return. Other chiefs were men who had become conspicuous through their proficiency in certain occupations, and had become leaders of men. Such were war chiefs, hunting chiefs, chiefs of the religious dances. A woman who was noted for wealth, or who gave more than one potlatch, was called a chief; and any man who gave a large potlatch, or was able to repeat his potlatches from time to time, was called a chief. Another class called chiefs were men who gave a great public feast when taking their ancestral names. These men corresponded to the chief of the Thompson Indians. Their rank was not hereditary.
>
> The child of a "chief," or rather of an influential person of this kind, could attain a rank equal to that of his father, only by his own exertion and worth. While the hereditary chiefs formed a nobility of rank, these people formed a nobility of merit. The hereditary chiefs were looked upon as the real chiefs of communities, even though other men called chiefs might have greater influence and power. [Teit 1906:255]

Higher-ranking St'át'imc families and their associated households appear to have used a number of strategies to maintain and reaffirm their position of power. Chiefs had the power to "supervise" the harvest of major berry patches. Elite families could also control access to the best fishing places along the Fraser River and its adjacent drainages. Teit suggests that, outside of the Lillooet area, elite families might have controlled hunting landscapes. The early ethnographer A.G. Morice likewise described the control of quarries. If certain families could exercise control over access to food and other desired resources, then these families could also control other forms of wealth, including rare foods, tools, and ornaments. Sam Mitchell, a Fountain elder, described the ownership of fishing places to Bouchard and Kennedy:

> Some dip-net fishing places at *Sh-HIT-tl* were owned by individuals, and the use of such spots was limited to the immediate members of that person's

family. However, after that particular family had obtained enough salmon, then anybody could use that fishing rock. [Bouchard and Kennedy 1977:67]

Competitive generosity was expressed in the villages through potlatching or gift-giving ceremonies. Although it is unclear how far back in the past these ceremonies go, potlatches might have marked a variety of occasions, included name-giving and coming-of-age ceremonies. Receipt of gifts generally obligated an individual or family to present gifts in the future. Wealth and power could be demonstrated through elaborate gift giving within and between communities. Ethnographers Kennedy and Bouchard describe the potlatch:

According to Teit (1906:258), "potlatches were given to one individual to another or by the chief of one clan to another." Potlatches were given at any time of the year to honour the memory of a dead relative, give ancestral names to children, or merely to increase the status of the host ... At these feasts it was necessary for the host to supply his guests with gifts of fresh meat ... the host sent parties of hunters into the hills to obtain deer for the potlatch guests. Occasionally, a whole deer was also tossed into the pit house to be randomly butchered by the guests, but usually the deer were butchered outside. This random butchering of ... a deer inside the pit house as part of a potlatch, constituted one aspect of a "scramble" ... As a result of the introduction of money into the Fraser River Lillooet economy during the nineteenth century, the items used as part of the potlatch scramble changed. Instead of mountain goat blankets, which formerly were "scrambled" for, long sticks imbedded with coins were tossed into the pit house, where they were immediately broken apart by the eager recipients ... Teit (1906:253, 257-259) claims that "clan masks," which represented the first ancestor or had references to some important incident in the first ancestor's life, were shown at large potlatches. Because of the mask's association with the ancestors and death, the host never wore the mask himself. Generally an old man was hired to wear the mask, sing the "clan songs," and dance or act the "clan legend." [Kennedy and Bouchard 1978:49]

The social importance of potlatching is more profoundly illustrated in the words of elder Sam Mitchell:

My old man used to tell (that they had potlatches) in the fall of the year ... If there's a death in the family and lots of people to help him, he and his family get together and go hunting deer (and) jerk it ... (A man potlatches if) he's chief and he wants to be recognized. "So and so chief want to be recognized." Everybody gathered, not just certain parties.

(The funeral potlatch is) not right away – maybe next year. The best of the game – September and October – fattest. They go out and get enough of it. It will last quite a while ... / If the chief dies will his son take the title at the potlatch? / Yes, that's it ... It will have to be announced. In them days, naturally the son would take the title. They give lots of grub ... That's why they give a potlatch: to announce. That's why these potlatches are. They didn't have any newspapers. [Romanoff 1992b:475-76]

Social Relations in the Ancient Villages

Reconstructing social relations from archaeological evidence is extremely difficult. Researchers typically develop arguments to explain specific data patterns. Housepits, for instance, are generally assumed to be the remnants of winter residences of one or more families. Based on the limited dating of housepits from Keatley Creek, Brian Hayden argues that some small houses might have been the site of special functions performed by shamans or secret societies. Large houses might have held more than one family. One clue is the presence of multiple activity areas around hearths. Ethnographies of peoples in the Interior and on the Coast suggest that family groups in large houses lived around a single hearth. They prepared food, worked on tools, and slept in the area, sometimes up on platforms. These family areas typically had storage space for winter food. Numerous hearths and storage facilities featuring redundant artifacts and food remains suggest the coexistence of more than one family within a single house (Figure 6.1).

Reconstructing the actions of individual persons and inheritance systems through archaeological data is almost impossible. Some archaeologists, however, have made strides in reconstructing the activities of different groups based on gender and, possibly, status. To a certain extent, the actions of men and women in ancient Mid-Fraser villages can be reconstructed by drawing upon 19th-century historical observations. In other words, archaeologists assume that if something was done in a specific way in the recent past, such as in the late 1800s, then that same practice likely occurred in the more remote past. This approach can be problematic because things do change. But it at least offers a starting point for looking at the contributions of different groups, such as men and women.

Ethnographies of the Mid-Fraser region suggest that women prepared food, made clothes, tended children, and foraged for a wide range of foods, and there is no doubt that women made stone tools associated with these activities. Men, in contrast, were more involved in making weapons and heavy-duty tools,

FIGURE 6.1 Life in the interior of Housepit 7 at Keatley Creek in the period before the village was abandoned around 800 to 900 years ago. Note the higher-status individuals on the right side of the floor. *Illustration by Eric S. Carlson*

hunting and fishing, and waging war. They made and used stone tools associated with these activities. There were exceptions to this general division of labour. Men sometimes helped prepare salmon and women participated in the hunt when necessary.

Recognizing the presence of hereditary versus achieved status in archaeological evidence is likewise difficult (Box 6.2). Most archaeologists agree that two lines of enquiry are necessary. First, there must be strong evidence of status distinctions in the household record. This evidence could, however, merely reflect status gained during the lifetime of an individual, not status inherited and handed down from generation to generation. Another approach is to look for evidence of the centralized control of the production and distribution of particular goods. A good example of this phenomenon is the manipulation of bead production and exchange by hereditary Chumash chiefs in southern California.

Second, evidence from burials can be used to identify inherited status in societies where wealth is passed on through the generations. Archaeologists generally look for signs of status differences – for example, elaborate artifacts or no artifacts at all – in child burials. On the central Northwest Coast, inherited status is indicated by cranial deformation – the purposeful modification of the child's skull to mark nobility. If the burial pattern of children matches that of older adults, then it is easier to make the argument that social distinctions were hereditary.

The Bell Site

Arnoud Stryd excavated housepits of several sizes at the Bell site that dated to between 1,000 and 2,000 years ago. Current dating suggests that the earlier occupations (ca. 1,800 to 1,400 years ago) favoured smaller houses while the largest houses appeared somewhat later (ca. 1,500 to 1,000 years ago). It is likely,

BOX 6.2 ARCHAEOLOGY METHODS: IDENTIFYING INEQUALITY

Social inequality is an element of all communities. In most cases, it is related to skill, experience, and the abilities of people. In other contexts, social differences become formalized and permanent. Reconstructing the level of status differences in the past is difficult. Burial practices provide one means. Burial goods can provide insight into social inequalities because treatment in death often reflects a person's status in life. In the Mid-Fraser Canyon, however, burials likely occurred away from villages since archaeologists have only identified a few sites. In addition, many archaeologists do not feel comfortable studying burials without the explicit interest and support of First Nations communities.

Beyond mortuary analysis, there is other evidence that archaeologists can use to identify status differences within housepit villages. For example, people and families of high and low status often had different access to foods. It is possible, if not probable, that some families ate more deer or more high-quality salmon than others and that some families had the capacity to store more foods, perhaps of more desirable types than others. Similarly, it is possible that some groups controlled access to key stone quarries or, potentially, entire landscapes. Archaeologists can measure these differences by documenting the distribution of food remains, storage features, and tool stone sources. Did differential control of food translate into the potential to acquire excess trade goods? This question can be answered through a careful consideration of variations in nonlocal materials and variations in artifact types and workmanship.

Similarly, did elite houses include powerful shamans? It is possible that the houses of powerful families were the locations of the community's ceremonial and religious events. Evidence of religious behaviour is extremely hard to tease from the record, however. Archaeologists must look at house floors for evidence of special areas for religious activities and for caches of items such as shamans' tools.

however, that houses of different sizes probably occurred simultaneously at some points. The arrangements of features on the floors of the Bell Site houses may reflect variation in the numbers of families residing in individual houses. Housepit 1, for example, is small and contains a single hearth and a single cache pit. It was, therefore, probably occupied by a single family. In contrast, Housepit 6 is slightly larger and has a central hearth but two sets of cache pits located on opposite sides of the house. It is possible that two families resided in the house and shared a single central hearth. Housepit 19 is quite large and has a complex arrangement of post-holes and rocks on its floor. The large size reflects the presence of multiple families. There are, however, only two small cache pits and a single central cluster of rocks, possibly associated with a hearth feature. From these data, it would appear that a minimum of two families resided in the house. An infant burial, located below the northwest portion of the floor of Housepit 19, includes an amazing assortment of items: 246 dentalium beads, 5 steatite pipe fragment pendants, an incised antler comb, a quartz crystal, a siltstone bear figure, chipped-stone flakes, and red ochre for painting. Although one burial is not enough to infer hereditary inequality, it is a provocative find, particularly in light of recent data from the nearby Keatley Creek site.

The Keatley Creek Site

Brian Hayden's excavations at Keatley Creek were explicitly oriented toward reconstructing ancient social organization, particularly social status relationships within and between houses (Figures 6.2 to 6.4). He explored this subject by excavating nearly the entire floors of large, medium, and small houses in the hope of seeing differences in subsistence, storage, and prestige goods. Similar to Stryd, Hayden recognized potentially high variation in household populations. Small houses such as Housepits 12 and 90 had only one hearth (if that) and one cache pit, suggesting a single-family residence. Housepit 3 contained clusters of cache pits and hearths in three corners of the house, which suggested the presence of up to three family units. Housepit 7, which has at least five hearth and cache pit clusters, is exceptionally complicated and possibly reflects a much larger population (Figure 6.5).

Interestingly, there are no major differences among the houses in terms of types of food. With the exception of Housepit 90, which is dominated by mammal bones, all house assemblages are dominated by salmon. There are, however, major differences in storage capacity. Housepit 7, the large house, has substantially more storage space than the others, even accounting for relative differences in floor area. Hayden argues that people in Housepit 7 had a much greater ability to generate surplus food and nonfood goods than did the families of the other houses.

FIGURE 6.2 Housepits of various sizes at the Keatley Creek site. Housepit 7 is on the lower left. Archaeologists believe these housepits could represent different social groups.

Photograph by Duggan Backhouse-Prentiss

Housepit 7 also contains more exotic and valuable items, including moose antler, hand mauls, nephrite tools, steatite pipes, steatite beads, a copper bead, clamshell, and mica. Housepit 3 contains some of these items, particularly pipes, but in greatly reduced numbers. The smallest houses contain the fewest items, though it is interesting that tiny Housepit 90 contains a hand maul and a nephrite adze. Hayden suggests that there is also variability among the hearth-centred areas in Housepit 7. He points out that the south group had the highest incidence of mammal bone. Fish bone is relatively rare throughout the west side of the house, whereas it is common in activity areas to the east. Hayden argues that people who lived in the eastern side needed the fish bones for late winter soups. Discarded tools for the manufacture of wood or antler implements are most common on the east side. Small arrow points are common on the west side, and larger, possibly atlatl, dart points are most common to the east. Hayden interprets these data in social terms and suggests that less well off people lived on the east side of the pithouse, where they used mostly old technologies (darts), did heavy tool manufacture, and ate substandard food. It should be noted, however, that this same data could also be interpreted as evidence for the presence of different

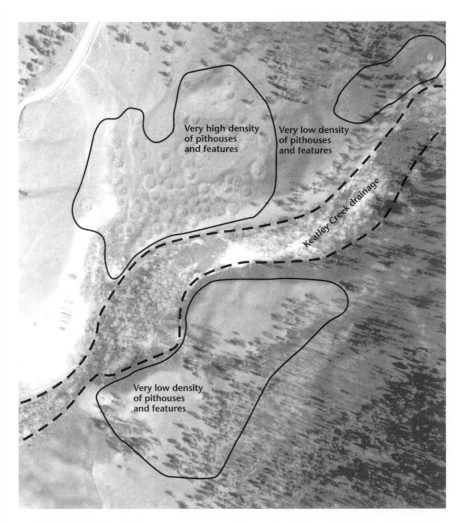

FIGURE 6.3 This aerial photograph illustrates variations in the number and size of housepits throughout the entire Keatley Creek site.

activity areas organized by a single household, rather than the physical and material division of an entire household.

Could Housepit 7 also have been a centre for sacred or ceremonial activities? The evidence is ambiguous at best. There is a large central space that could have been used for ceremonies, dances, and even feasts. Similar to the great whaler's house at Ozette, in northwestern Washington State, this space also has a unique hearth pit. Given the housepit's extensive caches, it is possible, following Hayden, that some sort of ceremonies might have occurred.

FIGURE 6.4 Keatley Creek village at its peak size, perhaps around 1,300 to 1,200 years ago.

Illustration by Eric S. Carlson

FIGURE 6.5 This plan view of Housepit 7 at the Keatley Creek site shows numerous fire hearths and storage features.

Redrawn from original map by J. Spafford

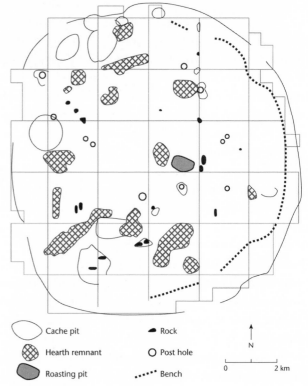

Cache pit   Rock

Hearth remnant   Post hole

Roasting pit   Bench

N

0   2 km

The dog bones found at Housepit 7 are more intriguing (Figure 6.6). When Hayden's crews exposed the central portion of the floor, they found an intact dog skull in the centre of the floor. Other excavations revealed a cluster of dog bones deep in a cache pit. Analysis of the bones by David Crellin suggests that the dogs had not been butchered but that one dog had been killed by a blow to the head. There is evidence of ravaging (or postmortem gnawing and destruction) by other dogs. Hayden argues that the dogs were part of ritual sacrifices like those held by the Koryak of Siberia. The Koryak would kill a dog with a blow to the head and then hang it on a pole for a period of time, perhaps until the other neighbourhood dogs had removed enough flesh that the bones could be gathered and placed in a safe place within the house. Crellin alternatively proposes that these dogs may not have been sacrificial animals but rather nuisance animals that were killed, ravaged, and then disposed of deep in a pit. Dog bones with cut marks were found in the rim deposits, suggesting that dogs were used as a food item. In addition, no caches of special shaman's items have been found at Housepit 7. So, while the house was likely used as a place for the occasional feast or even dance, it is not clear that it was also used for religious practices.

Based upon these three patterns, from a village of over one hundred houses, Hayden argues that the village was organized around single families and multi-

FIGURE 6.6 A dog skull exposed in a cache pit at Housepit 24 at the Bridge River site during excavations in 2008. Similar dog remains were found at the Keatley Creek site.

Photograph by Anna M. Prentiss

family corporate groups. There might have been higher- and lower-ranked corporate groups, which were marked by house size, storage capacity, and the ability to accumulate rare and hard-to-make goods. Hayden suggests that more elaborate artifacts, which he interprets as prestige items, were perhaps used to show off affluence and possibly to attract others to join the group. Taking this argument one step further, Hayden suggests that ranking might have existed within households as well. He speculates that families on the west side of Housepit 7 were better off than those on the east side: they had better food, more storage, and different tools. He places the south hearth group at the top rank because they had the best technologies, prestige goods, deer meat, and the optimal spot in the house (the south-facing side of the house faces the sun throughout the winter).

Our consideration of the Keatley Creek site suggests substantial change in social organization between the village's inception about 1,600 to 1,700 years ago and its abandonment around 800 to 1,000 years ago. We base this conclusion on data analyses that compare artifacts and faunal remains from dated strata in the Housepit 7 rim to similarly dated floors elsewhere in the village. The amount of botanical debris (burned plant materials) in the rim did not change for most of the occupation then suddenly jumped around 1,200 years ago. The numbers of fire-cracked rock fragments, which reflect hearth cooking, also increased dramatically. Assuming that each family cooked at the same rate with the same techniques before and after this time, the evidence suggests that more families were living in the big house after 1200 BP (before the present). The presence of prestige objects such as beads and pipes and potential prestige-related raw material such as obsidian, nephrite jade, and soapstone also increased significantly around 1,200 years ago. This pattern of change is not evident in the other houses. The small housepits were abandoned before 1200 BP, and we have no record of change at Housepit 3 because the rims were not excavated.

There are no signs that people in large houses had the capacity to accumulate excess material wealth before 1200 BP. Therefore, the wealth-based hereditary inequality described in ethnographies probably did not develop until after this time. Perhaps the early village at Keatley Creek was organized around households in which there was no formal ranking system; certain individuals could, however, earn high degrees of respect and even some limited authority. Perhaps some families maintained respected positions in the village that translated into social advantages for their children, but these distinctions are not easily measured in the archaeological record. Reciprocal sharing might have been a critical facet of village life. Thus, economic successes in the bigger houses perhaps offered benefits to all. But something happened to trigger a change, and we cannot begin to understand how this occurred until we explore the record from the Bridge River site.

The Bridge River Site

Like Keatley Creek, the Bridge River site is a large pithouse village located close to a river. Radiocarbon dating makes it clear that the village was substantial from its founding nearly 1,900 years ago to its abandonment between 1,200 and 1,100 years ago. Although the original village likely included no more than 7 structures, the last occupation included between 30 and 40 houses (Figure 6.7). In other words, the village grew by 300 percent or more in this period. It is likely that the Keatley Creek village also went through a similar growth pattern. Interestingly, Keatley Creek might have suffered a contraction in the numbers of its houses at about the same time that Bridge River was abandoned. The record from Housepit 7 suggests that more people packed into the remaining households.

There are also some tantalizing indicators of social change at Bridge River. Evidence for the first occupation indicates a full range of house sizes. Indeed,

FIGURE 6.7 Bridge River
village at its peak, around
1,200 to 1,300 years ago.
Illustration by Eric S. Carlson

one of the largest houses in the village is also one of the earliest. Geophysical mapping at the site also suggests that the houses had similar arrangements of hearth and cache pit features, suggesting multifamily group occupations. Recent excavations confirm the existence of activity areas around the household interior perimeters, much like the large houses at Keatley Creek, which contained hearths, cache pits, and discarded tools, flakes, and animal and plant remains. This evidence suggests the presence of multifamily corporate groups within single houses.

The spatial arrangements of the houses provide other insights into changing social conditions or practices that are hard to recognize in the limited Keatley Creek data. If we examine the history of the village, it appears that it grew in two clusters located on the north and south sides. At the height of its occupation, around 1,200 to 1,300 years ago, the village featured two semicircular arrangements of housepits. The larger north cluster had disproportionate numbers of distinctly large and relatively small housepits, a pattern also found by Hayden at Keatley Creek. The south house cluster also had smaller and larger houses, but the differences between the two were not substantial. This arrangement could mean that the highest-ranking houses were situated in the north group, rather than the south. We argue that this evidence suggests horizontal and vertical social complexity. The two arc-like arrangements of houses could represent the presence of at least two social groups, which could be based on clans, lineages, or something else entirely. The distinct differences in size could indicate wealth and power differentials between households. Many houses did produce typical prestige items, including nephrite jade wood-working tools; steatite, marble, dentalium, and copper beads; a copper pendant; steatite pendants; steatite pipes; quartz crystal; painted ground slate tools, and obsidian tools.

Research conducted in 2008 and 2009 offers new evidence about the history of social relations at Bridge River. The exposure of floor materials from multiple time periods provided the opportunity to examine hunting, storage, exchange or trade, the accumulation of wealth items, and interaction among residents. Ethnographers have a clear picture of what was necessary to maintain a successful traditional household in the Mid-Fraser Canyon and on the Northwest Coast. The house had to keep up its numbers to remain productive; its members needed not only to feed the residents but also to produce a subsistence surplus for use in exchange and potlatch ceremonies. Next, the residents had to retain rights to property, including segments of the landscape used for fishing, hunting, and gathering. Ownership or control of property is difficult to measure in the archaeological record but could be manifested in the presence of the frequent appearance of select mammalian species in middens (Figure 6.8), along with other preferred items such as stones attributable to particular quarry locales. The household would also have to produce a food surplus and store it in large household cache pits. The surplus could be used as backup food during hard times, but it was more often used in social contexts such as meeting trade obligations, developing debt relationships, and demonstrating generosity in giveaway ceremonies. Finally, the residents would have to actively exchange goods for nonlocal items such as high-quality tool stone such as obsidian and some cherts and chalcedonies. If the system functioned properly, the payoff was the maintenance of high population levels and the accumulation of wealth items and other highly valued items such as nephrite adzes.

Preliminary analysis of Bridge River data suggests that there was a village-wide correlation between densities of fire-cracked rock and total cache pit volume (per house), implying variation between houses in density of occupants. There was an independent correlation between indicators of mammalian hunting, the exchange of goods for nonlocal raw materials, and wealth objects. This means that the number of people in each household did not fully predict household affluence. Housepit 24 (Figure 6.9), a large house (about 16 metres in diameter) occupied during the period known as Bridge River 3 around 1,200 years ago, appears to have maintained large numbers of occupants along with frequent

FIGURE 6.8 Cluster of
butchered deer bones from
the Bridge River site, Period 3
occupation of Housepit 25.

Photograph by Anna M. Prentiss

indicators of wealth. Another house, Housepit 20, had the large size but not the same record of occupants or goods accumulation and exchange. No smaller houses were able to put the entire package together either. Housepit 16, for example, was a much smaller house, apparently occupied by a relatively high number of people. Despite its demographics, household members rarely ate deer and accumulated few valuable ornaments or tools made from exotic raw materials.

Housepit 24 also contained evidence of ceremonies or celebrations. Cache pits on its south side contained the remains of two large domestic dogs that had apparently been butchered for consumption in a single event (Figure 6.6). Discarded with the dog bones were other significant items, including a bear canine tooth and a dentalium shell bead. Another cache pit on the same floor contained piles of salmon cranial bones, a very rare occurrence at Bridge River. Salmon heads were valued for their oil content and could have been retained in

FIGURE 6.9 Housepit 24 at the Bridge River site, under excavation in 2008.

Photograph by Anna M. Prentiss

dried form either as a dietary supplement or as a feasting food. Given the nearby presence of the butchered dogs, feasting seems to be a possibility. Further, one of the village's largest outdoor fish/meat roasting pits is located just off the south rim of Housepit 24 and dates to the same occupation period.

These studies imply that, as at Keatley Creek, inequality came late to Bridge River; indeed, it developed just prior to the abandonment of the village. These findings raise the possibility that inequality, at least as measured by variations in material goods, was a partial by-product of escalating competition for dwindling food resources.

Did Higher-Order Multivillage Social Entities Exist?

Based on the existence of large pithouse villages and small hamlets in the Mid-Fraser Canyon, Brian Hayden and geologist June Ryder argued that the Classic Lillooet period of 1,000 to 2,000 years ago might have been characterized by multivillage polities or chiefdoms. This provocative idea needs to be explored further.

In his original ethnography of the Lillooet, James Teit stated that when a single clan was distributed across several villages, there might be only one presiding chief. Teit recognized that villages in the 18th and 19th centuries were generally smaller than those of the Classic Lillooet period. Since villages at about 1,100 to 1,300 years ago were significantly larger than those of more recent periods, it would be reasonable to expect similar, or perhaps more complex, social relationships between communities.

Archaeological research into the development of Mid-Fraser polities is in its infancy. We generally know how to look for settlement patterns that indicate the presence of social hierarchies, for example, disparities in the size of communities. There may also be indications of alliances between communities such as symbolic markers in artwork. More significantly, we seek archaeological indicators of differential power and authority among communities. For example, members of smaller communities might be expected to supply specific goods to elites in the larger villages or towns. Although this anticipated pattern departs from what we know from the ethnographies, it would confirm that some ancient societies could have been more socially complex than those of the eighteenth and nineteenth centuries. If small and somewhat ephemeral polities existed in the Lower Fraser Canyon, there is no reason that something a bit more stable could not have developed in the Mid-Fraser Canyon.

Why Did Social Complexity Develop in the Mid-Fraser Villages?

Archaeologists have been interested in explaining the rise of social complexity for many years. Some have proposed that complexity was linked to population growth, while others have argued that it was the result of individual initiative under either optimal or adverse conditions. The former argument suggests that things will remain the same unless they are forced to change by some external factor. Population growth, for example, required people to either extract more food from the environment or incorporate new foods into their diet to ensure a prosperous society. One by-product of a more complex society was that it required a social hierarchy or permanent leaders to control labour. Over time, as these leaders developed greater powers, the possibility of entrenched social inequality emerged. If this hypothesis is true, growth in the size and number of villages should have been accompanied in the archaeological record by more signs of social complexity.

It appears to us that the Mid-Fraser villages developed suddenly during a period of low regional population. Once founded, the villages expanded, but there was no significant social change until about 1,200-1,300 years ago, when the Bridge River village peaked in size and was subsequently abandoned and the socioeconomic structure of the Keatley Creek village was reorganized. The growth of social inequality at Keatley Creek may have come at a time of population *decline* in the Mid-Fraser region. The population pressure model may not be a perfect fit, but this does not mean that population growth of some kind did not play a role. For example, it is entirely possible that some form of population packing occurred at the Keatley Creek village, perhaps as people from other communities integrated with larger households. Data from Bridge River support the argument that peak social complexity may well have coincided with a significant rise in the village's population nearly 1,300 years ago. Thus, population factors may well have played a role in the emergence of inequality.

Some archaeologists have promoted the argument that cultural change was the consequence of aggressive individuals within ancient societies. There are two versions of this line of argument that are potentially applicable to the Mid-Fraser context. Adherents of the first argue that, under optimal resource conditions, certain individuals and their families collected surpluses and used them to make deals with less well off people. As they drove these people into debt, they propelled themselves to a higher status. If this was the case, then we should see evidence of full-scale inequality developing rapidly at the onset of the villages, when they enjoyed peak resources. In contrast, adherents of the second version of this argument argued that the people would not have been sucked into the machinations of ambitious individuals unless they had no other choice. Inequality likely emerged suddenly, during a short-term rough period such as a major reduction in either salmon or roots. In these situations, proto-elites likely offered handouts in return for agreements to repay goods and acknowledgment of their increasing control of the landscape.

The current data from the Mid-Fraser region suggest that the villages did not come about during the most optimal salmon period, around 3,000 years ago. Rather, the villages might have been founded during a period of slightly weaker but improving fish resources. At the same time, roots, berries, and deer were probably plentiful. The villages apparently grew as the fish resource improved. Radiocarbon dating suggests that the first hints of inter-household ranking – in other words, status inequality – appeared at Keatley Creek and Bridge River around 1,200 to 1,300 years ago. Paleofisheries data suggest that it was at about this point that fisheries production in the eastern Pacific Ocean peaked and rapidly declined. Independent research into fisheries production in the Columbia River by Jim Chatters and colleagues points to significant reductions in spawning salmon between about 1,200 and 600 years ago, a period that coincides with the villages' decline. Bridge River village was clearly abandoned by 1100 BP, while some houses at Keatley Creek lasted one or two more centuries. But the small houses at Keatley Creek were likely abandoned by this time, a phenomenon that would be expected during hard times. Ethnographic studies tell us that smaller households generally had a more difficult time than their larger counterparts during periods of food stress.

Inequality therefore emerged at about the same time that salmon resources peaked and declined. The great villages had likely enjoyed good times for as long as anyone could remember. There had been no reason to slow down population growth and village construction in the area. The resource calamity brought about significant changes and caused people to rethink their relationship to the land and to one another. It is likely that household heads sought to maintain their threatened houses by attracting more members. They did this by building up surpluses and flaunting their wealth through feasts and ceremonies, such as those that featured dogs around 1,200 years ago. This pattern of competition between households for viability triggered a pattern of increased differentiation between successful and not-so-successful households.

But why did hereditary inequality develop? Why didn't social relations, traditionally organized around cooperative arrangements such as food sharing, stay the same? If hereditary inequality did emerge, as the evidence at the Keatley Creek and Bell sites suggests, it might have been due to this drastically rearranged social landscape. If we imagine household chiefs before 1200 BP, we think of individuals who were responsible for making good decisions to ensure healthy economies and peaceful communities. If meeting these conditions meant sharing, then the use of wealth to increase one's status at the expense of one's neighbours would not have been welcomed, especially since members of neighbouring households were biologically and economically interconnected. However, once resources began to decline (either through natural fluctuations, as in the case of salmon, or through overhunting, as in the case of deer and other small mammal and plant species), it is possible that some individuals began to develop strategies to ensure the survival of their households. Ownership, or at least control of key places on the landscape, would be one strategy. Some families might have always preferred some locales over others; perhaps these preferences became more formalized in tough times, as corporate groups laid claim to fishing rocks, berry patches, deer-hunting locales, and the like. To protect their family members, heads of household perhaps then decided to formalize a system of inheritance, whereby only members of the original family had the right to wealth, places, rank, and even the use of certain household symbols (such as crest animals) and stories. Within this scenario, new people, moving in from collapsed households elsewhere, were likely excluded from property ownership and fell into the ranks of free commoners.

Perhaps competition for household viability under conditions of regional subsistence stress intensified the harvest of local resources. If this indeed happened, surviving communities were likely pushed beyond their economic limits. The final alternative was the abandonment of the largest Mid-Fraser villages.

7
The Abandonment and the Return

They watched in silence as the big house burned. Ash floated like black feathers from the sky and stuck to the people's skin and clothes. A timber crashed to the floor. The people had lived in this house for countless generations. They had survived tough winters and war. But now it was all gone.

The woman cleared her eyes and turned away to survey the valley. A few small villages dotted the east side of the big river. They too would be abandoned. Her husband had worked with their household heads and the chief at the big village at Keatley Creek. Together, they had shared food, fended off marauders from the north and east, and traded with people on the Coast. But she, along with everyone else, was exhausted and tired of living like salmon packed too tight in a cache pit. Her children had heard the old stories, stories of salmon runs so strong you could walk across their backs, but they had never known anything but hard work. Constant cooking and foraging, and garbage piled everywhere, on the roof and in the old storage pits that once housed dried deer meat and roots. The garbage attracted bugs and dogs, which ran in packs and got so violent they had to be killed, their remains stuffed into garbage pits or buried outside the village.

But now it was all gone. They did not plan to rebuild this time. They would move on. The woman looked forward to life in a new village in a new valley, to a new house and fewer people, to a place where her children could play as they picked berries.

Today, significant changes in the settlement and subsistence systems of past cultures are often viewed as a form of cultural collapse, an interpretive construct that simultaneously implies elements of economic upheaval and an almost tragic change in social systems. The term *cultural collapse* is used by people in a number of ways, many of which implicitly romanticize cultural transformations in the past. Archaeological models have, historically, represented dramatic culture change as being the result of external causes, such as environmental change. Alternatively, some researchers have explored the importance of factors internal to human social systems, such as warfare, political upheaval, and economic decision making. Reflecting upon the magnitude of cultural shifts is at once highly complicated and critical to labelling, describing, and understanding change. At what point, for example, can one confidently argue that a culture shift should be labelled abandonment or some less romantic case of downscaling? Although it is not usually stated explicitly, the term *abandonment* encompasses moments of rapid and irreversible culture change, in contrast to cultural transformations that are less dramatic.

The collapse and abandonment of human settlements are of interest to archaeologists, scientists, and the general public. It is not hard to find books that discuss some of the more famous cases: the collapse of the Mayans, the rise and fall of the Roman Empire, or the disaster on Rapa Nui (Easter Island). There are, however, hundreds of other equally fascinating cases. People are fascinated with collapse and abandonment because these episodes offer insight into problems suffered by contemporary society. And, it must be acknowledged, some of us simply have a morbid fascination with bad times. What were they like? What happened to the people?

In this chapter, we use the term *abandonment* to denote the complete depopulation of a village, at least as it can be reconstructed from the archaeological record. We do not want to imply that village abandonment meant regional abandonment. Rather, the abandonment of particular villages more often accompanied the reorganization of land-use practices, as might occur when a group of people ceases a semi-sedentary existence in large population aggregates in favour of more frequent residential moves and smaller-scaled groups.

The Mid-Fraser Abandonment

We know that the large villages of the Mid-Fraser Canyon were abandoned between 800 and 1,100 years ago. Archaeologists have debated the timing, scope, and process of abandonment since the early 1990s. The villages of the Mid-Fraser Canyon likely contained the highest density of persons anywhere in the Pacific Northwest region during the late prehistoric period. The breakup of these villages must have drastically altered exchange networks and, by extension, subsistence patterns, social relations, and security throughout the entire region. We examine the evidence for economic collapse and the abandonment of villages in the Mid-Fraser area. Why were these villages abandoned? Were the villages reoccupied later? If so, what were they like (Box 7.1)?

The population peak in the Mid-Fraser arguably occurred around 1,200 to 1,300 years ago. After this point, there was a steady decline in human population, as demonstrated by abandoned villages and a decline in the frequency of other smaller archaeological sites. Current data suggest that the first big abandonment came at Bridge River. The Bridge River village peaked about 1,200 years ago, when it comprised 30 simultaneously occupied houses. As many as 800 to 1,000 people lived in the settlement, which was large by hunter-gatherer

BOX 7.1 HOW DO ARCHAEOLOGISTS RECONSTRUCT POPULATION GROWTH AND DECLINE?

Archaeologists monitor the rise and fall of human populations using several methods and different scales. From a methodological perspective, the strongest approach involves direct evidence. Like census takers who go from door to door in a neighbourhood, archaeologists can count the number of burials from a certain period of time or, at a larger scale, the number of cemeteries. Changes in the number of burials over time indicate changing population levels, but they can also indicate changes in preferred burial places. The absence of burial data for the Mid-Fraser Valley makes it impossible to develop accurate population estimates.

Archaeologists can use other indirect lines of evidence. For example, if our census takers cannot knock on each door and find out how many people live at each house, they can count the number of houses and use the average number of people from known houses to calculate how many people live in the neighbourhood. In a general way, this is the challenge archaeologists face: how does one use indirect lines of evidence – such as the number of houses, the frequency of salmon bones, the amount of stones produced by fire hearths – to reconstruct a

picture of changes in the intensity of human occupation in the past?

Archaeologists can use these methods to reconstruct population changes at the scale of the house, settlement, or region. At the broadest scale, researchers document the number of sites that date from a particular time and look for periods when there is a significant drop in the number of settlements, an indication that people moved away. Another way to do this is to examine the frequency of houses within dated sites, an approach that provides detailed estimates of the actual number of people living at different periods. This approach, however, requires extensive and expensive radiocarbon dating of charcoal or bone samples from a significant sample of houses. In modern political polling, it is necessary to understand household and neighbourhood data to accurately understand voting patterns within a city. In the Mid-Fraser Canyon, the Bridge River site is the only settlement in which archaeologists have undertaken a systematic sampling and dating program that provides a detailed sense of when structures throughout the village were occupied and how they varied in size.

standards. After the peak, the village was empty for a period of at least five hundred years. Other villages were occupied to the south of Bridge River, in the Seton drainage. When archaeologist Mike Rousseau conducted test excavations at a small site at the east end of Seton Lake, the occupation dates corresponded to those of Bridge River. Some pithouses from the Bell and Fountain sites also date to the same time frame. There are only a few radiocarbon dates from the Bell site, and given its large size, it is possible that the village was occupied longer, perhaps like neighbouring Keatley Creek.

Archaeologists have extensively excavated only a limited number of pithouses at Keatley Creek village, some of which have been dated with scientific techniques. Although the investigators noted the problems of dating large complex housepits, such as Housepit 7, their research provides a rough understanding of when individual houses were founded and when they were abandoned. Not enough housepits have been dated, however, to understand the overall growth patterns in the village. If we use Bridge River as a model, then we can see that the village could have grown from possibly fewer than a dozen to potentially over 25 simultaneously occupied houses and a population of around a thousand people. If a chiefdom-like polity existed in the Mid-Fraser, could this have been its centre? Although not as large, could other contemporary villages have been more affluent and influential? Excavations at the Bridge River site have produced more wealth items per capita than at Keatley Creek. Regardless of the answers to these questions, all of these sites, including Keatley Creek, were eventually abandoned.

To summarize, current data suggest that the Mid-Fraser abandonment came in at least two phases. Bridge River, possibly Bell, and some smaller settlements were abandoned first, followed two to three centuries later by Keatley Creek and, possibly, other associated small sites. There are other major villages in the area that have not been investigated. Much of the Fountain, Pavilion, and Lillooet town site villages were destroyed by modern development. Other large villages exist at Kelly, McKay, and Leon creeks to the north, Kwoiek Creek to the south, and upper Seton Lake to the west. Inaccessibility has, however, prevented any significant work at these places. Interestingly, large housepit villages located even farther to the north, near the mouth of the Chilcotin River, also date to the same general time frame as the Lillooet area villages. Collectively, these data do suggest a significant pattern of village abandonment. However, further research is needed to develop a better understanding of this phenomenon.

Why Abandonment?

In 1991, Brian Hayden and June Ryder published an important article in which they argued that the Mid-Fraser abandonments had occurred as the result of a single catastrophic landslide. The landslide had occurred near Texas Creek around one thousand years ago, at about the same time the villages were abandoned. Hayden and Ryder argued that the slide created a long-lasting dam that backed up to the Fraser River and formed steep falls that prevented salmon from passing into the Lillooet area (Figure 7.1). They suggest that even if the river wore down the dam in a few years, the blockage would have had adverse effects on the salmon runs that would have lasted for generations. If the villages were heavily dependent on salmon, then the sudden loss of this critical resource would have caused the collapse of local economies and mass famine. They believe that the failure of the salmon runs to regenerate kept people away from the area for centuries.

Hayden and Ryder's model makes sense if a number of assumptions are accepted, including the assumption that the Mid-Fraser villages were abandoned simultaneously, that the economy was inflexibly centred on salmon, that the slide occurred just before village abandonment, that the dam lasted long enough to prevent several salmon runs from getting through and, finally, that the salmon runs could not have regenerated in anything less than about 300 years, the period associated with substantial population losses in the Mid-Fraser Canyon.

There are enough facts, however, to suggest an alternative hypothesis more consistent with the available data. First, it is now clear that the villages were not abandoned at once; in some cases, reduced populations continued to live in some villages after 1000 BP (before the present). The record from the Keatley Creek site suggests that people, at least in this village, diversified their economy. The inhabitants of Keatley Creek appear to have eaten a significant quantity of mammals and plants during the period between 1,200 and 800 years ago. Thus, declining salmon runs might not have been the coup de grâce at this village. But it is possible that villages such as Bridge River were more dependent on the fish resource.

It is also important to point out that the Texas Creek land slide has yet to be dated. Although there is a chance that it could have occurred 1,000 years ago, Ian Kuijt argues that it could have happened substantially earlier and would have left a greater footprint on the landscape. If the dam lasted as long as Hayden and Ryder claim, it should have produced a substantial reservoir of water that would have left lacustrine or lake bottom sediments on the Lillooet terraces. There is, however, no evidence. Sediments of the Lillooet terraces are fluviatile or stream bed in nature.

If there was a short-term landslide that blocked the Fraser River, fisheries data show that the salmon numbers would have returned to normal levels within several years. Salmon are remarkably reproductive creatures; barring overfishing, as we've witnessed in the 20th century, or some form of major change within

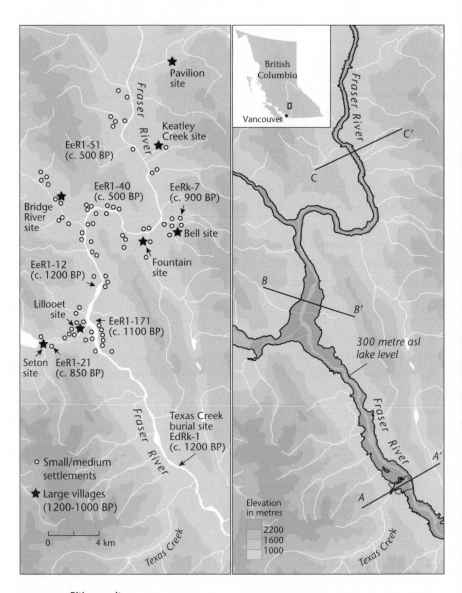

FIGURE 7.1 Pithouse sites in the Mid-Fraser region. The map on the right shows the hypothesized extent of the Texas Creek landslide.

Redrawn from maps by Ian Kuijt

the Pacific Ocean, we need to look to some other explanation for regional abandonment.

We argue that cultural shifts in the Mid-Fraser Canyon were not an isolated event. Rather, it is clear that the period from 1,200 to 800 years ago was one of significant change at the regional level. Archaeologists need to re-examine the widely held assumption that the region's so-called cultural collapse was related to a single hydrological event and devote more attention to explaining why a similar shift – from large aggregate pithouse villages to smaller pithouse occupations – occurred in several, if not most, areas of the Plateau after 1200 BP. We are not suggesting that landslides and associated hydrological events did not periodically happen. We are suggesting that there is not adequate evidence to link the abandonments to this one event.

To fully understand abandonment, we must step back and look at the wider region. Was abandonment a local phenomenon, or were there major changes elsewhere in the Pacific Northwest? There is growing evidence for population downscaling in all areas of the region, not just the Mid-Fraser Canyon (Box 7.2). There are, for example, signs of major cultural reorganization within the Columbia River drainage. In the Lower Columbia region, particularly around The Dalles, settlements shifted from more permanent pithouses to small and ephemeral mat lodges. Neither the Mid-Columbia nor the Lower Snake River valleys contained large settlements during this time. There are, interestingly enough, indicators of increased violence throughout the region, such as more small, fortified settlements and evidence of projectile wounds in cemetery remains. The large villages of the Upper Columbia, Kutenai, and Slocan drainages fluoresced briefly before they were abandoned by 750 BP. Similar processes appear to have been underway on the Coast. The Marpole area of the central Coast, for instance, contains signs of depopulation, warfare, and abandonment.

When viewed in a regional context, the Mid-Fraser abandonments are not unique; rather, they are part of a regional pattern. But what could have caused such a shakeup throughout this extensive landscape? Could a major resource common to the Coast and the Interior have failed? Researchers interested in reconstructing past ecosystems have looked at the remains of fish and other organisms from deep cores at various places in the eastern and northeast Pacific. Evidence from marine research around Vancouver Island – such as increased counts of fish bones and diatoms – suggests that ocean waters became increasingly productive between about 1,800 and 1,200 years ago. Although salmon bones from archaeology sites are not included in these data, salmon numbers do correlate with productive seas. We therefore have no reason to doubt that salmon were abundant. This fact is certainly supported by evidence for abundant salmon harvests in the Mid-Fraser and Columbia River valleys and signs of cooler temperatures in the region, including the growth of the Lillooet glacier, a steady reduction in Plateau forest fires, and pollen levels in forest systems.

What would happen if the salmon runs suddenly became less predictable and, if present, much smaller? People would necessarily have to work harder to make up the deficit by collecting other foods in larger numbers. There are some signs from the Keatley Creek village that salmon declined suddenly. A number of highly processed dog bones were recovered from Housepit 7 that dated to this time. Although the pattern quickly shifts to deer as the favoured prey, it is possible that dogs were eaten under emergency conditions.

Taking this scenario one step further, let's imagine that each year the average household surplus for stored winter salmon decreased and that, as a result, some villages simply did not have a sufficient surplus for the group. This situation would have led to serious and immediate problems. Perhaps this happened at Bridge River. The people, in response, may have packed into other villages such as Keatley Creek, where the people were simply hanging on. Now, with more mouths to feed, people had to collect food from the local area even more intensively and likely caused major reductions in preferred prey species. There are some hints that access to preferred root resources declined during this period. For example, people no longer roasted roots in the Keatley Creek village. If the sources were farther away, the people would have roasted them close to their collection contexts rather than hauling them home. Furthermore, if roots became

BOX 7.2 THE WORLD AT 1200 BP: CHANGING ENVIRONMENTAL CONDITIONS

To what extent were past moments of cultural florescence and abandonment linked to global environmental changes? This is a complicated question. In North America, the timing of periods of cultural florescence and abandonment, such as those experienced in the pithouse villages of the Mid-Fraser, is strikingly similar to that of the environmental changes. Depopulation in the Interior was part of a larger trend that occurred in other areas of the world and correlated with warmer temperatures and drought, particularly in many areas of western North America.

Data from the eastern Pacific Ocean suggest that marine productivity peaked about 1,200 years ago and then declined to below-average levels. Warm sea conditions do not favour a strong upwelling of microscopic nutrients and can result in major declines in the number and health of predators up the food chain. Warm and dry conditions on land adversely affect the spawning of anadromous fish such as salmon and result in reduced numbers of fry. Archaeologist James Chatters recognized a major drop in the number of salmon at sites on the Columbia Plateau during this period. Clearly, similar changes also occurred on the Canadian Plateau.

Other areas of North America also saw major cultural changes. Climate change helped harder to get, people would start to look for other carbohydrate sources. Rising numbers of pine nuts in the strata (layers) of Housepit 7 at Keatley Creek after 1200 BP support this theory.

It would have been even easier to overexploit mammalian species. The data from Keatley Creek suggest that deer had to be hunted at greater distances between 1,200 and 800 years ago. Deer bones at Housepit 7 from this period consist almost entirely of lower limbs, whereas earlier strata include representations of most parts. Archaeologists have recognized a similar signature at the Bridge River site. The exclusive presence of lower limbs most likely means that animals were butchered in the field. Only smoked meat and hides (with lower limbs attached) were returned to the village.

Considering all of the data, it appears that the Mid-Fraser villages suffered first from a regional decline in salmon, which was linked to major changes in the Pacific Ocean. The villages then experienced deterioration in local land resources, which was followed by attempts to intensify the use of some food sources and the overexploitation of others. Only a restricted number of villages could survive. With economies on the edge, it would not have taken much to precipitate the final abandonment of packed villages. We will probably never know what the final events were – deteriorating salmon resources, collapsed deer populations, failure of root resources, or some combination of the three. We do not know whether the villages were abandoned suddenly or gradually, over

some people and regions and hurt others. In northern latitudes, warm conditions permitted the Norse people to establish farms on Greenland. The same warm conditions favoured the expansion of maize farming onto the northern Great Plains and supported the intensified agricultural economy of North America's first city, now known as Cahokia. In contrast, farming systems in the American Southwest failed during this same period because of droughts that lasted for decades, bringing about changes in long-established ways of life. Stormy conditions in northwestern Alaska a thousand years ago led to the collapse of the Ipiutak culture, which had focused on seal and caribou hunting, and its replacement by groups who focused on whaling. This period of replacement and reorganization helped to precipitate the famous Thule expansion, which brought Inupiat speakers to the North American Arctic.

Global warming at around 1000 BP had complex effects on ecosystems and human groups in and around the Pacific Ocean. Following a period of climatic instability that extended from 1,200 to 800 BP, human groups in the Gulf of Alaska benefitted from significant growth in salmon populations, while those people on the Northwest Coast and in the Interior, including the Fraser and Columbia River drainages, suffered major reductions.

decades. Whatever happened, the great villages were fully abandoned by about 800 or 900 BP.

Relocation

Although sections of the Mid-Fraser Canyon were probably not occupied for at least a century after the collapse of the major villages, this does not mean that the entire region was abandoned. A few families perhaps established smaller communities along or near the canyon, while others returned occasionally for short seasonal visits. But it would take centuries before ideal conditions would return. So where did the majority of people go?

Many researchers have pointed out that hunter-gatherers and foragers maintain kinship-based alliances and trade partnerships with many people from neighbouring groups. They are, in short, economically and socially connected to people in other areas, at times several hundred miles away and separated by major rivers and mountain ranges. Early white explorers in British Columbia commented that peoples in the Mid-Fraser region had extensive regional contacts and had married into families on the Pacific Northwest Coast and other neighbouring regions. One possibility is that the villagers moved southwest to the Coast Range. This, traditionally, was a core Lillooet area and might have held more families that were willing to accept people who were moving away from the Mid-Fraser villages. It is also possible that salmon runs in the Lower Lillooet area were not affected as badly as those located farther in the Interior.

Some people likely remained within or near the Mid-Fraser Canyon. Villages probably split up as individual families took up residence in new locations such as upland valleys. The number of root-roasting ovens actually rose during this period in places such as Hat Creek Valley, located to the east of the Fraser Canyon. Were families scratching out a living in smaller groups that moved seasonally to take advantage of resources? This would not be unheard of among hunter-gatherers. For example, when the caribou populations of northern Alaska collapsed around 1900, Eskimo groups in the interior moved to the coast. But a few families survived in the Brooks Range by moving frequently between areas with caribou and places with sheep, fish, moose, and other food sources. It is also possible that groups living in more distant areas, such as the Thompson drainage, regularly travelled into the Mid-Fraser area to collect roots. More archaeological research is needed to answer these questions more fully.

The Late Villages

It is generally accepted that the cultural patterns of the final centuries before European contact were probably similar to what is described in the ethnographies and travel accounts of the 1800s and early 1900s. We know that many of the more ancient villages were reoccupied at a smaller scale during the final three hundred years of the pre-colonial period. New villages were also established in the Lillooet area. Accounts by European explorers such as Simon Fraser suggest that some of these villages were fortified. Although some of the villages were sizable, none reached the heights achieved during the Classic Lillooet period.

Oral histories describe the return of people to traditional villages, but the time frame remains unclear. Elder Baptiste Ritchie placed the return of people to Mount Currie after a mythical great flood: "After awhile *In-CHEE-nim-kan* returned to Mount Currie; the meadows here were better after the flood. He found that a lot of the people had moved to Mount Currie because their own land was now covered with rocks. They settled along the Lillooet River" (Bouchard and Kennedy 1977:12).

Excavations at the Bridge River site revealed over a dozen houses that dated to the final pre-colonial and early colonial periods, around 500 to 200 years ago. The houses were distributed in a roughly linear pattern that ran north to south through the village (see Figures 4.13 and 7.2). Preliminary evidence allows us to

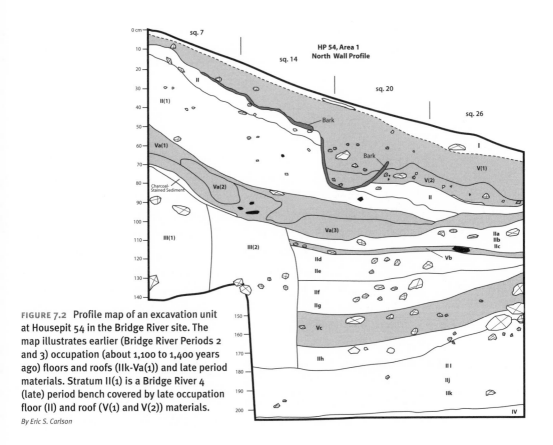

FIGURE 7.2 Profile map of an excavation unit at Housepit 54 in the Bridge River site. The map illustrates earlier (Bridge River Periods 2 and 3) occupation (about 1,100 to 1,400 years ago) floors and roofs (IIk-Va(1)) and late period materials. Stratum II(1) is a Bridge River 4 (late) period bench covered by late occupation floor (II) and roof (V(1) and V(2)) materials.
By Eric S. Carlson

FIGURE 7.3 Housepit 20 was a large housepit occupied during Bridge River 2, 3, and 4 periods. Note the smoky background from Coast Range forest fires in 2009.

Photograph by Anna M. Prentiss

draw several conclusions. First, Bridge River was a major village in the Classic Lillooet period. It was established before 1100 BP, as is seen in the high number of simultaneously occupied houses throughout the Late Period. Late Period villages had extremely large and very small houses and many showed signs of wealth and status distinctions similar to those described in ethnographies. Smaller housepits contained little more than a few chipped-stone tools, highly fragmentary animal bones, and fire-cracked rock, a common remnant of cooking. In contrast, the larger houses contain more markers of wealth (Figure 7.3).

There might also have been clusters of smaller and larger houses in different parts of the village. Three sets of smaller housepits, each with side entrances and conjoined by tunnels, likely existed during the Late Period in the southeast corner of the village (Figure 7.4). The meaning of this pattern has yet to be deciphered, but the houses could have been residences for special persons or visitors from another social group or clan.

The Bridge River site also contains abundant evidence of outdoor roasting ovens and cache pits (Figure 7.5). Immediately before the abandonment about

FIGURE 7.4 View of excavations at Housepit 11 at the Bridge River site in 2009. The side entrance to the housepit is clearly visible in the foreground.

Photograph by Anna M. Prentiss

FIGURE 7.5 University of Montana students conducting test excavations in an external pit feature (roasting oven or cache pit) at Bridge River during the 2003 field season.

Photograph by Anna M. Prentiss

1,100 years ago, the Bridge River people had begun to engage in frequent outdoor cooking events that featured meat, fish, and berries. This activity reappeared with the reoccupation of the village after about 400 BP. As in the earlier period, the largest pits were located at the north end of the village, whereas the south end featured a larger number of smaller ovens. In addition, and in contrast to the earlier occupation, Late Period people appear to have built food storage cache pits outside their houses. Indeed, it is rare to find cache pits inside houses throughout the Late Period.

It is important to note that stone technologies did not significantly change between the time of the abandonment and reoccupation of the site. Although the Late Period saw an increase in the use of ground slate tools, manufacturing techniques and styles did not change. The same could be said for other stylistically sensitive items such as arrow points and other soapstone and nephrite items. Given that these stone tool industries are unique – especially the production of slate knives and scrapers, which was accomplished using a combination of chipping, grinding, and sawing – it is possible that the village might well have been reoccupied by descendants of the original occupants.

In places where soil conditions favoured preservation, excavations have revealed abundant salmon remains for the Late Period. Contemporary ethnographic informants point out that a large deer population can be found from late winter to early summer within walking distance of the Bridge River site. The availability of this resource might have offered important advantages to the village's hunters.

The people who reoccupied the Bridge River village were once again powerful. Salmon were available in vast numbers, and the people occupied a central position in a vast trade network that extended from Alaska to California and from the West Coast to the Great Plains. The wealthiest houses accumulated a variety of trade items and art objects, including copper pendants, jade adzes, and dentalium beads. They even accumulated European trade goods before the arrival of Europeans on the Pacific Coast.

Many questions surround the final occupation of the Keatley Creek village. At the moment, the diverse archaeological evidence from different periods of time makes it a challenge for archaeologists to talk about village-scale patterns. Brian Hayden and colleagues have excavated a number of small housepits located on the periphery of the village. These houses often have standard residential materials in the form of discarded tools, animal bones, hearths, and cache pits, and they were likely residential in nature. Housepit 104 contained a Lahal gaming piece and a large quantity of sandstone flakes and tool fragments. Sandstone tools were typically used to make nephrite jade items. The same house contained an impressively high number of large billet flakes, which are normally associated with the manufacture of knives and spear points. The house also contained a large assortment of faunal remains, which Hayden interpreted as being related to feasting. Finally, the excavators found a fragment of coiled basketry, along with abundant charred needles and grasses. Housepit 106 contained a line of boulders around a portion of the wall, a rectangular floor-plan shape, and a unique funnel-shaped hearth located at the centre of the pithouse. Relatively few artifacts were recovered, but they included a goose bone drinking tube, a cervid tooth bead, and a chipped-stone "tomahawk." Some mammal bones rested in the floor in vertical positions. Recent research at Housepit 109 resulted in the recovery of a small pit on the edge of the house that contained five cut and polished long bone cylinders from at least one dog. They also found a fragmentary bone comb or scratcher, possibly shaped in a canid form, and an articulated wolf paw on the floor.

Once again breaking new ground, Hayden argued that such houses could have been ritual structures: they hold evidence of unique activities; they contain the special property of ritual specialists or secret societies; and they have special structural characteristics such as unique hearths, roof materials, and floor plans. He also speculated that the roasting features could have been used for ritual feasting activities. Hayden's provocative arguments have not yet been subjected to adequate independent testing or debate in the archaeological literature. More importantly, radiocarbon dating tells us that the majority of these structures are not contemporaneous with structures such as Housepit 7. The relatively late date of these structures – between about 150 and 300 years ago – and the lack of comparative excavated structures from within Keatley Creek's core village area hint at a range of activities clearly not related to the original major occupation of the site. At a minimum, it is possible that a wide range of activities occurred in small isolated houses at Keatley Creek, and that we do not yet fully understand how these activities fit in with earlier practices and the broader occupation of the village.

Given the lack of systematic sampling and dating at the Keatley Creek site, many questions remain regarding occupation patterns and village organization, particularly during the final occupation period. Excavators in 1989 found a hearth and scattered domestic debris (food remains, flakes, and stone tools) in sediments on the surface of the collapsed roof of Housepit 7. They interpreted the remains as a camp in the crater of the abandoned housepit. In 1999 and 2002, however, new excavations by University of Montana teams outside the rim of the house revealed extensive household debris scattered in a single sheet midden similar to the outdoor debris found around European frontier homesteads. A hearth excavated just below this layer dated to between 300 and 400 BP. All told, these new data suggest that the camp in Housepit 7 might actually have been a thin floor from a shallow housepit reoccupation. Similar patterns of thin floors covering more ancient deposits were also found at Bridge River. If this is the case, it is possible that the Keatley Creek site was reoccupied by some yet-to-be-defined residential group and that the small houses on the periphery functioned in some way associated with this group.

If the centre of Keatley Creek was never reoccupied as an aggregated village, and if the domestic debris around Housepit 7 is nothing more than remnants from temporary camps, then something interesting must have been happening in the small houses. It is possible that the Keatley Creek area came to be viewed as a special place, a place where people who still lived in the area came to recall stories of great deeds or happenings that had occurred long ago. Similar places, such as the Hill of Tara in Ireland and Stonehenge in England, exemplify the cultural reuse of land and space through time. The giant city of Teotihuacan, in the basin of Mexico, collapsed so totally around 1300 BP that knowledge of the civilization and its inhabitants was almost completely lost. Later, Toltec and Aztec people regarded the ruins as a sacred place where the sun and the moon were born. People travelled great distances to visit the sacred landscape of Teotihuacan, to commune with the ancient gods who lived so close to the place.

Regardless of these mysteries, it is clear that a vibrant and complex culture re-emerged in the Mid-Fraser Canyon during the final centuries before European contact. These people were undoubtedly the direct ancestors of the St'át'imc.

8
A Broad Perspective
Looking Back, Looking Forward

Not long ago, historian Trefor Smith lamented that Aboriginal and non-Aboriginal children in Lillooet schools were not taught the history of the St'át'imc people. Noting that St'át'imc history "is hidden at their doorstep," Smith sought to rectify this problem by writing a popular overview of St'át'imc history and culture. In this book, we returned to this metaphorical doorstep and attempted to look further into that which is hidden or, more appropriately, that which is buried beneath the ground just beyond that doorstep. Indeed, the archaeological record, along with oral histories and historical accounts, provides a robust means of describing the long-term history of the indigenous peoples of the Middle Fraser Canyon and surrounding lands. In the broadest of terms, this record provides direct material evidence for the comings and goings of past peoples and some of the processes that led to the development of St'át'imc culture.

Looking Back

The archaeological record of the Mid-Fraser Canyon provides insight into the complex cultural history of the region's indigenous peoples, especially the St'át'imc. Although there is abundant evidence for cultural change and the exchange of goods and ideas from surrounding regions, we also recognize that there was significant cultural continuity within the region. Ancestors of today's St'át'imc people survived periods of significant global climate change, dramatic changes in the nature of wild food resources, and complex interactions with neighbouring groups. Thus, traditional St'át'imc culture is a product of the long-term history we describe.

The Earliest Inhabitants

One of the most important lessons from Mid-Fraser archaeology is that First Nations have lived here for a long time. There is direct archaeological evidence that people lived in the Mid-Fraser area for at least eight thousand to nine thousand years, and it is entirely possible that future research will push these dates back even further. The earliest people, defined by archaeologists as part of the Nesikep tradition, were hunter-gatherers who moved seasonally throughout the Interior and had different cultural practices from those of people of more recent times. They were apparently successful, for they lived on the land for thousands of years with relatively little change. Sites from this period are small and suggest that people lived in small camps and engaged in special activities, such as stone tool production. These early people apparently ate more wild game than fish and placed their camps near the best hunting spots. They used large and well-made spear tips accompanied by small blade insets for hunting. A plethora of specialized scraping, cutting, and drilling tools were designed to process hides, make clothing, and build shelters. It is most likely that everyone was equal when it came to the ownership of goods, and they probably shared food and other resources.

This early culture persisted until around 4,000 years ago and then disappeared. The disappearance of the Nesikep tradition came at time of great cultural and ecological change throughout the Pacific Northwest. Like other groups in the region, it is possible that the Nesikep found their way of life severely threatened by the changes occurring around them. Perhaps their economies were unable to change. Whatever happened, the Nesikep cultural pattern vanished from the region.

Meanwhile, a cultural revolution was occurring on the Northwest Coast. People had begun to settle into more sedentary communities, where they supported themselves by harvesting and storing fish, shellfish, sea mammals, and a variety of plant species. These tasks required new ways of organizing labour and resulted in altered social arrangements. Isolated family groups no longer moved about seeking an immediate return from hunting and fishing. New forms of advance planning led to annual migrations to key fishing sites and periods of hard work by all members of the group, who caught and processed enough salmon to feed significant numbers of people for extended periods of time. It was a strategy that helped the people survive new, colder conditions.

This new collector strategy appeared in the Mid-Fraser area around 3,500 years ago. Archaeologists call this culture the Shuswap horizon, and the people of this period resided in small camps and villages that contained clusters of semi-subterranean dwellings called pithouses. Dug into the ground up to a metre or more, the houses were generally small, though on rare occasions they were large enough to hold one to two extended families. Storage pits in the floors and the presence of large numbers of processed salmon suggest that food storage was practised much as it was on the Coast. People still employed darts and throwing-sticks or atlatls for hunting, but they also possessed a wide array of fishing tools similar to those of the coastal cultures. Other tools included heavy wedges and stone mauls or hammers for splitting and working wood, tools that were also typical of the coastal context. Although it is subject to further study, this evidence may support the argument that some people moved into the Interior from the Coast. Certainly, there was no one there to stop them. And with new technologies and the collector strategy of resource harvesting and storage, these new people were equipped to flourish in a place that had grown too harsh for the more mobile Nesikep peoples, who lacked storage technologies.

The Shuswap horizon was the real beginnings of what archaeologists call the Plateau Pithouse tradition, a period in which Aboriginal groups relied on the use of pithouses, focused on salmon, and generally lived in villages of multiple extended families. This tradition dominated the region for over three thousand years and formed the cultural backbone of the historical St'át'imc culture. Between 3,000 and 1,800 years ago, the Mid-Fraser Canyon was only sparsely inhabited. Over time, however, large groups of people started to aggregate annually at the junction of the North and South Thompson rivers to the east. Simultaneously, a new complex collector cultural pattern emerged in the Fraser Valley and elsewhere on the Northwest Coast. People began to live in large multifamily groups in permanent villages made up of many large houses. Some sites featured pithouses, others, above-ground wooden structures. The new pattern permitted house groups to at once protect resources near their settlement and move farther afield to collect more distant foods. The new pattern probably also promoted new leadership structures, including household heads or chiefs charged with maintaining the more complex political system. One byproduct of this development was that these heads might also have garnered a higher and more permanent degree of respect and status among household members than had any senior members of society before them.

The Emergence of Housepit Villages

The complex collector pattern appeared in the Mid-Fraser Valley a little after 2000 BP (before the present). The new villages were initially small, probably comprising no more than two to three houses. But the houses were large and were likely populated by more people than were housed in earlier Plateau pithouses. People relied on salmon in these early villages, and the presence of large numbers of roasting pits in nearby localities such as Hat Creek suggest that people intensively harvested and cooked root foods. Their technologies included a wide range of chipped-stone knives, piercers, and scrapers; bows and arrows; ground slate, nephrite, and steatite tools and ornaments; and a variety of other items, including birch bark basketry, digging sticks, and fishing nets.

Researchers have only a limited understanding of early village social organization. It is clear, however, that inter-household ranking, as marked by the differential accumulation of prestige goods and control of food resources, was not present at this time. There was variation in house size, and it is possible that the leaders of individual households wielded greater authority than in earlier periods. However, ancient social rules might have made it mandatory to share resources within and between houses, thereby reducing the archaeological visibility of any elite statuses (if they existed at all).

The number of people living in villages increased substantially around 1,200 to 1,300 years ago. Evidence from the Bridge River site suggests the possibility of a 300 to 400 percent increase in the numbers of houses. Keatley Creek village might have been much the same. The pattern of village growth correlates with indicators of rising marine productivity in the eastern Pacific. Interestingly, people started to abandon Mid-Fraser villages when there was sudden drop in marine productivity, perhaps implying a major reduction in access to salmon. Although the Bridge River village was abandoned between 1,200 and 1,100 years ago, the large village at Keatley Creek might have survived longer. There is evidence that select house groups grew in size at this time, and it is during this period that the material trappings of social inequality – such as the accumulations of prestige-related goods and raw materials in larger houses – appear.

There might not have been a single trigger for social inequality, but we can identify several interconnected factors that contributed toward it. One factor was population growth. It is quite likely that many people packed into larger housepits when there was restricted access to salmon. Simultaneous declines in local plant and animal resources might have required longer foraging trips to gather resources. This situation perhaps contributed to heightened tensions among household members. Mortality rates among villagers could also have increased as food became less available and people more mobile. At times, maintaining the household would have required the recruitment of new members, perhaps from other failed houses or from recently abandoned villages. To guarantee access to food, formal control of key places also became important. Household heads perhaps took measures to protect their family line and develop new rules to control access to household property. If this theory is correct, then we have a situation in which access to land, stories, and a wide range of material things was linked to inherited privileges. This marked the beginning of a pattern of ascribed (or inherited) inequality that would re-emerge during the late pre-historic and contact periods.

It is clear that the Mid-Fraser villages did not suddenly collapse a thousand years ago. Bridge River was abandoned by 1100 BP, while Keatley Creek was abandoned by around 800 BP. This and other evidence suggests that there was no single catastrophic event, such as a landslide, that brought about the cultural changes seen after 1000 BP. So what did happen? The pattern of abandonments in the Mid-Fraser mirrors a similar process that occurred in the complex villages of the eastern Great Basin (Utah and eastern Nevada) at this time. The pithouse villages associated with the Fremont culture also failed in this region, and there is no evidence for a single calamity. Rather, drought-induced crop failure and overhunting by the residents of burgeoning villages created depressions in key wild resource populations, especially deer. Suffering from increasingly harsh conditions, village after village failed, their inhabitants moving away. The Fremont culture disappeared completely.

Our understanding of what happened to the Fremont culture provides a model for explaining the decline of the Mid-Fraser villages: their abandonment was a form of cultural reorganization in reaction to climatic changes. Through a stroke of bad luck (weak eastern Pacific marine resources), a critical food source (salmon in the Fraser River) weakened, and people responded by intensely harvesting alternative foods that required them to travel longer and longer distances for the same return. With fluctuations between good and bad years, this pattern could have persisted for a while. In the long run, however, there was less and less food to go around each year. We will probably never be able to identify what triggered abandonment – perhaps a bad salmon catch, failed deer hunts, collapsed root populations, increased raiding, or simply better opportunities elsewhere – we can, however, say that broader regional ecological conditions and social relations undoubtedly played major roles.

Data from Keatley Creek and other sites highlight that reduced numbers of people continued to live sporadically in or near the Mid-Fraser Canyon in the centuries after the major villages were abandoned. On the landscape, this would have appeared as a single pithouse here, another a few miles down the river, and so on. Archaeologists have yet to satisfactorily answer the question of where the remainder of the people went. Educated guesswork suggests that these people moved in with other groups, perhaps to the west, in the mountains or, conversely, to the east, on the open Plateau. Another possibility is that many families simply stopped living in pithouses and started living in tents and migrating on a seasonal basis. Ephemeral camps and food-gathering and -processing sites could have popped up throughout region, but they remain largely invisible to the archaeologist. We do know that a similar development occurred on the Plateau several millennia earlier. When Pithouse I collapsed around 4000 BP, small residual groups crossed the Columbia Basin, leaving behind occasional hearths and stone tools.

Although they were dispersed for some time after the final abandonment, people returned to the Mid-Fraser in the centuries before the appearance of Europeans. Droughts gave way to cooler and wetter conditions. Salmon fishing improved. Other food resources became more stable. The stage was set for a renaissance in the Mid-Fraser Valley and the re-emergence of large, vibrant villages. Villages appeared in multiple locales including the Bridge River Valley, at the Lillooet townsite, in the Seton drainage, near Fountain, and farther upstream near Pavilion. The Keatley Creek village probably never returned to its former glory, but it is clear that people occupied it periodically. Warfare might have been a significant issue during this period. Early European explorers even documented the presence of palisades in some places on the Plateau. The Bridge River people still speak of past troubles with the Chilcotin to the north. Ethnographies from the 1900s suggest that villages were organized in clan-like groups and that status inequality was organized along hereditary lines.

By AD 1774, the year that Spanish explorer Juan Pérez visited Haida Gwaii (the Queen Charlotte Islands), people in the Mid-Fraser Canyon had seen both good and bad times. Nothing, however, prepared them for the developments of the coming century. They learned of the coming of the Europeans second-hand as they became involved in the fur trade. The first white person recorded to have visited the Mid-Fraser was Simon Fraser during his historic expedition down the Fraser River. On June 14, 1808, he met with the St'át'imc chiefs and sought to encourage trade relations between the peoples. Fraser himself initiated an exchange but apparently did not do so well at the hands of the shrewd St'át'imc chiefs. Regardless, trade with the newcomers quickly linked the St'át'imc people with global socioeconomic and political processes. In the mid-1800s, gold miners moved into the region. The smallpox epidemic came shortly after and led to significant losses of human life. Under conditions of population losses due to sickness, failed salmon runs led to famine. Perhaps even worse, the colonial government passed laws that restricted the people's rights to their traditional lands. More epidemics followed. Tough times had come to the Mid-Fraser Canyon.

Into the Present: The St'át'imc People Today

Despite all these hardships and challenges, the St'át'imc have survived. To do this, they incorporated new technologies and new resources into their traditional annual cycles in the 19th century. Although traditional practices such as fishing, hunting, and gathering continued, many people sought employment in farming, mining, and wage labour. But this transition was not easy. Christian churches were established, and priests condemned traditional spiritual practices. Despite its intended goal of integration, the Indian Act of 1876 effectively separated "Indian" people from the rest of Canadian society. As agents of the government, Indian agents determined how, when, and why people used the land, elected chiefs, or made use of band funds. Survival in this new bureaucratized world required education. Characteristic of all First Nations at this time, the St'át'imc were not generally provided with access to schools, and when they were, the schools were dark, dreary places of harsh discipline.

Beyond the cultural challenges of this new world, developments in the 19th century brought about significant environmental changes. The construction of dams and hatcheries destroyed salmon runs, and the government sought to restrict traditional salmon trade. Logging had an adverse effect on forests and wetlands, and First Nations groups were forced away from the best locations for living and fishing. Even after the Second World War, the so-called Indian schools continued the government's assault on traditional culture and language.

It was only in the 1970s that things started to change. The closure of the Indian schools and the demise of the Indian agent system were major steps in this process. During the 1980s and '90s, the federal government and courts finally began to recognize Aboriginal rights and title. In 2008, the prime minister of Canada apologized in public for the mistreatment of First Nations. But the struggle for rights continues. Today's St'át'imc chiefs and councillors maintain active negotiations with government and corporate entities to improve the lives of their people. Beyond recovering access to land and resources, community development is important. Even a cursory look at recent developments on reserves such as Xwisten or Bridge River illustrates this. Chiefs, administrators, councillors, and elders are playing significant roles in the renaissance of traditional St'át'imc culture. For the first time, Lillooet schools have a traditional language program, and children are learning about their heritage. Cultural tourism has been initiated and is centred on visits to important cultural places, including the ancient pithouse villages and fishing sites.

Sadly, many of the ancient sites have been destroyed over the last 150 years. The Lillooet townsite sits on one of the ancient villages, and development around Seton Lake has adversely affected other sites. Farming and housing construction have damaged the traditional villages at Fountain, Pavilion, and Bridge River, and livestock have done similar harm at Keatley Creek. Some villages have been affected in recent decades by illegal artifact collecting or looting. Despite the possibility of stiff fines, looting has occurred at Bridge River, Keatley Creek, and a host of smaller and lesser-known sites.

Looking Forward: The Challenge of the Future

Collectively, we are left with a significant challenge: how do we learn from the past and apply these lessons to the future? Despite the adverse effects of modern development, the ancient Mid-Fraser villages remain a priceless legacy of St'át'imc history and traditional culture. These sites are of regional, indeed global, importance: they provide a record of cultural stability and change in complex hunter-gatherer societies. At its peak, perhaps around 1,200 to 1,300 years ago, the Mid-Fraser Canyon might have held over ten thousand people. Archaeological research in the villages has recorded the means by which these ingenious people survived and flourished during periods of significant climate change and social upheaval. These lessons of survival and adaptation are essential in today's world, as we struggle with an unpredictable future that once again includes global warming and socio-political unrest. Archaeological research in the 21st century will give the ancient people of the Middle Fraser Canyon the opportunity to speak again. We have much to learn.

Appendix
The St'át'imc Language

Leora Bar-el

St'át'imcets (speech of the people of the Fraser River) is the name of the language spoken by the St'át'imc people (Matthewson 2005:5). There are two St'át'imcets dialects: Lower (Mount Currie) and Upper (Fountain). The terms correspond to the geographic areas in which the dialects are spoken (van Eijk 1997:xxviii).

St'át'imcets belongs to the Northern Interior branch of the Salish language family, which consists of 23 languages that are, or once were, spoken in British Columbia, Washington, Idaho, Montana, and Oregon (Czaykowska-Higgings and Kinkade 1998:1).

Sound Inventory
St'át'imcets has 44 consonantal sounds and 8 vowel sounds (van Eijk 1997:3). The sound inventories of Salish languages contain many consonant sounds that are not found in English. Some recurring features of St'át'imcets sounds are glottalization, labialization, retraction, and stress.

Glottalization
Glottalized stop consonants (e.g., *p', k', q*) and affricate consonants (e.g., *t', ts'*), both of which are also called ejectives, are pronounced with a buildup of air pressure in the vocal tract when the glottis (vocal cords) is closed and air is

---

Sincere thanks are owed to Henry Davis, Jan van Eijk, and Lisa Matthewson for invaluable feedback.

trapped between the glottis and an articulator (e.g., the lips or tongue). When the larynx is raised and the articulator released, an audible popping sound is produced. Glottalized resonant consonants (e.g., *m', n', l', y', w*) are produced by either constricting the vocal cords to produce a creaky voice effect or by closing the vocal cords completely at the beginning or end of the consonant. Glottalization is related to the glottal stop sound found frequently in St'át'imcets and occasionally in English. This sound is made by closing the glottis and then opening it again (as in the sound between the vowels in the English word *uh-oh*, or at the beginning of the word *apple*). The phonetics and phonology of glottalized resonants in St'át'imcets have been discussed in the literature (see Bird and Caldecott 2004; Bird et al. 2008; Caldecott 2004). Glottalization is indicated orthographically in St'át'imcets by *'* after the consonant symbol, e.g., *p', m'*. Glottalized resonants have varying pronunciations in St'át'imcets (see Davis 2009 for a detailed discussion).

Labialization (Rounded Consonants)

Rounded consonants are those consonants that are pronounced with the lips rounded. Rounding is indicated orthographically in St'át'imcets by *w* following the consonant, for example, *kw, qw*. In St'át'imcets, we find rounded velar consonants *(kw, k'w, cw)* and uvular consonants *(qw, q'w, xw, gw, g'w)*. Note that in the St'át'imcets orthography, the marking of rounding is omitted before rounded vowels (e.g., *u, o*) since it is predictable (Davis 2009; Matthewson 2005).

Retracted Sounds

Some St'át'imcets consonants (e.g., *l, l', s, ts, ts*) and vowels (e.g., *a, e, i, u*) are retracted. These sounds are pronounced with the tongue raised and pulled farther back in the mouth and with greater tension of the tongue muscles. Retraction in consonants is indicated orthographically in St'át'imcets with underlining (e.g., *l, s, ts*), while retraction in vowels is represented in the practical orthography by different vowels (e.g., *ao, v, ii, o*). Vowels are always retracted when they occur immediately before a uvular consonant *(q, q', qw, q'w, x, xw, g, g', gw, g'w)*. Furthermore, the glottal stop *(7)* is transparent to retraction. As a result, the nonretracted vowels are used orthographically in these cases. The phonetics and phonology of retraction in St'át'imcets has been discussed extensively in the literature (see, for instance, Davis 2006, 2009; Namdaran 2006; Shahin 2002; Bessell 1998; van Eijk 1997).

Stress

A stressed syllable is one that is more prominent than the others in a word. Stress usually correlates with a higher pitch, an increase in loudness or length. Caldecott

(2009) presents a detailed description and analysis of stress in St'át'imcets (see also van Eijk 1997 and Davis 2006, 2009). Stress is indicated orthographically in St'át'imcets by placing ´ on top of the vowel of the stressed syllable (e.g., *ú, á*). Note that stress is sometimes predictable (e.g., in monosyllabic words) and thus is sometimes omitted from the orthographic representation (see Matthewson 2005:13; van Eijk 1997:5; and Davis 2009 for further discussion).

Writing Systems

There have been four orthographies (writing systems) used to document the St'át'imc language.

An earlier orthography developed by Randy Bouchard in 1970 and slightly revised in 1973 is used, according to van Eijk (1997:251), by only the oldest generation of speakers, many of whom have passed away. This orthography appears in the two versions of Bouchard's paper "How to Write the Lillooet Language." A comparison chart with the current practical orthography (developed by van Eijk and detailed below) is given in van Eijk (1978:44).

The orthography used in Bouchard and Kennedy (1977) was designed as a rough guide to pronunciation for English speakers. It varies from both Bouchard's previous orthography and current orthographies. No key is given in Bouchard and Kennedy, and thus the pronunciation of some forms cannot be reconstructed, especially because many are personal or geographical names (personal communication with Jan van Eijk, May 2010). However, it is apparent that the capitalization Bouchard uses in this publication represents stress (the prominence of one syllable over others, see above).

In his published grammar of the Lillooet language, van Eijk uses a version of the Americanist Phonetic Alphabet, described in detail in van Eijk (1997). A correspondence with the practical orthography and discussion can be found in Matthewson (2005:11-14) and in van Eijk (1997:251-52).

The practical orthography that is in general use in both the Upper and Lower St'át'imc communities as well as by linguists in various linguistic publications on the St'át'imc language was developed by Jan van Eijk in conjunction with the Mount Currie community in 1974 and is discussed in van Eijk (1978). This orthography is used in Matthewson's (2005) compilation of oral narratives of St'át'imcets speakers, in Davis' (2006) teaching grammar of the language, and in the intermediate St'át'imcets dictionary developed by members of the St'át'imc community (Davis 2009).

Pronunciation Guide

The following charts (adapted from descriptions in Davis 2009; Matthewson 2005; and van Eijk 1997) list the symbols used in the current St'át'imcets (ST') practical orthography, a brief description of their pronunciation, and their corresponding representations in the Americanist Phonetic Alphabet (APA) and International Phonetic Alphabet (IPA). When separate symbols for IPA and APA are not given, the symbol(s) should be understood as being the same in both alphabets. In some cases, more than one symbol appears, and they are separated by a slash. They should be understood as variants of the same symbol. Where the ST' symbol and the APA symbol differ from that used in van Eijk (1997), the differences are noted in the "Linguistic symbols" column with *JVE* (see also discussion in Matthewson 2005:13-14). Refer to Davis (2009) for detailed discussion of St'át'imcets pronunciation.

The charts below are presented in two sections: consonants and vowels. The consonants are ordered according to the symbols of the English alphabet, with the exception of the glottal stop, which appears first. For sounds that are found in English, example words are given. For other sounds, a brief description, along with the linguistic terms used to describe those sounds, is given. Audio recordings of the sounds represented by the IPA symbols below can be found on the International Phonetic Association's website. Audio recordings of St'át'imcets words can be found on the First Voices website. Sample recordings of both dialects are archived on the site as Northern St'át'imc and Líl'wat.

CONSONANTS

ST' symbol	Pronunciation	Linguistic symbols (APA and IPA)
7	The glottal stop is made by closing the vocal cords and then opening them again. We find this sound in English in between the vowel sounds in the word *uh-oh*.	[ʔ]
c	This is a voiceless velar fricative, which is pronounced in roughly the same place of the mouth as the English *k*, though slightly more forward, but as though you were blowing through it, as in the final sound in the German word *ich*.	[x]
cw	This is pronounced like the *c* (see above), but with rounded lips.	[xʷ]
g	This is a voiced uvular fricative, a sound not found in English but found in languages such as French, Dutch, and German. It is a continuous sound pronounced in the same place as St'át'imcets' *q* (see below), which is farther back in the mouth than the English *k*, but with vibrating vocal folds.	[ʁ], JVE: [ʕ]¹

g'	This is pronounced in the same way as the *g* (see above), but with glottalization.	[ʁ̇] / [ʁ'], JVE: [ʕ']
gw	This is pronounced in the same way as the *g* (see above), but with rounded lips.	[ʁʷ], JVE: [ʕʷ]
g'w	This is pronounced in the same way as the *gw* (see above), but with glottalization.	[ʁ̇ʷ] / [ʁ'ʷ], JVE: [ʕ'ʷ]
h	Pronounced like the English *h* (as in the initial sound of the English words *happy, hot*).	[h]
k	Pronounced like the English *k* (as in the initial sound of the English words *key, keep*).	[k]
k'	Pronounced like the English *k* (see above), but with glottalization, which results in a popping sound.	[k̓] / [k']
kw	Pronounced like the English *k* (see above), but with with rounded lips (as in the English words *quarter, quick*).	[kʷ]
k'w	Pronounced like the English *kw* (see above), but with glottalization, which results in a popping sound.	[k̓ʷ] / [k'ʷ]
l	Pronounced like the English *l* (as in the initial sound of the English words *lip, lake*).	[l]
ḻ	Pronounced like the English *l* but retracted, pronounced with the tongue root slightly farther back in the mouth (similar to the English *l* when it occurs at the end of syllables, as in the English words *fool, hill*).	APA: [ḻ] / [ḻ], IPA: [ḻ]², JVE: [ḻ]
l'	Pronounced like the English *l* (see above), but with glottalization.	[l̓] / [l']
ḻ'	Pronounced like the English *l* (see above), but with glottalization.	APA: [ḻ'] / [ḻ̓], IPA [ḻ'], JVE: [ḻ']
lh	This is a lateral fricative that is pronounced by "blowing through" the sound *l*, touching the tongue to the ridge behind your teeth and pushing air along both sides of the tongue, without any vibrations of the vocal cords.	APA: [ɬ] / [ɬ], IPA: [ɬ], JVE: [ɬ]
m	Pronounced like the English *m* (as in the initial sound in the English words *mother, many*).	[m]
m'	Pronounced like the English *m* (see above) but with glottalization. This is similar to some pronunciations of *m* in the English word	[m̓] / [m']

	something, or the *m* of the English word *uh-uh* when pronounced with the lips closed.	
n	Pronounced like the English *n* (as in the initial sound in the English words *not, nap*).	[n]
n'	Pronounced like the English *n* (see above), but with glottalization.	[ṅ] / [n']
p	Pronounced like the English *p* (as in the initial sound in the English words *pit, play*).	[p]
p'	Pronounced like the English *p* (see above), but with glottalization, which results in a popping sound.	[ṗ] / [p']
q	This is a voiceless uvular stop that is similar to the English *k* but pronounced farther back in the mouth. It is pronounced by touching the uvula (the cone-shaped fleshy bit hanging in the back of the mouth) to the back of the tongue.	[q]
q'	Pronounced like the *q* (see above), but with glottalization, which results in a popping sound.	[q̇] / [q']
qw	Pronounced like the *q* (see above), but with rounded lips.	[qʷ]
q'w	Pronounced like the *qw* (see above), but with glottalization, which results in a popping sound.	[q̇ʷ] / [q'ʷ]
r	This is a voiced velar fricative. It is pronounced in the same place as the St'át'imcets *c* above, but with vibrating vocal cords.	[ɣ]
r'	Pronounced like the *r* (see above), but with glottalization.	[ɣ̇] / [ɣ']
s	Pronounced like the English *sh* (as in the initial sound in the English words *shoe, shade*).	APA: [š], IPA: [ʃ], JVE: [s][3]
s̲	Pronounced like the English *s* (as in the initial sound in the English words *sit, sack*).	APA: [s̲] / [ṣ] IPA: [ṣ][4], JVE: [s][5]
t	Pronounced like the English *t* (as in the initial sound in the English words *top, tap*).	[t][6]
t'	This is a glottalized lateral affricate. It is pronounced as a combination of a glottalized *t* at the onset, but with a lateral fricative *lh* release. It is similar to the medial sound in the English word *meatless.*	APA: [ƛ̓], IPA: [tɬ']
ts	Pronounced like the English *ch* (as in the initial and final sound of the English word *church*).	APA: [č], IPA: [tʃ], JVE: [c][7]

ts	Pronounced like the final sound in the English word *cats*.	APA: [c̱] / [c̨]
		IPA: [tʂ][8], JVE: [c̨][9]
ts'	Pronounced like the final sound in the English word *cats*, but with glottalization, which results in a popping sound.	APA: [c̓] / [c̓],
		IPA [ts'][10]
w	Pronounced like the English *w* (as in the initial sound of the English words *woman, wash*).	[w]
w'	Pronounced like the English *w* (see above), but with glottalization.	[ẇ] / [w']
x	This is a voiceless uvular fricative that is pronounced in the same place as the *q* above, but as though you were continuing it. It is like the sound made when clearing your throat.	APA: [x̌], IPA [χ]
xw	Pronounced like the *x* (see above), but with rounded lips.	APA: [x̌ʷ],
		IPA [χʷ]
y	Pronounced like the English *y* (as in the initial sound of the English words *yes, you*).	APA: [y], IPA [j]
y'	Pronounced like the English *y* (see above), but with glottalization.	APA: [ẏ], IPA [j']
z	Pronounced somewhere in between the English *z* (as in the initial sound of the English words *zip, zoo*) and the voiced *th* (as in the initial sound of the English words *this, there,* but NOT like the initial sound of the English words *thin or thick*).	[z][11]
z'	Pronounced like the *z* (see above), but with glottalization.	[ż] / [z']

NOTES:

1 The JVE symbol is a voiced pharyngeal fricative, which is found in Southern Interior Salish languages, such as Okanagan and Moses Columbia. Van Eijk (1997: 253n2) suggests that *g* in St'át'imcets "resembles the uvular trill in French 'rouge' or German 'rot,' but is ... pronounced further back." The status of *g* as a uvular resonant is confirmed in Namdaran's (2006) phonetic study. The symbol is included here since it is used in van Eijk's orthography. See also the glottalized and rounded variants.

2 Retraction is also represented in the IPA with underlining (e.g., [l̠]).

3 See Matthewson (2005:13-14) for discussion of [s] and [c] versus [ṣ] and [č].

4 Note that the IPA symbol for English *s* in *sit* is [s].

5 Van Eijk (1997:3, and personal communication with the author, May 2010) suggests that the APA/IPA symbol for St'át'imcets *s̱* is [s̺].

6 Caldecott (2009) lists the IPA symbol for St'át'imcets *t* as [t̺], which corresponds to Davis' (2009) description of this sound as being slightly farther forward in the mouth than English *t*.

7 See Note 4.

8 Note that the IPA symbol for *ts* sound in the English word *cats* is [ts] and the APA symbol is [c].

9 Van Eijk (1997:3, and personal communication with the author, May 2010) suggests that the APA/IPA symbol for St'át'imcets *ts̲* is [ɕ] (see also Footnote 5).

10 Following Namdaran (2006), Caldecott (2009) includes a retracted version of this sound in her inventory of St'át'imcets sounds, which is not included in van Eijk (1997), Matthewson (2005), or Davis (2009).

11 Note that the IPA symbol for the *th* sound in the English word *this* is [ð]. The difference in pronunciation of the St'át'imcets *z* strongly correlates with dialect variation: it is closer to [z] in the Upper dialect and closer to [ð] in the Lower dialect.

As Davis (2009:4.2.6) notes, the pronunciation of vowels in St'át'imcets is "highly sensitive to the consonants that surround them." As well, variation among speakers in vowel pronunciation is also observed. Thus, the guide below gives a general description of the pronunciation of the eight vowels in the language. However, to master correct pronunciation of St'át'imcets vowels, it is, as Davis states, "essential to understand how different consonants affect vowel quality." For example, all St'át'imcets vowels are produced with lip rounding when they immediately precede a rounded consonant.

VOWELS

ST' symbol	Pronunciation	Linguistic symbols (APA and IPA)
a	Pronounced somewhere in between the English vowel sounds in the words *led* and *bad*.	[æ] / [ɛ]; JVE [a][1]
ao	Pronounced like the beginning of the vowel sound in the English word *buy*.	APA: [a̲], IPA: [a][2] JVE: [a̲]
e	Generally pronounced like the short reduced vowel found in the English words *about*, *Canada* (but can vary depending on the neighbouring consonants – see above).[3]	[ə] (schwa)
v	Pronounced like the vowel sound in the English words *cut*, *luck*.	APA: [ə̲], IPA: [ʌ] JVE: [ə̲]
i	Pronounced like the vowel sound in the English words *bait*, *fate* (but without the *y* sound after the vowel), but also like the vowel sound in the English words *beet*, *steam* (but without the *y* sound after the vowel).	[e] [i][4]

ii	Sometimes pronounced like the vowel sound in the English words *led*, *end* (like St'át'imcets *a* above). Sometimes pronounced like the vowel sound in the English words *bait*, *fate*, but without the *y* sound after the vowel (like one of the pronunciations of St'át'imcets *i* above). Pronunciation is dependent on the neighbouring sounds.	APA: [i̱], IPA: [ɛ], [e], JVE: [i̱]
u	Pronounced like the vowel sound in the English words *coat*, *code* (but without the *w* sound that follows the vowel, and thus closer to the pronunciation described for St'á'timcets *o* below); also pronounced like the vowel sound in the English words *coot*, *shoe* (but without the *w* sound that follows the vowel).	[o] [u]⁵
o	Pronounced like the vowel sound in the English words *cord*, *short*.	APA: [u̱], IPA: [ɔ], JVE: [u̱]

NOTES:

1 Caldecott (2009) lists the IPA symbol for St'át'imcets *a* as [æ]; van Eijk states that *a* is "broadly" [ɛ].

2 Caldecott (2009) lists the IPA symbol for St'át'imcets *ao* as [ɑ].

3 H. Davis (personal communication with the author, November 2010) suggests that in its least marked form, St'át'imcets *e* is pronounced like the vowel sound in the English word *sit*, which is represented with the symbol [ɪ] in both the APA and IPA.

4 The two sounds here also correspond to a dialect difference: [i] in the Upper dialect and [e] in the Lower dialect (see Davis 2009; Caldecott 2009). Caldecott (2009) lists the IPA symbol for St'át'imcets *i* as [ɪ].

5 The two sounds here also correspond to a dialect difference: [u] in the Upper dialect and [o] in the Lower dialect (see Davis 2009; Caldecott 2009).

SAMPLE WORDS

Orthographic representation	IPA	Gloss
St'át'imc	[ʃtl'ɛ́tl'imx]	ʃtl'ɛ́tl'imx
Líl'wat	[líl'wɛt]	Mount Currie
s7ístken	[ʃʔíʃtkən]	pithouse
scet' (Sh-HIT-tl in the Bouchard and Kennedy orthography)	[ʃxətl']	fishing rocks near Fountain Reserve

Notes on Sources

Chapter 1: Introduction

The British Columbia Interior Plateau has been described in many publications. A good source book is Cannings and Cannings (1996). Alexander (1992a, 1992b) provides an excellent overview of the Mid-Fraser landscape from the standpoint of food and nonfood resources used by the St'át'imc.

There are a number of key sources on the St'át'imc people. The classic St'át'imc ethnography is Teit (1906). Additional insight can be gained from several of Teit's other ethnographies (e.g., 1900, 1909). Kennedy and Bouchard have written a number of significant ethnographic works (e.g., Bouchard and Kennedy 1977; Kennedy and Bouchard 1978, 1992, 1998). Additional studies were undertaken by Romanoff (1985, 1992) and Turner (1992). Diana Alexander (1992b, 2000) led ethnoarchaeological studies of St'át'imc land use and subsistence practices during the 1980s and '90s.

Smith (1998) provides an accessible review of St'át'imc history. Kennedy and Bouchard (1998) provide another short history. A more exhaustive review of British Columbia First Nations history during the 18th and 19th centuries can be found in Fisher (1977).

There are many introductory archaeology textbooks that cover the basics of archaeological terminology, methods, and theories. Several recent examples include Fagan (2009), Feder (2004), and Renfrew and Bahn (2008). The systematics of Canadian Plateau culture history is covered by Richards and Rousseau (1987), Rousseau (2004), and Stryd and Rousseau (1996).

Archaeologists have discussed inference in many publications (e.g., Watson 2008). Famous examples of those that outline major issues and provide recognized frameworks include Binford (1981, 1983, 2001), Hodder (1982, 1992), and Wobst (1978). Bettinger (1992) provides a useful review, specifically in reference to hunter-gatherers. Carlson et al. (2010) summarize issues associated with archaeological inference and artistic creations.

Archaeologists who study hunter-gatherers approach the record from a wide range of theoretical perspectives (see Bentley, Maschner, and Chippindale 2008 for an extensive review of theory in archaeology) that are often ecologically oriented (see, e.g., Bettinger 1992 and

Kelly 1995). However, there is increasing interest in understanding hunter-gatherers from new historical, cultural, and evolutionary viewpoints (see, e.g., Prentiss et al. 2009 and Sassaman and Holly 2011).

Chapter 2: Before the Villages

Niles Eldredge (e.g. 1985, 1999) has published many significant works on evolutionary process. Important early investigations in Plateau archaeology were conducted by Borden (1961), Butler (1961, 1965), and Sanger (1970). The most recent thoughts on the origins of the Western Stemmed and Old Cordilleran cultural traditions can be found in Beck and Jones (2010), Chatters et al. (2012), and Prentiss and Clarke (2008).

Middle Holocene climate change is a complex subject that is summarized for the Plateau region by Chatters (1995, 1998) and Chatters, Butler, and Scott et al. (1995).

Most field research concerning the Nesikep tradition has been conducted in cultural resource management contexts. Kuijt (1989), Stryd and Rousseau (1996), and Rousseau (2004) provide overviews of this research. Prentiss and Kuijt (2004) provide summary data from a number of sites. Research on the Old Cordilleran has been conducted primarily in the coastal context and is most often associated with academic (non-Cultural Resource Management) projects. Matson and Coupland (1995) provide a good summary of much of this material. Additional sources include Chatters et al. (2010), Matson (1996), and Pokotylo and Mitchell (1998).

Prentiss and Chatters (2003a, 2003b, and see also Chatters 2009; Chatters and Prentiss 2005; and Prentiss 2009) present evidence for a dramatic cultural evolutionary process in the Middle Holocene period, throughout the Pacific Northwest region. They point to the development of unique cultural patterns in many key areas, including the Columbia Plateau (Chatters 1995), the Canadian Plateau (Prentiss and Kuijt 2004), the Gulf Islands and Fraser Valley (Lepofsky et al. 2009; Matson and Coupland 1995; Ormerod 2002; Schaepe 2003), and Haida Gwaii (Christensen and Stafford 2005; Mackie and Acheson 2005). There has not yet been a published counterargument to Prentiss and Chatters' diversification and decimation hypothesis. Although many archaeologists of the Pacific Northwest seem to rely on an implicit assumption of continuous and gradual change, data from the region suggest a far more punctuated pattern. We believe that although some interpretive details of specific cultural patterns may change, the wider pattern of rapid Middle Holocene diversification followed by equally sudden cultural constriction will likely hold up under further research.

The earliest groups to use a collector-like strategy on the central Coast are identified by archaeologists as the Locarno Beach phase. The term *collector* is derived from the work of Lewis Binford (1980; see also Ames 2002). The best sources on the Locarno Beach phase are probably broad summaries of regional prehistory (Ames and Maschner 1999; Matson and Coupland 1995) and Matson (1989). Early collectors on the Plateau are recognized as the Pithouse II culture of the Columbia Plateau (Chatters 1995; Prentiss, Chatters, and Lenert et al. 2005), the Shuswap horizon of the Canadian Plateau (Prentiss and Kuijt 2004; Richards and Rousseau 1987; Rousseau 2004), and the Upper Columbia Collector I period (Goodale et al. 2004, 2008). Discussion and debates over the interpretation of the Baker site can be found in Prentiss and Kuijt (2004), Rousseau (2004), Stryd and Rousseau (1996), and Wilson (1992). Chisholm (1986) outlines the results of isotope studies supporting higher salmon consumption by Shuswap horizon collectors.

Chapter 3: The Early House Societies

Our short review of Fraser Valley paleoecology and archaeology draws most heavily on the important work of Dana Lepofsky, Michael Blake, and colleagues. Lepofsky et al. (2009) provide an overview of major village sites. Lepofsky et al. (2000) is the primary open literature publication of the Scowlitz or Qithyil site. Lepofsky et al. (2005) provide a detailed review of Fraser Valley and southern Coast Range paleoecology and culture history from 1,000 to 3,000 years ago. Lenert (2007) is the best source on the Katz site.

The Marpole phase of central Northwest Coast prehistory has been extensively studied and remains extremely important for a complete understanding of regional prehistory. Unfortunately, given the focus of this book on Canadian Plateau archaeology, we are unable to provide it with detailed coverage. Some key sources on the Marpole phase include Burley (1980), Burley and Knüsel (1989), Grier (2001), Matson (1983), and Matson and Coupland (1995).

The archaeology of early villages associated with the Graham tradition on Haida Gwaii is summarized by Mackie and Acheson (2005). Research by Andrew Martindale and colleagues in the Prince Rupert Harbour area has been critical for refining our understanding of the culture history of this important segment of the Northwest Coast. Some recent theses and publications include Martindale and Marsden (2003), Ruggles (2009), and Stewart et al. (2009).

Our discussion of Canadian Plateau archaeology during the period between 1,500 and 2,500 years ago draws heavily from field studies presented by Wilson and Carlson (1980). We also rely on regional overviews in Pokotylo and Mitchell (1998), Prentiss, Chatters, and Lenert, et al. (2005), Richards and Rousseau (1987), and Rousseau (2004). Debates about the Plateau interaction sphere are discussed in Hayden and Schulting (1997) and Rousseau (2004).

The Columbia Plateau archaeology of the same period is summarized in Ames et al. (1998), Andrefsky (2004), Chatters (2004), and Prentiss, Chatters, and Lenert, et al. (2005). The best discussion of Columbia Basin bison hunting is Chatters, Campbell, and Smith et al. (1995; see also Chatters 2004). Chatters (2004) summarizes evidence for violence on the Plateau. Archaeology of the Upper Columbia drainage and the Slocan Narrows site is summarized by Goodale et al. (2004, 2008).

Chapter 4: The Rise of the Mid-Fraser Villages

The best sources on the construction of traditional Mid-Fraser house forms include Alexander (2000), Kennedy and Bouchard (1978, 1998; Bouchard and Kennedy 1977), and Teit (1900, 1906). Ames (2006) offers an important perspective on issues associated with the persistence of Northwest Coast households. Recent reviews of Northwest Coast household archaeology include Matson et al.(2003) and Sobel et al. (2006).

Arnoud Stryd's (1973) PhD dissertation remains the best source on the archaeology of the Bell site. A review of known Mid-Fraser villages with and without significant excavation can be found in Morin et al. (2008-9).

Hayden and Cannon (1982) review the archaeological implications of the corporate group concept. A good recent review of the archaeology of the Ozette site is found in Samuels (2006).

Archaeological research at the Keatley Creek site has been published extensively. Hayden (2000a, 2000b) provides overviews of work conducted in the core village by teams from

Simon Fraser University. Hayden reviews the results of his dating studies in several publications (1997, 2000c, 2005; Hayden and Mathewes 2009). The revised stratigraphic assessments and the dating of Keatley Creek deposits by University of Montana teams are found in Prentiss et al. (2003) and Prentiss, Lenert, Foor and Goodale (2005). Harris (2004) analyzes and describes Subhousepit 3 in depth.

Early research at the Bridge River site can be found in Stryd (1974, 1980). Detailed results of geophysical investigations and archaeological testing and radiocarbon dating at Bridge River are outlined in Prentiss et al. (2008).

The issues of packing and warfare in Plateau villages are discussed in Chatters (2004). Mid-Fraser warfare is discussed by Cannon (1992) and Sakaguchi et al. (2010). Kew (1992) discusses variability in Mid-Fraser salmon populations and its implications for traditional fishing.

The population pressure model of village growth in the Pacific Northwest is best explicated by Cohen (1981). Lohse and Sammons-Lohse (1985) apply a version of this argument to the Columbia Plateau. Hayden (1981; see also Hayden and Mathewes 2009) provides a technological determinist model of village emergence.

Macroevolutionary perspectives on culture change and village development are outlined in Prentiss et al. (2009). The concepts of locked cultural strategies and punctuated change are discussed by Chatters (2009), Kuijt and Prentiss (2009), Prentiss (2009), and Prentiss and Lenert (2009). Prentiss, Chatters, and Lenert et al. (2005) and Prentiss (2009) discuss the rise and spread of complex collectors.

Chapter 5: Hunting, Gathering, and Fishing

We consulted a number of references on Pacific salmon. A good general overview of salmon biology is found in Quinn (2005). Important works on salmon fishing in the Mid-Fraser region include Kew (1992), Kennedy and Bouchard (1978, 1992), Romanoff (1985), and Teit (1900, 1906).

The effects of climate and oceanographic conditions on salmon populations are discussed in Finney et al. (2002, 2010), Benson and Trites (2002), and Mueter, Peterman, and Pyper (2002). Evidence for variability in eastern Pacific marine productivity and its potential effects on fish stocks during the later Holocene period is presented in many sources, including Finney et al. (2002), Hay et al. (2007), Patterson et al. (2005), and Tunnicliffe et al.(2001). Evidence for climate change and its impact on Columbia Basin salmon populations during the Holocene period is presented in Chatters, Butler, and Scott et al. (1995).

Traditional hunting practices are reviewed by Alexander (1992b, 2000), Romanoff (1992), and Teit (1900, 1906).

A number of works explore Mid-Fraser ethnobotany and paleoethnobotany. Nancy Turner has published the essential works on western Canadian Plateau ethnobotany (e.g., Turner 1992, 1997; Turner et al. 1990). Important publications on paleoethnobotany include Lepofsky (2000), Lepofsky and Peacock (2004), Peacock (1998), and Pokotylo and Froese (1983).

Ethnographic descriptions of traditional technology are found in Alexander (1992b, 2000), Bouchard and Kennedy (1977), Kennedy and Bouchard (1978), 1992, 1998), Magne (1985), Morice (1893), and Teit (1900, 1906, 1909).

Hayden's approach to subsistence at Keatley Creek resulted in innovative research into variability in housepit subsistence economies. Important sources include Hayden (1997), Kusmer (2000a, 2000b), Lepofsky (2000), and Lepofsky et al. (1996).

Evidence for temporal change in subsistence at Keatley Creek is presented in Lepofsky and Peacock (2004) and Prentiss et al. (2007). Bridge River subsistence analyses are currently in process, and no formal publications have yet been produced.

Discussion of Mid-Fraser villages as gateway communities is found in Hayden et al. (1985). Chisholm (1986) outlines the results of isotope analyses of human remains from the Late Period that suggest the regular consumption of salmon.

Chapter 6: Living Together

Complex hunter-gatherers in the western Arctic are described by Sheehan (1985). The Chumash people at the time of European contact are described in detail by Gamble (2008). The Calusa are known from the work of Marquardt (1991).

There is an extensive literature on ranked societies. Ames (2008) provides a good archaeological overview. Concepts of scale and organization in ranked societies are discussed by Johnson (1982). Price and Feinman (1995) and Arnold (1996b) (and chapters therein) provide good discussions of archaeological issues associated with the development of social status inequality and ranking. Historical and evolutionary perspectives on social change are provided in Prentiss et al. (2009) and Sassaman and Holly (2011). Arnold (1996a) and Sassaman (2004) provide good reviews of archaeological research into complex hunter-gatherer societies. Recent thoughts on the development of inequality are summarized in Bowles et al. (2010). Egalitarianism in hunter-gatherer contexts is best explicated in Lee's (1969) famous article, "Eating Christmas in the Kalahari."

Social organization in traditional villages of the Mid-Fraser region is discussed in Alexander (2000), Hayden (1994, 1995, 1997; Hayden et al. 1985), and Teit (1900, 1906). Social complexity in the Lower Fraser Canyon is proposed by Schaepe (2006). Higher-order political organizations in the Mid-Fraser are proposed by Hayden and Ryder (1991). Schulting (1995) reviews evidence from burials.

Evidence for variability in the social standing of pithouses at Keatley Creek is reviewed by Hayden (1997, 2000b). This conclusion is based on a number of studies, including Hayden et al. (1996), Hayden and Spafford (1993), Lepofsky et al. (1996), and Spafford (1991). Debates over the timing and causality of social inequality at Keatley Creek have developed from studies by Prentiss and colleagues at Housepit 7 (Prentiss et al. 2003, 2007; Prentiss, Lenert, Foor, and Goodale 2005), suggesting a later development. Studies about dog remains are reviewed by Crellin (1994) and Crellin and Heffner (2000).

Research at the Bridge River site has produced evidence of growth and the emergence of complex society (Prentiss et al. 2008). Ongoing research into social evolution at Bridge River has yet to be published in the primary literature.

Chapter 7: The Abandonment

Collapse is a popular topic among archaeologists and the general public. An excellent analysis is provided by Tainter (1988). Kirch (1997, 2000) reviews Polynesian examples (including Rapa Nui).

Hayden and Ryder (1991) proposed the major abandonment of Mid-Fraser villages. The most precise dating of these abandonments is found in Prentiss et al. (2003, 2008). Additional evidence is compiled and presented by Lenert (2001). Kuijt (2001) suggests an alternative to Hayden and Ryder's landslide-induced abandonment hypothesis. Hayden and Ryder (2003) favour explanatory frameworks based on regional earthquakes and presumed disasters elsewhere. Kuijt and Prentiss (2004) and Prentiss et al. (2007) point to subsistence resource depression as a significant issue associated with abandonment.

Abundant evidence exists for a significant regime change in the eastern Pacific around 1,100 to 1,200 years ago that reduced fish populations, including salmon (Finney et al. 2002; Hay et al. 2007; Patterson et al. 2005; and Tunnicliffe et al. 2001). A variety of other data sources – including Columbia River hydrology and fisheries, glaciology, pollen studies, and fire histories – provide strong evidence for regional warming and drought during the Medieval Warm period, which extended from around 1,200 to 650 years ago (see, e.g., Chatters, Butler, and Scott et al. 1995; Chatters and Leavell 1995; Hallett and Walker 2000; Reyes and Clague 2004). Medieval Warm period village abandonments elsewhere on the Plateau and central Coast are discussed in Chatters (2004); Goodale et al. (2008); Kuijt (2001); Kuijt and Prentiss (2004); Matson and Coupland (1995); and Prentiss, Chatters, and Lenert et al. (2005).

The Bridge River site features a relatively extensive late pre-European and early European contact period village (Prentiss et al. 2008). Keatley Creek also appears to have been occupied during the Late Period. The most extensive work on the Keatley Creek site emphasizes the existence of small structures on the margins of the major village (see, e.g., Hayden and Adams 2004; Morin 2006; Muir et al. 2008). Many other smaller sites were undoubtedly occupied during the Late Period as well (see Morin et al. 2008-9; Rousseau 2004; Sakaguchi et al. 2010; and Stryd 1973, 1974, 1980).

Chapter 8: A Broad Perpective

Trefor Smith (1998) offers an accessible history of the St'át'imc. Kennedy and Bouchard (1998) provide additional historical documentation.

Janetski (1997) provides a good example of Fremont subsistence intensification, resource depression, and village abandonment.

Simon Fraser's journal is published in Lamb (1960).

References

Alexander, Diana. 1992a. "Environmental Units." In *A Complex Culture of the British Columbia Plateau,* ed. Brian Hayden, 47-98. Vancouver: UBC Press.

—. 1992b. "Prehistoric Land Use in the Mid-Fraser Area Based on Ethnographic Data." In *A Complex Culture of the British Columbia Plateau,* ed. Brian Hayden, 99-176. Vancouver: UBC Press.

—. 2000. "Pithouses on the Interior Plateau of British Columbia: Ethnographic Evidence and Interpretation of the Keatley Creek Site." In *The Ancient Past of Keatley Creek,* vol. 2, *Socioeconomy,* ed. Brian Hayden, 29-66. Burnaby: Archaeology Press.

Ames, Kenneth M. 2002. "Going by Boat: The Forager-Collector Continuum at Sea." In *Beyond Foraging and Collecting: Evolutionary Change in Hunter-Gatherer Settlement Systems,* ed. Ben Fitzhugh and Junko Habu, 19-52. New York: Kluwer Academic/Plenum.

—. 2006. "Thinking about Household Archaeology on the Northwest Coast." In *Household Archaeology on the Northwest Coast,* ed. Elizabeth A. Sobel, D. Ann Trieu Gahr, and Kenneth M. Ames, 16-36. Ann Arbor: International Monographs in Prehistory Archaeological, Series 16.

—. 2008. "The Archaeology of Rank." In *Handbook of Archaeological Theories,* ed. R. Alexander Bentley, Herbert D.G. Maschner, and Christopher Chippindale, 487-514. Lanham: Altamira Press.

Ames, Kenneth M., Don E. Dumond, Jerry R. Galm, and Rick Minor. 1998. "Prehistory of the Southern Plateau." In *Handbook of North American Indians,* vol. 12, *The Plateau,* ed. Deward E. Walker Jr., 103-19. Washington, DC: Smithsonian Institution.

Ames, Kenneth M., and Herbert D.G. Maschner. 1999. *Peoples of the Northwest Coast: Their Archaeology and Prehistory.* London: Thames and Hudson.

Andrefsky, William, Jr. 2004. "Materials and Contexts for a Culture History of the Columbia Plateau." In *Complex Hunter-Gatherers: Evolution and Organization of Prehistoric Communities on the Plateau of Northwestern North America,* ed. William C. Prentiss and Ian Kuijt, 23-35. Salt Lake City: University of Utah Press.

Arnold, Jeanne E. 1996a. "The Archaeology of Complex Hunter-Gatherers." *Journal of Archaeological Method and Theory* 3: 77-126.

–, ed. 1996b. *Emergent Complexity: The Evolution of Intermediate Societies*. Ann Arbor: International Monographs in Prehistory.

Beck, Charlotte, and George T. Jones. 2010. "Clovis and Western Stemmed: Population Migration and the Meeting of Two Technologies in the Intermountain West." *American Antiquity* 75, 81-116.

Benson, Ashleen J., and Andrew W. Trites. 2002. "Ecological Effects of Regime Shifts in the Bering Sea and Eastern Pacific Ocean." *Fish and Fisheries* 3, 95-113.

Bentley, R. Alexander, Herbert D.G. Maschner, and Christopher Chippindale, eds. 2008. *Handbook of Archaeological Theories*. Lanham: Altamira Press.

Bessell, Nicola. 1998. "Phonetic Aspects of Retraction in Interior Salish." In *Salish Languages and Linguistics: Theoretical and Descriptive Perspectives,* ed. Ewa Czaykowska-Higgins and M. Dale Kinkade, 125-52. New York: Mouton de Gruyter.

Bettinger, Robert L. 1992. *Hunter-Gatherers: Archaeological and Evolutionary Theory*. New York: Plenum.

Binford, Lewis R. 1980. "Willow Smoke and Dog's Tails: Hunter-Gatherer Settlement Systems and Archaeological Site Formation." *American Antiquity* 45, 4-20.

–. 1981. *Bones: Ancient Men and Modern Myths*. New York: Academic Press.

–. 1983. *In Pursuit of the Past*. London: Thames and Hudson.

–. 2001. *Constructing Frames of Reference*. Berkeley: University of California Press.

Bird, Sonya, and Marion Caldecott. 2004. "Timing Differences in St'át'imcets Glottalised Resonants: Linguistic or Biomechanical?" In *Proceedings of the 10th Australian International Conference on Speech Science and Technology,* Macquarie University, Sydney, Australia, 328-33.

Bird, Sonya, Marion Caldecott, Fiona Campbell, Bryan Gick, and Patricia Shaw. 2008. "Oral-Laryngeal Timing in Glottalised Resonants." *Journal of Phonetics* 36, 492-507.

Borden, Charles. 1961. *Fraser River Archaeological Project: Progress Report*. Anthropology Papers No. 1. Ottawa: National Museum of Man.

Bouchard, Randy. 1973. "How to Write the Lillooet Language." British Columbia Indian Language Project, Victoria.

Bouchard, Randy, and Dorothy I.D. Kennedy, eds. 1977. *Lillooet Stories*. Sound Heritage Series 6, 1. Victoria: Aural History, Provincial Archives of British Columbia.

Bowles, Samuel, Eric A. Smith, and Monique Borgerhoff Mulder. 2010. "The Emergence and Persistence of Inequality in Premodern Societies." *Current Anthropology* 51, 7-17.

Burley, David V. 1980. *Marpole: Anthropological Reconstructions of a Prehistoric Northwest Coast Culture Type*. Burnaby: Simon Fraser University, Department of Anthropology.

Burley, David, and Christopher Knüsel. 1989. "Burial Patterns and Archaeological Interpretation: Problems in the Recognition of Ranked Society in the Coast Salish Region." In *Development of Hunting-Fishing-Gathering Maritime Societies along the West Coast of North America,* ed. Blukas Onat. Seattle: Washington State University Press.

Butler, B. Robert. 1961. *The Old Cordilleran Culture in the Pacific Northwest, with an Appendix by Earl Swanson Jr*. Occasional Papers 5. Pocatello: Idaho State College Museum.

–. 1965. "The Structure and Function of the Old Cordilleran Culture Concept." *American Anthropologist* 67, 1120-31.

Caldecott, Marion. 2004. "A Preliminary Look at Glottalized Resonants in St'át'imcets." In *Studies in Salish Linguistics in Honour of M. Dale Kinkade,* ed. Donna B. Gerdts and Lisa Matthewson, 43-57. University of Montana Occasional Papers in Linguistics, no. 17. Missoula: University of Montana.

–. 2009. "Non-Exhaustive Parsing: Phonetic and Phonological Evidence from St'át'imcets." Doctoral dissertation, University of British Columbia.

Cannings, Richard, and Sydney Cannings. 1996. *British Columbia: A Natural History.* Vancouver: Greystone Books.

Cannon, Aubrey. 1992. "Conflict and Salmon on the Interior Plateau of British Columbia." In *A Complex Culture of the British Columbia Plateau,* ed. Brian Hayden, 506-24. Vancouver: UBC Press.

Carlson, Eric, Anna Marie Prentiss, Ian Kuijt, Nicole Crossland, and Art Adolph. 2010. "Visually Reconstructing Middle Fraser Canyon Prehistory: Redefining a Process." *SAA Archaeological Record* 10, 29-33.

Chatters, James C. 1995. "Population Growth, Climatic Cooling, and the Development of Collector Strategies on the Southern Plateau, Western North America." *Journal of World Prehistory* 9, 341-400.

–. 1998. "Environment." In *Handbook of North American Indians,* vol. 12, *The Plateau,* ed. D.E. Walker, 29-42. Washington, DC: Smithsonian Institution Press.

–. 2004. "Safety in Numbers: The Influence of the Bow and Arrow on Village Formation on the Columbia Plateau." In *Complex Hunter-Gatherers: Evolution and Organization of Prehistoric Communities on the Plateau of Northwestern North America,* ed. William C. Prentiss and Ian Kuijt, 67-83. Salt Lake City: University of Utah Press.

–. 2009. "A Macroevolutionary Perspective on the Archaeological Record of North America." In *Macroevolution in Human Prehistory: Evolutionary Theory and Processual Archaeology,* ed. Anna M. Prentiss, Ian Kuijt, and James C. Chatters, 213-34. New York: Springer.

Chatters, James C., Virginia L. Butler, M.J. Scott, D.M. Anderson, and D.A. Neitzel. 1995. "A Paleoscience Approach to Estimating the Effects of Climatic Warming on Salmonid Fisheries of the Columbia Basin." *Canadian Special Publication in Fisheries and Aquatic Sciences* 21, 489-96.

Chatters, James C., Sarah K. Campbell, G.D. Smith, and P.E. Minthorn. 1995. "Bison Procurement in the Far West: A 2100 Year Old Kill Site on the Columbia Plateau." *American Antiquity* 60, 751-63.

Chatters, James C., Steven Hackenberger, Brett Lenz, Anna M. Prentiss, and Jayne-Leigh Thomas. 2012. "The Paleoindian to Archaic Transition in the Pacific Northwest: In Situ Development or Ethnic Replacement?" In *On the Brink: Transformations in Human Organization and Adaptation at the Pleistocene-Holocene Boundary in North America,* ed. C. Britt Bousman and Bradley J. Vierra. College Station: Texas A & M Press (In Press).

Chatters, James C., and Daniel Leavell. 1995. "Harding Lake: A Study of Fire, Succession, and Sedimentation since 350 AD in the Subalpine Fir Forests of the Yaak River, Northwestern Montana." Applied Paleoscience Research Report P-4, Richland, Washington.

Chatters, James C., and William C. Prentiss. 2005. "A Darwinian Macro-Evolutionary Perspective on the Development of Hunter-Gatherer Systems in Northwestern North America." *World Archaeology* 37, 46-65.

Chisholm, Brian S. 1986. "Reconstruction of Prehistoric Diet in British Columbia Using Stable-Carbon Isotope Analysis." PhD diss., Simon Fraser University.

Christensen, T., and J. Stafford. 2005. "Raised Beach Archaeology in Northern Haida Gwaii: Preliminary Results from the Cohoe Creek Site." In *Haida Gwaii: Human History and Environment from the Time of the Loon to the Time of the Iron People,* ed. Daryl W. Fedje and Rolf W. Mathewes, 245-73. Vancouver: UBC Press.

Cohen, Nathan. 1981. "Pacific Coast Foragers: Affluent or Overcrowded." *Senri Ethnological Studies* 9, 275-95.

Crellin, David F. 1994. "Is There a Dog in the House? The Cultural Significance of Pre-historic Domesticated Dogs in the Mid-Fraser River Region of British Columbia." Master's thesis, Simon Fraser University.

Crellin, David F., and T. Heffner. 2000. "The Cultural Significance of Domesticated Dogs in Prehistoric Keatley Creek Society." In *The Ancient Past of Keatley Creek,* vol. 2, *Socio-economy,* ed. Brian Hayden, 151-66. Burnaby: Archaeology Press, Simon Fraser University.

Czaykowska-Higgins, Ewa, and M. Dale Kinkade, eds. 1998. *Salish Languages and Linguistics: Theoretical and Descriptive Perspectives.* Berlin: Mouton de Gruyter.

Davis, Henry. 2006. "A Teacher's Grammar of Upper St'át'imcets." Unpublished manuscript, University of British Columbia.

–. 2009. "Introduction." In C. Alexander, B. Frank, G. Ned, D. Peters, and R. Whitley. *Ta Nqwal'uttenlhkálha,* vol. 2, *Intermediate,* ed. H. Davis. Lillooet: Upper St'át'imc Language, Culture and Education Society.

Elredge, Niles. 1985. *Unfinished Synthesis: Biological Hierarchies and Modern Evolutionary Thought.* New York: Oxford University Press.

–. 1999. *The Pattern of Evolution.* New York: W.H. Freeman and Company.

Fagan, Brian. 2009. *In the Beginning.* New York: Pearson.

Feder, Kenneth. 2004. *Linking to the Past: A Brief Introduction to Archaeology.* Oxford: Oxford University Press.

Finney, Bruce P., Jurgen Alheit, Ya-Christian Emeis, David B. Field, Dimitri Gutierrez, and Ulrich Struck. 2010. "Paleoecological Studies of Variability in Marine Fish Populations: A Long-Term Perspective on the Impacts of Climate Change on Marine Ecosystems." *Journal of Marine Systems* 79, 316-26.

Finney, Bruce P., Irene Gregory-Eaves, Marianne S.V. Douglas, and John P. Smol. 2002. "Fisheries Productivity in the Northeastern Pacific Ocean over the Past 2,200 Years." *Nature* 416, 729-33.

Fisher, Robin, 1977. *Contact and Conflict: Indian-European Relations in British Columbia, 1774-1890.* Vancouver: UBC Press.

Gamble, Lynn H. 2008. *The Chumash World at European Contact: Power Trade and Feasting among Complex Hunter-Gatherers.* Berkeley: University of California Press.

Goodale, Nathan B., Ian Kuijt, and Anna M. Prentiss. 2008. "Demography of Prehistoric Fishing-Hunting People: A Case Study of the Upper Columbia Area." In *Recent Advances in Paleodemography: Data, Techniques, and Patterns,* ed. Jean-Pierre Bocquet-Apel, 179-207. New York: Springer-Verlag.

Goodale, Nathan B., W.C. Prentiss, and Ian Kuijt. 2004. "Cultural Complexity: A New Chronology of the Upper Columbia Drainage Area." In *Complex Hunter-Gatherers: Evolution and Organization of Prehistoric Communities on the Plateau of Northwestern North America,* ed. William C. Prentiss and Ian Kuijt, 36-48. Salt Lake City: University of Utah Press.

Grier, Colin. 2001. "The Social Economy of a Prehistoric Northwest Coast Plankhouse." PhD diss., Arizona State University.

Hallett, Douglas J., and R.C. Walker. 2000. "Paleoecology and Its Application to Fire and Vegetation Management in Kootenay National Park, British Columbia." *Journal of Paleolimnology* 24, 401-14.

Harris, Lucille E. 2004. "Subhousepit 3: Assessing the Role of a Small Semi-Subterranean Mat Lodge in Late Plateau Horizon Settlement Strategies." Master's thesis, University of Montana, Missoula.

Hay, Murray B., Audrey Dallimore, Richard E. Thomson, Stephen E. Calvert, and Reinhard Pienetz. 2007. "Siliceous Microfossil Record of Late Holocene Oceanography and Climate along the West Coast of Vancouver Island, British Columbia (Canada)." *Quaternary Research* 67, 33-49.

Hayden, Brian. 1981. "Research and Development in the Stone Age: Technological Transitions among Hunter-Gatherers." *Current Anthropology* 22, 519-48.

–. 1994. "Competition, Labor, and Complex Hunter-Gatherers." In *Key Issues in Hunter-Gatherer Research,* ed. Ernest S. Burch and Linda J. Ellana, 223-39. Oxford: Berg Press.

–. 1995. "Pathways to Power: Principles for Creating Socioeconomic Inequalities." In *Foundations of Social Inequality,* ed. T. Douglas Price and Gary M. Feinman, 15-86. New York: Plenum Press.

–. 1997. *The Pithouses of Keatley Creek.* Fort Worth: Harcourt Brace College Publishers.

–. 2000a. *The Ancient Past of Keatley Creek.* Vol. 1, *Taphonomy.* Burnaby: Archaeology Press, Simon Fraser University.

–. 2000b. *The Ancient Past of Keatley Creek.* Vol. 2, *Socioeconomy.* Burnaby: Archaeology Press, Simon Fraser University.

–. 2000c. "Dating Deposits at Keatley Creek." In *The Ancient Past of Keatley Creek,* vol. 1, *Taphonomy,* ed. Brian Hayden, 35-40. Burnaby: Archaeology Press, Simon Fraser University.

–. 2005. "Emergence of Large Villages and Large Residential Corporate Group Structures among Complex Hunter-Gatherers at Keatley Creek." *American Antiquity* 70, 169-74.

Hayden, Brian, and Ron Adams. 2004. "Ritual Structures in Transegalitarian Communities." In *Complex Hunter-Gatherers: Evolution and Organization of Prehistoric Communities on the Plateau of Northwestern North America,* ed. William C. Prentiss and Ian Kuijt, 84-102. Salt Lake City: University of Utah Press.

Hayden, Brian, Edward Bakewell, and Robert Gargett. 1996. "World's Longest-Lived Corporate Group: Lithic Analysis Reveals Prehistoric Social Organization Near Lillooet, British Columbia." *American Antiquity* 61, 341-56.

Hayden, B., and A. Cannon. 1982. "Corporate Group as an Archaeological Unit." *Journal of Anthropological Archaeology* 1, 132-58.

Hayden, B., M. Eldridge, and A. Eldridge. 1985. "Complex Hunter-Gatherers in Interior British Columbia." In *Prehistoric Hunter-Gatherers: The Emergence of Cultural Complexity,* ed. T. Douglas Price and James A. Brown, 191-99. New York: Academic Press.

Hayden, Brian, and Rolf Mathewes. 2009. "The Rise and Fall of Complex Large Villages on the British Columbian Plateau: A Geoarchaeological Controversy." *Canadian Journal of Archaeology* 33, 281-96.

Hayden, Brian, and June Ryder. 1991. "Prehistoric Cultural Collapse in the Lillooet Area." *American Antiquity* 56, 50-65.

–. 2003. "Cultural Collapses in the Northwest: A Reply to Ian Kuijt." *American Antiquity* 68, 157-160.

Hayden, Brian, and Rick Schulting. 1997. "The Plateau Interaction Sphere and Late Prehistoric Cultural Complexity." *American Antiquity* 62, 51-85.

Hayden, Brian, and James Spafford. 1993. "The Keatley Creek Site and Corporate Group Archaeology." *BC Studies* 99: 10-139.

Hodder, Ian. 1982. *The Present Past: An Introduction to Anthropology for Archaeologists.* New York: Pica Press.

–. 1992. *Theory and Practice in Archaeology.* London: Routledge.

Janetski, Joel C. 1997. "Fremont Hunting and Resource Intensification in the Eastern Great Basin." *Journal of Archaeological Science* 24, 1075-88.

Johnson, Gregory A. 1982. "Organizational Structure and Scalar Stress." In *Theory and Explanation in Archaeology*, ed. Colin Renfrew, M.J. Rowlands, and B.A. Segraves, 389-421. New York: Academic Press.

Kelly, Robert L. 1995. *The Foraging Spectrum: Diversity in Hunter-Gatherer Lifeways*. Washington, DC: Smithsonian Institution.

Kennedy, Dorothy I.D., and Randy Bouchard. 1978. "Fraser River Lillooet: An Ethnographic Summary." In *Reports of the Lillooet Archaeological Project*, No. 1, *Introduction and Setting*, ed. Arnoud H. Stryd and Stephen Lawhead, 22-55. National Museum of Man, Mercury Series. Ottawa: Archaeological Survey of Canada, Paper No. 73.

–. 1992. "Stl'átl'imx (Fraser River Lillooet) Fishing." In *A Complex Culture of the British Columbia Plateau*, ed. Brian Hayden, 266-354. Vancouver: UBC Press.

–. 1998. "Lillooet." In *Handbook of North American Indians*, vol. 12, *Plateau*, ed. Deward E. Walker Jr., 174-90. Washington, DC: Smithsonian Institution.

Kew, Michael. 1992. "Salmon Availability, Technology, and Cultural Adaptation in the Fraser River Watershed." In *A Complex Culture of the British Columbia Plateau*, ed. Brian Hayden, 177-221. Vancouver: UBC Press.

Kirch, Patrick V. 1997. "Microcosmic Histories: Island Perspectives on Global Change." *American Anthropologist* 99, 30-42.

–. 2000. *On the Road of the Winds*. Berkeley: University of California Press.

Kuijt, Ian, 1989. "Subsistence Resource Variability and Culture Change during the Middle-Late Prehistoric Cultural Transition on the Canadian Plateau." *Canadian Journal of Archaeology* 13, 97-118.

–. 2001. "Reconsidering the Cause of Cultural Collapse in the Lillooet Area of British Columbia: A Geoarchaeological Perspective." *American Antiquity* 66, 692-703.

Kuijt, Ian, and Anna Marie Prentiss. 2009. "Niche Construction, Macroevolution and the Late Epipaleolithic of the Near East." In *Macroevolution in Human Prehistory: Evolutionary Theory and Processual Archaeology*, ed. Anna Marie Prentiss, Ian Kuijt, and James C. Chatters, 253-74. New York: Springer.

Kuijt, Ian, and William C. Prentiss. 2004. "Villages on the Edge: Pithouses, Cultural Change, and the Abandonment of Aggregate Pithouse Villages." In *Complex Hunter-Gatherers: Evolution and Organization of Prehistoric Communities on the Plateau of Northwestern North America*, ed. William C. Prentiss and Ian Kuijt, 155-70. Salt Lake City: University of Utah Press.

Kusmer, Karla D. 2000a. "Animal Resource Utilization and Assemblage Formation Processes at Keatley Creek." In *The Ancient Past of Keatley Creek*, vol. 1, *Taphonomy*, ed. Brian Hayden, 135-64. Burnaby: Archaeology Press.

–. 2000b. "Archaeological Analysis at Keatley Creek: Socioeconomy." In *The Ancient Past of Keatley Creek*, vol. 2, *Socioeconomy*, ed. Brian Hayden, 119-34. Burnaby: Archaeology Press.

Lamb, W. Kaye, ed. 1966. *Simon Fraser: Letters and Journals, 1806-1808*. Toronto: MacMillan.

Lee, Richard Borshay. 1969. "Eating Christmas in the Kalahari." *Natural History* (December), 1-4.

Lenert, Michael. 2001. "Calibrated Radiocarbon Dates and Culture Change: Implications for Socio-Complexity in the Mid-Fraser Region, British Columbia." *Northwest Anthropological Research Notes* 35, 211-28.

—. 2007. "Coast Salish Household and Community Organization at Sxwoxwiymelh: An Ancient Sto:lo Village in the Upper Fraser Valley, British Columbia." PhD diss., University of California, Los Angeles.

Lepofsky, D. 2000. "Site Formation Processes at Keatley Creek." In *The Ancient Past of Keatley Creek,* vol. 1, *Taphonomy,* ed. Brian Hayden, 105-34. Burnaby: Archaeology Press.

Lepofsky, Dana, Michael Blake, Doug Brown, Sandra Morrison, Nicole Oakes, and Natasha Lyons. 2000. "The Archaeology of the Scowlitz Site, SW British Columbia." *Journal of Field Archaeology* 27, 371-416.

Lepofsky, Dana, Douglas Hallett, Kenneth P. Lertzman, and Rolf Mathewes. 2005. "Climate Change and Culture Change on the Southern Coast of British Columbia, 2400-1200 B.P." *American Antiquity* 70, 267-94.

Lepofsky, Dana, Karla Kusmer, Brian Hayden, and Ken Lertzman. 1996. "Reconstructing Prehistoric Socioeconomies from Paleoethnobotanical and Zooarchaeological Data: An Example from the British Columbia Plateau. *Journal of Ethnobiology* 16, 31-62.

Lepofsky, Dana S., and Sandra Peacock. 2004. "A Question of Intensity: Exploring the Role of Plant Foods in Northern Plateau Prehistory." In *Complex Hunter-Gatherers: Evolution and Organization of Prehistoric Communities on the Plateau of Northwestern North America,* ed. William C. Prentiss and Ian Kuijt, 115-39. Salt Lake City: University of Utah Press.

Lepofsky, Dana, David M. Schaepe, Anthony P. Graesch, Michael Lenert, Patricia Ormerod, Keith Thor Carlson, Jeanne E. Arnold, Michael Blake, Patrick Moore, and John J. Clague. 2009. "Exploring Stó:lō-Coast Salish Interaction and Identity in Ancient Houses and Settlements in the Fraser Valley, British Columbia." *American Antiquity* 74, 595-626.

Lohse, E.S., and D. Sammons-Lohse. 1986. "Sedentism on the Columbia Plateau: A Matter of Degree Related to Easy and Efficient Procurement of Resources." *Northwest Anthropological Research Notes* 20, 115-36.

Mackie, Quentin, and Steven Acheson. 2005. "The Graham Tradition." In *Haida Gwaii: Human History and Environment from the Time of the Loon to the Time of the Iron People,* ed. Daryl W. Fedje and Rolf W. Mathewes, 274-302. Vancouver: UBC Press.

Magne, Martin P.R. 1985. *Lithics and Livelihood: Stone Tool Technologies of Central and Southern Interior British Columbia.* National Museum of Man, Mercury Series. Ottawa: Archaeological Survey of Canada, Paper No. 133.

Marquardt, William H. 1991. "Politics and Production among the Calusa of South Florida." In *Hunters and Gatherers: History, Evolution, and Social Change,* ed. Tim Ingold, David Riches, and James Woodburn, 161-88. New York: Berg.

Martindale, Andrew R.C., and Susan Marsden. 2003. "Defining the Middle Period (3500 BP to 1500 BP) in Tsimshian History through a Comparison of Archaeological and Oral Records." *BC Studies* 138-39: 13-50.

Matson, R.G. 1983. "Intensification and the Development of Cultural Complexity: The Northwest versus Northeast Coast." In *The Evolution of Maritime Cultures on the Northeast and Northwest Coasts,* ed. Ronald Nash, 125-48. Burnaby: Simon Fraser University, Department of Archaeology, Publication No. 11.

—. 1989. "The Locarno Beach Phase and the Origins of the Northwest Coast Pattern." In *Development of Hunting-Fishing-Gathering Maritime Societies along the West Coast of North America,* ed. Blukas Onat. Pullman: Washington State University Press.

—. 1996. "The Old Cordilleran Component at the Glenrose Cannery Site." In *Early Human Occupation in British Columbia,* ed. Roy L. Carlson and Luke Dalla Bona, 111-22. Vancouver: UBC Press.

Matson, R.G., and Gary Coupland. 1995. *The Prehistory of the Northwest Coast*. San Diego: Academic Press.

Matson, R.G., Gary Coupland, and Quentin Mackie. 2003. *Emerging from the Mist: Studies in Northwest Coast Culture History*. Vancouver: UBC Press.

Matthewson, Lisa. 2005. *When I Was Small – I Wan Kwikws: A Grammatical Analysis of St'át'imc Oral Narratives*. Vancouver: UBC Press.

–. 2008. "Psychology." In *Wenácw Iz': Sqwéqwel's sLaura = True Stories by Laura Thevarge*, ed. Lisa Matthewson, Christiana Christodoulou, John Lyon, and Martin A. Oberg. Vancouver: University of British Columbia Working Papers in Linguistics, Vol. 22.

Morice, A. 1893. *Notes Archaeological, Industrial and Sociological on the Western Denes*. Transactions of the Royal Society of Canada, 1892-1893.

Morin, Jesse. 2006. "Non-Domestic Architecture in Prehistoric Complex Hunter-Gatherer Communities: An Example from Keatley Creek on the Canadian Plateau." Master's thesis, University of British Columbia.

Morin, Jesse, Ryan Dickie, Takashi Sakaguchi, and Jamie Hoskins. 2008-9. "Late Prehistoric Settlement Patterns and Population Dynamics along the Mid-Fraser." *BC Studies* 160, 9-35.

Mueter, Franz J., Randall M. Peterman, and Brian J. Pyper. 2002. "Opposite Effects of Ocean Temperature on Survival Rates of 120 Stocks of Pacific Salmon (Ocorhychus spp.) in Northern and Southern Areas." *Canadian Journal of Fisheries and Aquatic Science* 59, 456-63.

Muir, Robert, Jonathan Sheppard, Mykol Knighton, Heather Newton, and Ryan Dickie. 2008. "The 2006 Excavations of HP 109 Keatley Creek Site." Report on file, Archaeology Branch, Government of British Columbia, Victoria.

Namdaran, Nahal. 2006. "Retraction in St'át'imcets: An Ultrasonic Investigation." Master's thesis, University of British Columbia.

Ormerod, Patricia L. 2002. "Reading the Earth: Multivariate Analysis of Feature Functions at X̱á:ytem (The Hatzic Rock Site, DgRn23), British Columbia." Master's thesis, University of British Columbia.

Patterson, R. Timothy, Andreas Prokoph, Arun Kumar, Alice S. Chang, and Helen M. Roe. 2005. "Late Holocene Variability in Pelagic Fish Scales and Dinoflagellate Cysts along the West Coast of Vancouver Island, NE Pacific Ocean." *Marine Micropaleontology* 55, 183-204.

Peacock, Sandra L. 1998. "Putting Down Roots: The Emergence of Wild Plant Food Production on the Canadian Plateau." PhD diss., University of Victoria.

Pokotylo, David L., and P.D. Froese. 1983. "Archaeological Evidence for Prehistoric Root Gathering on the Southern Interior Plateau of British Columbia: A Case Study from the Upper Hat Creek Valley." *Canadian Journal of Archaeology* 7, 127-57.

Pokotylo, D.L., and D. Mitchell. 1998. "Prehistory of the Northern Plateau." In *Handbook of North American Indians*, vol. 12, *Plateau*, ed. Deward Walker, 81-102. Washington, DC: Smithsonian Institute.

Prentiss, Anna Marie. 2009. "The Emergence of New Socioeconomic Strategies in the Middle and Late Holocene Pacific Northwest Region." In *Macroevolution in Human Prehistory: Evolutionary Theory and Processual Archaeology*, ed. Anna Marie Prentiss, Ian Kuijt, and James C. Chatters, 111-32. Springer: New York.

Prentiss, Anna Marie, and David S. Clarke. 2008. "Lithic Technological Organization in an Evolutionary Framework: Examples from North America's Pacific Northwest Region." In *Lithic Technology: Measures of Production, Use and Curation*, ed. William Andrefsky, 257-85. Cambridge: Cambridge University Press.

Prentiss, Anna Marie, Guy Cross, Thomas A. Foor, Dirk Markle, Mathew Hogan, and David S. Clarke. 2008. "Evolution of a Late Prehistoric Winter Village on the Interior Plateau of British Columbia: Geophysical Investigations, Radiocarbon Dating, and Spatial Analysis of the Bridge River Site." *American Antiquity* 73, 59-82.

Prentiss, Anna Marie, Ian Kuijt, and James C. Chatters, eds. 2009. *Macroevolution in Human Prehistory: Evolutionary Theory and Processual Archaeology.* Springer: New York.

Prentiss, Anna Marie, and Michael Lenert. 2009. "Cultural Stasis and Change in Northern North America: A Macroevolutionary Perspective." In *Macroevolution in Human Prehistory: Evolutionary Theory and Processual Archaeology,* ed. Anna Marie Prentiss, Ian Kuijt, and James C. Chatters, 235-52. Springer: New York.

Prentiss, Anna Marie, Natasha Lyons, Lucille E. Harris, Melisse R.P. Burns, and Terrence M. Godin. 2007. "The Emergence of Status Inequality in Intermediate Scale Societies: A Demographic and Socio-Economic History of the Keatley Creek Site, British Columbia. *Journal of Anthropological Archaeology* 26, 299-327.

Prentiss, William C., and James C. Chatters. 2003a. "Cultural Diversification and Decimation in the Prehistoric Record." *Current Anthropology* 44, 33-58.

–. 2003b. "The Evolution of Collector Systems on the Pacific Coast of Northwest North America." *Senri Ethnological Studies* 63, 49-82.

Prentiss, William C., James C. Chatters, Michael Lenert, David S. Clarke, and Robert C. O'Boyle. 2005. "The Archaeology of the Plateau of Northwestern North America during the Late Prehistoric Period (3500-200 B.P.): Evolution of Hunting and Gathering Societies." *Journal of World Prehistory* 19, 47-118.

Prentiss, William C., and Ian Kuijt. 2004. "The Evolution of Collector Systems on the Canadian Plateau." In *Complex Hunter-Gatherers: Evolution and Organization of Prehistoric Communities on the Plateau of Northwestern North America,* ed. William C. Prentiss and Ian Kuijt, 49-66. Salt Lake City: University of Utah Press.

Prentiss, William C., Michael Lenert, Thomas A. Foor, and Nathan B. Goodale. 2005. "The Emergence of Complex Hunter-Gatherers on the Canadian Plateau: A Response to Hayden." *American Antiquity* 70, 175-80.

Prentiss, William C., Michael Lenert, Thomas A. Foor, Nathan B. Goodale, and Trinity Schlegel. 2003. "Calibrated Radiocarbon Dating at Keatley Creek: The Chronology of Occupation at a Complex Hunter-Gatherer Community." *American Antiquity* 68, 719-35.

Price, T. Douglas, and Gary M. Feinman, eds. 1995. *Foundations of Social Inequality.* New York: Plenum.

Quinn, Thomas P. 2005. *The Behavior and Ecology of Pacific Salmon and Trout.* Bethesda: American Fisheries Society.

Renfrew, Colin, and Paul Bahn. 2008. *Archaeology: Theories, Methods and Practice.* London: Thames and Hudson.

Reyes, A.V., and J.J. Clague. 2000. "Stratigraphic Evidence for Multiple Advances of Lillooet Glacier, Southern Coast Mountains, British Columbia." *Canadian Journal of Earth Science* 41, 903-18.

Richards, Thomas H., and Mike K. Rousseau. 1987. *Late Prehistoric Cultural Horizons on the Canadian Plateau.* Burnaby: Department of Archaeology, Simon Fraser University, Publication Number 16.

Romanoff, Steven. 1992a. "Fraser Lillooet Salmon Fishing." In *A Complex Culture of the British Columbia Plateau,* ed. Brian Hayden, 222-265. Vancouver: UBC Press.

–. 1992b. "The Cultural Ecology of Hunting and Potlatches among the Lillooet Indians." In *A Complex Culture of the British Columbia Plateau,* ed. Brian Hayden, 470-505. Vancouver: UBC Press.

Rousseau, Mike K. 2004. "A Culture Historic Synthesis and Changes in Human Mobility, Sedentism, Subsistence, Settlement and Population on the Canadian Plateau from 7000 to 200 BP." In *Complex Hunter-Gatherers: Evolution and Organization of Prehistoric Communities on the Plateau of Northwestern North America,* ed. William C. Prentiss and Ian Kuijt, 3-22. Salt Lake City: University of Utah Press.

Ruggles, Angela J. 2009. "Is Home Where the Hearth Is? Evidence for an Early Non-Domestic Structure on the Dundas Islands of North Coastal British Columbia." Master's thesis, University of British Columbia.

Sakaguchi, Takashi, Jesse Morin, and Ryan Dickie. 2010. "Defensibility of Large Prehistoric Sites in the Mid-Fraser Region on the Canadian Plateau." *Journal of Archaeological Science* 37, 1171-1185.

Samuels, Stephan R. 2006. "Households at Ozette." In *Household Archaeology on the Northwest Coast,* ed. Elizabeth A. Sobel, D. Ann Trieu Gahr, and Kenneth M. Ames, 200-32. Ann Arbor: International Monographs in Prehistory Archaeological Series 16.

Sanger, D. 1970. "The Archaeology of the Lochnore-Nesikep Locality." *Syesis* 3 (Supplement 1): 1-146.

Sassaman, Kenneth E. 2004. "Complex Hunter-Gatherers in Evolution and History: A North American Perspective." *Journal of Archaeological Research* 12, 227-80.

Sassaman, Kenneth E., and Donald Holly, eds. 2011. *Hunter-Gatherer Archaeology as Historical Process.* Tucson: University of Arizona Press.

Schaepe, David M. 2003. "Validating the Mauer House." In *Archaeology of Coastal British Columbia: Essays in Honor of Professor Phillip M. Hobler,* ed. by Roy Carlson, 113-52. Burnaby: Archaeology Press.

–. 2006. "Rock Fortifications: Archaeological Insights into Precontact Warfare and Sociopolitical Organization among the Sto:lo of the Lower Fraser Canyon B.C." *American Antiquity* 71, 671-706.

Schulting, Rick J. 1995. *Mortuary Variability and Status Differentiation on the Columbia-Fraser Plateau.* Burnaby: Archaeology Press.

Shahin, Kimary. 2002. *Postvelar Harmony.* Amsterdam/Philadelphia: John Benjamins.

Sheehan, Glenn W. 1985. "Whaling as an Organizing Focus in Northwest Alaskan Eskimo Society." In *Prehistoric Hunter-Gatherers: The Emergence of Cultural Complexity,* ed. T. Douglas Price and James A. Brown, 123-54. Orlando: Academic Press.

Smith, Trefor, 1998. *Our Stories Are Written upon the Land: A Brief History of the Upper St'át'imc, 1800-1940.* Lillooet: Upper St'át'imc Language, Culture and Education Society.

Sobel, Elizabeth A., D. Ann Trieu Gahr, and Kenneth M. Ames. 2006. *Household Archaeology on the Northwest Coast.* Ann Arbor: International Monographs in Prehistory, Archaeological Series 16.

Spafford, James, 1991. "Artifact Distributions on Housepit Floors and Social Organization in Housepits at Keatley Creek." Master's thesis, Simon Fraser University, Burnaby.

Stewart, Kathlyn M., Frances L. Stewart, and Gary Coupland. 2008. "Boardwalk, Northern Northwest Coast, Canada: A New Face to an Old Site. *Canadian Journal of Archaeology* 33: 205-33.

Stryd, Arnoud H. 1972. "Housepit Archaeology in Lillooet, British Columbia: The 1970 Field Season." *BC Studies* 14, 17-46.

–. 1973. "The Later Prehistory of the Lillooet Area, British Columbia." PhD diss., University of Calgary.

–. 1974. "Lillooet Archaeological Project: 1974 Field Season." Cariboo College Papers in Archaeology 1.

–. 1980. "A Review of Recent Activities Undertaken by the Lillooet Archaeological Project." *The Midden* 122, 5-20.

Stryd, Arnoud H., and Mike K. Rousseau. 1996. "The Early Prehistory of the Mid-Fraser-Thompson River Area." In *Early Human Occupation in British Columbia,* ed. Roy L. Carlson and Luke Dalla Bona, 177-204. Vancouver: UBC Press.

Tainter, Joseph A. 1988. *The Collapse of Complex Societies.* Cambridge: Cambridge University Press.

Teit, James. 1900. *The Thompson Indians of British Columbia,* ed. Franz Boas. Memoirs of the American Museum of Natural History, Jesup North Pacific Expedition, vol. 1, 165-391.

–. 1906. *The Lillooet Indians.* Memoirs of the American Museum of Natural History, Jesup North Pacific Expedition, vol. 2, 193-300.

–. 1909. *The Shuswap Indians.* Memoirs of the American Museum of Natural History, Jesup North Pacific Expedition, vol. 4, 443-758.

Tunnicliffe, V., J.M. O'Connell, and M.R. McQuoid. 2001. "A Holocene Record of Marine Fish Remains from the Northeastern Pacific." *Marine Geology* 174, 197-210.

Turner, Nancy J. 1992. "Plant Resources of the Stl'átl'imx (Fraser River Lillooet) People: A Window into the Past." In *A Complex Culture of the British Columbia Plateau,* ed. Brian Hayden, 405-69. Vancouver: UBC Press.

–. 1997. *Food Plants of Interior First Peoples.* Vancouver: UBC Press.

Turner, Nancy J., Laurence C. Thompson, M. Terry Thompson, and Annie Z. York. 1990. *Thompson Ethnobotany: Knowledge and Use of Plants by the Thompson Indians of British Columbia.* Victoria: Royal British Columbia Museum, Memoir 3.

van Eijk, Jan. 1978. *Ucwalmicwts.* Mount Currie, BC: Ts'zil Publishers.

–. 1997. *The Lillooet Language: Phonology, Morphology, Syntax.* Vancouver: UBC Press.

Watson, Patty Jo. 2008. "Processualism and After." In *Handbook of Archaeological Theories,* ed. R. Alexander Bentley, Herbert D.G. Maschner, and Christopher Chippindale, 29-38. Lanham: Altamira Press.

Wilson, Ian. 1992. "Excavations at the Baker Site EdQx 43, Monte Creek Permit 97-107." Report on file, Archaeology Branch, Victoria, BC.

Wilson, Robert L., and Catherine Carlson. 1980. *The Archaeology of Kamloops.* Burnaby: Department of Archaeology, Simon Fraser University, Publication No. 7.

Wobst, H. Martin. 1978. The Archaeo-Ethnology of Hunter-Gatherers, or the Tyranny of the Ethnographic Record in Archaeology. *American Antiquity* 43, 303-9.

Index

artifacts: defined, 15, 20, 22; distributions on floors, 23; Fraser Delta, 73b; grave goods, 51; Keatley Creek, 190-91; in Lochnore-Nesikep area, 32; of Nesikep tradition, 33, 34f, 35f; prestige goods, 167, 169; Shuswap horizon, 61f; and status differentiation, 160; stone, 21-22, 41, 60. *See also* ecofacts

artwork: carved ladders/poles, 89-90; of Charles culture, 49, 54; Early Plateau, 78; Locarno Beach, 55. *See also* Carlson, Eric; O'Boyle, Robert

B

Baker site, 62-63

Bar-el, Leora, 201a-209a

Bell site, 69m, 94, 95f, 160-61, 180, 182m

Bella Bella, 50

bighorn sheep, 8f

bison, 79-80, 82

Blue Jackets Creek, 50-51

Borden, Charles, 31, 40f, 54

Bouchard, Randy, 93, 155, 156-57

Bridge River, 2, 4m

Bridge River site, 69m, 87m, 103-10, 103f, 104f, 105m, 108m, 109f, 182m; dog bones, 166f; Housepit 11, 189f; Housepit 16, 15f; Housepit 20, 16f, 170; Housepit 24, 169-71, 171f; Housepit 54, 187f; tools, 133f

Bridge River village: abandoned, 151, 174, 197; food preparation, 149f; growth, 150, 168-69, 168f, 179, 196; large *vs.* small houses, 169-71, 188; Late Period, 187-88; pithouse rebuilding, 12; population, 180; social change, 167-68, 173; subsistence diversification, 147-48; time span, 147-48, 167

burials, 51; changes in numbers, 179b; grave goods, 73b, 94, 160, 161; Qithyil cemetery, 72

C

cache pits, 15f, 16f, 59f, 125f, 128; Baker site, 62; Bell site, 161; Bridge River site, 166f, 170-71, 187, 190; Cohoe Creek site, 51; Keatley Creek site, 145

caches, above-ground, 125, 128, 161

camas, 52, 80

Canadian Plateau, 43, 72, 74-79; artifacts, 34f, 35f; villages, 69m. *See also specific archaeological sites; specific regions; specific villages*

carbohydrates, 128-31; rabbit starvation and, 62

carbon-14 dating. *See* radiocarbon dating

Carlson, Eric, 25, 35f, 36f, 88f, 109f, 125f, 127f, 135f-139f, 145f, 149f, 159f, 164f, 168f, 187m

Charles culture, 42m, 49; artwork, 49, 54; climate change and, 53-54; Eayam phase, 49-50; parallels with Locarno Beach groups, 56

Chatters, Jim, 31, 32, 46, 48, 82, 111, 113, 173-74, 184b

climate, 42f; and food resources, 43, 75, 80, 116; Neoglacial period, 52-54

climate change: and cultural reorganization, 197; European contact and, 199; and food resources, 29, 67-68, 74, 86, 148-49; in Fraser Valley, 66; of Neoglacial period, 65-66; positive and negative effects, 184b-185b; and subsistence patterns, 147-48

Clovis tradition, 32

Cohoe Creek, 50-51

Columbia Basin, 46, 48, 56, 80

Columbia Plateau, 32, 79-82; bison, 79-80; tools, 133f, 134f; villages, 69m

complex collecting, 71-72, 73b, 94, 114, 195

Cross, Guy, 103, 107b

cultural: bias, 25; categories, 154b; collapse, 178; decimation, 52-54; diversification, 45-52; iconography, 6, 7f. *See also specific iconic items*

cultural chronologies: Mid-Fraser Canyon villages, 98-102, 103-10, 113-14; types defined, 18

cultural features, 15, 20; benches, 87-88, 90; carved ladders/poles, 89; fish-drying racks, 6, 7f; Keatley Creek site, 161; magnetometry and, 107b; outdoor ovens, 148, 149f, 187, 190; roasting pits, 75; spatial organization and, 92, 161. *See also* cache pits; hearths culture: concepts of, 28b; environment and, 43-44, 52-54. *See also specific cultures; specific traditions*

culture change, 12, 14, 28b; aggregation, 110-14; causes, 45; climatic change and, 66; conservative learning environment and, 46b-47b, 113-14; cultural context and, 44-45; explanatory models, 30-31; factors, 172-75, 178; hindrances, 113-14; independent invention *vs.* transmission, 56; interpretation of, 178; isolation and, 51-52; patterns of, 33; status differentiation, 152-53, 166-67; subsistence diversification, 144-48; subsistence diversity, 115; wide-ranging, 183. *See also* social organization, changed; status differentiation

D

Dalles, The, 43, 78, 81, 112

dating: archaeological sites, 17-18; Bridge River abandonment, 173-74; Bridge River village, 107-10, 168f, 179b; Keatley Creek village, 98-100, 164f, 173-74, 180; social change, 172-74

deer, 126-28

Dietz, Ali, 148

diversification. *See* culture change

documentation: horizontal/vertical, 16-17; innovative, 98

E

ecofacts: animal bones, 20, 47, 48, 145; defined, 15; dog bones, 23, 165, 166f, 170; food remains, 145-46, 147-48, 161, 162; preservation of, 10, 12

ecological hotspots/ecotones, 48, 50, 69, 111, 112f

edible plants, 6, 60, 62, 68, 74f, 128; berry-producing, 52-53, 129-31; geophytes, 6, 129, 132; roots, 52, 60, 80, 129, 130

Eldredge, Niles, 31

electrical conductivity, 19, 20b, 107b

environmental conditions. *See* climate; climate change

Eskimo people, 75, 116

ethnocide, 10

ethnography, 22, 24, 25. *See also* records, ethnographic; *individual ethnographers*

F

fish-drying racks, 6, 7f, 26f, 122f, 123, 138f, 139f

fishing: nets, 120, 121f, 135f; sites, 65, 72; techniques, 120-21, 121f, 135f, 137f

food preparation/processing, 127f; berries, 130-31; deer, 127-28, 127f; game, 127-28, 127f; roots, 60, 75, 129; salmon, 6, 7f, 26f, 49, 122f, 123, 124b, 136f, 137f, 138f, 139f

food resources: accessibility, 65, 116, 149-50, 184-85; climate change and, 184b, 185b; fires and, 52-53, 67, 68; game, 8f, 80, 82, 125-28; and hereditary inequality, 174-75; overexploitation, 185; seasonal, 44, 115-16, 117, 118f, 131-32; and subsistence diversity, 115; and village growth/viability, 29-30, 148-50, 151-52. *See also* edible plants; salmon

food storage, 49, 51, 59f, 124, 125f. *See also* cache pits; caches, above-ground

foodways, traditional: Bridge River, 147-48; core foods, 117-30; Fraser Valley, 67-68; Keatley Creek, 144-47; Scowlitz, 71; seasonal round, 44, 115-16, 117, 118f, 131-32; Shuswap horizon, 60; subsistence technology, 131-44; and village growth, 148-50. *See also* food resources; subsistence practices

foraging: broad-spectrum, 41; collector strategy, 54-56, 57, 59, 62, 68-69, 131-32, 194; complex collecting, 71-72, 73b, 94, 114, 195; daily *vs.* delayed return, 53; mobile, 52; mobile serial, 50; seasonal round, 44, 115-16, 117, 118f, 131-32; sedentary, 46, 50, 52; serial, 48-49, 52; task-group mobility, 50-51, 69-71, 72, 82

Fountain Ridge, 42f

Fountain site, 180, 182m

Fraser, Simon, 93, 198

Fraser Delta tradition: Locarno Beach phase, 48m, 54-56, 68-69; Marpole phase, 66m, 67-72, 73b

Fraser River, 2, 3f, 4m, 5m, 7f, 31f, 40f; feeding creeks, 6

Fraser Valley: plank house villages, 68-69; population decline, 72; settlements, 67b; social networks, 71

Fremont culture, 197

pithouses: Bridge River *vs.* Keatley Creek, 88, 104, 107; ceremonial activities, 152, 160b, 163, 165, 170-71; construction of, 12, 13f, 46-47, 59, 88-89, 90b-91b; cross-section view, 13f; interior organization, 86-88; Lochnore phase, 62-63; rebuilding, 78, 88f, 104, 107; ritual structures, 72, 191; seasonal cycle and, 90-91; Shuswap horizon, 60; spatial organization, 86, 91-92, 168-69

plank house villages: extent of, 73b; Fraser Valley, 68-69; Northwest Coast, 67b; Scowlitz, 70-71, 70f

Plateau Interaction Sphere, 78-79

Plateau Pithouse tradition, 18, 194-96; Shuswap horizon and, 48m

Pokotylo, David, 74-75

population: decline, 72, 179, 198; expansions, 32, 113; and social change, 172-73

Prentiss, Anna, 100-1, 101f, 103, 107b, 147

property rights, 1, 9-10, 68, 71, 112, 150, 152, 156-57, 169, 174, 196, 199

Q

Qithyil. *See* housepit village sites, Scowlitz

R

radiocarbon dating, 18, 70; Bridge River site, 104, 167; Keatley Creek site, 99-100, 100-1, 103-4, 191; Mid-Fraser villages, 180; of status differentiation, 173

records: archaeological, 10, 50, 51; archaeological *vs.* ethnographic, 67b; ethnographic, 31, 78, 87-89, 90b-91b, 92, 117, 119-21, 123-31, 125b, 140-44, 140b-141b, 155-58; mortuary, 82, 160, 160b, 179b; oral history, 25, 187; of subsistence practices, 117

rim middens. *See* middens, rim

Ritchie, Baptiste, 87-89, 187

Romanoff, Steven, 120-21, 123, 124-25, 158

Rousseau, Mike, 62, 75-76, 79, 180

Ryder, June, 110, 171-72, 180-81

S

s7ístken. *See* pithouses

salmon, 6; and culture change, 147, 173-74; decline, 115, 184-86, 184b; eggs, 124;

fishing sites, 118f, 119, 121, 121f, 123, 137f; fishing techniques, 120-21, 121f; fluctuations, 52, 67-68, 80, 183-84; heads, 123, 124b, 170-71; and mobility, 116; nets, 120, 121f, 135f; oil, 124b; processing, 26f, 49, 122f, 123, 124b, 136f, 137f, 138f, 139f; resilience, 181, 183; species, 119b, 120-21; top food, 117; and village placement, 68, 75, 111

Samson, William, 124-25

Sanger, David, 31-32, 59, 60

Schaepe, David, 155

Schulting, 78

Scowlitz site, 69m, 69-70, 70-71, 70f

sedentism, 154b, 194; and task-group mobility, 50-51

sediment layers, 12, 16, 19-22, 43, 52, 67, 88-90, 92, 107b, 181, 187f

Seton Lake, 4m, 5m, 87m

Seton Lake site, 180, 182m

Shuswap people, 62-63

Six Mile Rapids, 75, 87m, 111, 112f, 117, 118f

Skoglund's Landing site, 51

Slocan Narrows, 69m, 80-81, 81m

Smith, Trefor, 193

Snake River Plateau, 32

social complexity. *See* status differentiation

social organization: of Bell site village, 160-61; Bridge River village, 167-71; changed, 166-67, 171; clans, 10, 95, 142, 153-55, 154b, 157, 169, 172; Coast Salish, 71; corporate groups, 94-95, 166; division of labour, 158-59; Early Nekisep, 38; of early villages, 196; egalitarian *vs.* ranked, 73b, 152-53, 154b; Haida Gwaii, 51; horizontal and vertical, 153-54, 168-69; of hunter-gatherers, 154b; increased violence, 82, 198; inheritance systems, 158; intergroup relations, 71, 78-79, 111, 174-75, 177, 186; Keatley Creek, 165-67; kinship, 154-55; Lochnore, 39; multivillage, 171-72; ranked, 113; social change, 152-53, 167-68; Stó:lō, 155-56

St'át'imc Nation, 1-2; collaboration with archaeologists, 1, 25; cultural continuity, 24; political organization, 8-9, 10

St'át'imc people: collector strategy, 131-32; culture, 195; direct ancestors, 186-92, 193;

Printed and bound in Canada by Friesens

Set in Trajan, Meta, and Garamond
by Artegraphica Design Co. Ltd.

Text design: Irma Rodriguez

Copy editor: Lesley Erickson

Proofreader and indexer: Dianne Tiefensee

Cartographer: Eric Leinberger